Port Isaac's
Fisherman's
Friends

· PORT ISAAC'S · FISHERMAN'S FRIENDS

SAILING AT EIGHT BELLS

with ROBERT UHLIG

**SIMON &
SCHUSTER**

London · New York · Sydney · Toronto · New Delhi

A CBS COMPANY

First published in Great Britain by Simon & Schuster UK Ltd, 2011
A CBS COMPANY

1 3 5 7 9 10 8 6 4 2

Simon & Schuster UK Ltd
1st Floor
222 Gray's Inn Road
London WC1X 8HB

www.simonandschuster.co.uk

Simon & Schuster Australia, Sydney
Simon & Schuster India, New Delhi

A CIP catalogue record for this book
is available from the British Library.

ISBN 978-0-85720-442-4

Typeset in Bembo by M Rules
Printed and bound by CPI Group (UK) Ltd, Croydon, CR0 4YY

CONTENTS

FOREWORD

As it happens, I know Port Isaac quite well. I holiday just up the coast from there every year and I fell, like every other grockle, for its almost unseemly quaintness. With its steep, narrow streets, white-washed cottages, fishery, fudgery, pub, pasties, pottery, post office and perplexing Pisky Gift Shop, it's everyone's ideal of what a fishing village should be. So seduced by its allure have I been that I've bought several artworks from the 'Secrets' gallery half-way down the steep incline of Fore Street. I've also parked on the shingle of the harbour beach itself, wondering if this wasn't some elaborate ploy by the locals to flood the posh cars of the incomers with salty water.

Port Isaac has become widely known as the location for the *Doc Martin* TV series starring middle-aged man no longer behaving badly, Martin Clunes, and also as the chosen weekend retreat of flamboyant painter and decorator Laurence Llewellyn Bowen. And yet the fact that there is now international recognition for this nigh-on perfect corner of Cornwall is due to a wholly less picturesque phenomenon. On Friday nights, around eight bells (or eight o' clock to those of you unfamiliar with seafaring parlance), startled tourists have for many years been unsettled by the accumulation of burly-looking men of no fixed hairstyle in matelot jerkins conglomerating on the quayside. Initially nervous glances will be exchanged by the visitors as they try to ascertain whether this band of locally sourced brothers are the neighbourhood militia

intent on inflicting mindless violence on the trespassers or just a homoerotic nautically themed troupe of coastal Morris men.

Gradually, however, these less than dapper dogs of the sea and
shore, these sturdy, stout-hearted stevedores, clear their throats – and
not just to expectorate onto the esplanade. The by-now jostling
throng, their initial fear giving way to curiosity, gather expectantly as
these gregarious *garçons de la plage* inhale deeply. And then something
wondrous happens. Like a well-lubricated Leviathan emerging from
the drunken deep, a tsunami of song sweeps over the seafront. Hard
men who have battled the elements at sea, folded jumpers for twelve
hours at a time in the gift shop, or grappled with clay at the wheel to
make an ornamental cake stand, hurl themselves headlong into harmony with scant regard for their own safety. Seasoned sea shanties
from down all the days ring out and echo through the alleyways and
alcoves that once swarmed with smugglers. The day trippers begin to
smile, to clap, to sway from side to side. It's as if there is nowhere in
the world they would rather be. Like a jigsaw, all the bits seem to have
dropped into place. We have stumbled on something very special
and we all know it.

The story of Port Isaac's Fisherman's Friends is modern folklore.
Like *The Calendar Girls*, it is the tale of the local that went global. It
is the success story that is all the sweeter, as no one saw it coming
or dared to dream it could happen. And who could begrudge them
their journey from shoreline to stadium, from cove to concert hall,
from rock pool to recording contract, from slipway to the studio, from
fishing boat to the Folk Awards, from rigging to the Royal Albert
Hall, from gift emporium to Glastonbury, from pasty shop to platinum-
selling albums, from wharf to the world stage, from bladderwrack to
there and back? From The Golden Lion to … another pub on the other
side of the pond.

I like them enormously as guys, although I have to say that spending any time with them incurs a very expensive round, as I found
to my cost in that hotel bar in Exmouth. But the joy they give and
get from their singing never fails to warm the heart, even if they stray

a bit too high in key occasionally, as no one has thought to buy a pitch pipe. No matter. They don't claim to be the world's best singers but the sound they make is as unique and special as the place they have in our hearts. This then is their story. Cheers lads. It can't be my round again surely.

Mark Radcliffe
Bound for South Australia 25 May 11

CHAPTER ONE

GLASTONBURY

Cleavey brought the news. From the sparkle in his eye and the twitch of his waxed walrus moustache – it always does that when he's trying to suppress a smile – we could tell it was good.

'Lads,' he said. 'You aren't going to believe this. They want us to play at Glastonbury.'

Us? A bunch of hairy-arsed Cornish fishermen, potters, builders and bakers with a collective age of 561. At *Glastonbury*? The mother of music and arts festivals.

Somehow it didn't seem right, but apparently it was. Just another strange twist in our fishing-net-to-riches tale of how the world blew into our tiny, remote village bringing fame and fortune to a group of mates who had never sought it.

The day had started much like any other Thursday evening in late-winter Port Isaac. Shortly before six o'clock, front doors slammed across the village as an ochre sun set behind Lobber Point. Beneath it, shadows stretched over the harbour, where our fishing boats bobbed on a low tide and the still air chilled.

From up on the hills and down in the valley we came. Cleavey and Rowey from close by the stream. Two of the Brown brothers and Trevor from high on the cliff. Johnny Mac and Jeremy Brown from near the village hall on Trewetha Lane. Nigel Sherratt from Cupcakes, his tea shop at the heart of the village. And from St Kew, John Lethbridge made the long trek. His farm is all of three miles inland, so we think of him as a bit of an outsider really.

Through the narrow lanes between whitewashed and slate-hung houses, down Shuggie's Ope and Squeeze-ee-belly Alley, our footsteps converged until we reached the Platt. Piled high with rusty chains, old anchors, lobster pots and all the paraphernalia of the sea, this cobbled fishing quay has for the past two decades been the centre of our lives. A place where we ten reprobates have gathered on summer evenings to sing sea shanties and Cornish tunes. A place where we've shared the simple joys of song, stories and beer beside a big plywood sign that says: *Fisherman's Friends. Shanty Singers. Tonight. Sailing Time: Eight Bells Me Hearties* . . .

But this was a winter's evening and the village was quiet, so our journey continued a few steps beyond the Platt. Up Roscarrock Hill to a slate-roofed former Methodist chapel, now the home of our tenth member, Billy Hawkins. A sign beside the door said a lot about the man inside. *Pottery*, it said. *Opening hours: Dreckly* – that's Cornish for *mañana*, but without the same sense of urgency.

A knock on the door. Laughter and golden light spilled out on to the granite step. Pints of ale and lager in hand, one by one we entered. Inside, friendly nods, warm smiles and warmer words as each of the Fisherman's Friends arrived for our weekly rehearsal. And as usual, before the singing and the hollering and the rollicking could start, time for the announcements and arrangements that keep the show on the road – what some people might call housekeeping, but what we call trouble and bother.

'Just wait a minute,' said one voice. 'Cleavey's on the way and I think he's got something to say.'

Just then, Jon Cleave arrived. Six foot one inch of bonhomie, charm and wit. A natural storyteller who knows more stories than the rest of us have forgotten, Jon's fruity deep bass lends itself to public announcements. That's why, as our master of ceremonies, he introduces all the songs and the singers on the Platt. That night it was no different.

'Lads,' he said. 'You aren't going to believe this . . .'

And, well, you know the rest.

Silence. We all looked at each other. No jumping in the air or whooping and hollering all over the place. After all, we're not quite young kids in a band that's always dreamed of playing Glastonbury. We're middle-aged men with middle-aged aches, pains and concerns. More socks and rugs and rock'n'roll than the usual sex and drugs combination. But we do know a gift horse when we see one. So before anyone could say anything, John Brown piped up.

'Do we have to?' he said. 'It's a bit of an effort.'

'What do you mean?' said Bill. 'This is a good opportunity.'

John shrugged. 'You know me. I'm not big on festivals.' It's true. Celebrity culture has completely passed John by. And the only music he likes is shanties. 'You know, I wouldn't bother going to see David Cameron, or even the Queen, if I thought I had to queue up and wait in a field with thousands of people to see 'em. Not my thing at all.'

'But just think of the prestige.'

'You can have my prestige, Bill. And I'll have your share of the money.'

'Oh, hang on now,' said Bill.

But the truth was none of us was going to get paid. For a bunch of relative unknowns such as the Fisherman's Friends, being asked to play Glastonbury was an honour that most of us felt we couldn't turn down. Sure, we'd hit the headlines when we signed a multi-album deal with Universal. And yes, our first album went straight into the top ten – a unique achievement for a British a cappella sea shanty group. But compared with the other names on the bill at Glastonbury – Stevie Wonder, Pet Shop Boys, Ray Davies or Dizzee Rascal – we were minnows. And at Glastonbury, minnows don't get paid.

The largest crowd we regularly played to was the few hundred who squeezed on to the Platt every Friday summer evening. At Glastonbury, there'd be something like 180,000 people – several times more than we'd sung to in all our twenty years. That's why, when we were given a wish list of festival bookings, most of us immediately plumped for Glastonbury. It was the one we'd all heard of.

Back then, Cleavey had thought we were overreaching ourselves by wanting to play the world's most prestigious music festival. He thought we should set our sights a bit lower. 'Bloody Glastonbury,' he'd said, shaking his head and looking baffled. 'Why for Christ's sake do you want to do that? It's ridiculous.'

And maybe Cleavey was right. It *was* a ridiculous ambition. After all, only Cleavey had ever been anywhere near a big festival. And that was as a policeman on the Glastonbury perimeter in the 1980s.

But we were determined. This might be our only chance, so we should shoot for the top, someone said.

Cleavey gave way. 'Oh well, put it down,' he'd said, thinking that would be the end of it. So we had. And now they'd got back to us. Not that it convinced Johnny Mac.

'They're only trying to keep us interested,' said the Macster, who's not so much a cynic as a realist. 'They'll get in touch later and there'll be some excuse. "No room for a load of old guys singing sea shanties," they'll say. Or maybe they'll only offer us some crummy little stage beside the beer tent.'

We needed to know more, so phone calls were made to find out what appearing at Glastonbury would involve. The answer came: there were three main stages and we'd be on one of them. It was called the Acoustic Stage. It was big and prestigious. A proper job.

That's when we realised we weren't going to be singing to a handful of people at the back of a remote field. And that's when the fear struck.

A few months later and it's the last Sunday in June. A glorious summer dawn is breaking over Port Isaac but most of the village is still asleep as we clamber aboard a white minibus. Jeremy Brown's wife has made two egg-and-bacon pies and there's a few cans of beer in plastic bags, but they're strictly not to be touched until the journey home. Feeling like little kids filled with a volatile mixture of excitement and dread, we begin the long journey up country, out of the valley, over the cliffs and along the edges of the moors to some fields in a Somerset valley.

By late morning, with plenty of time to spare before our slot on the Acoustic Stage, we are approaching Glastonbury when the call goes out.

'Stop!' It's John Brown. And it's urgent. 'Stop, I said.'

'We're only three miles from the performers' entrance gate,' says Johnny Mac, 'and for some reason you want us to stop?'

'We've got to have our breakfast,' says John, pointing at a roadside shack.

The bus pulls over and we pile out into the sunshine, then into a nondescript café, Johnny Mac grinning as he shakes his head. He's a Yorkshireman, our token incomer. He's been in Port Isaac so long we regard him as one of us now, but in all those years he hasn't lost his Yorkshire bluffness or his caution with money. It's often said that a Yorkshireman is a Scotsman with all the generosity squeezed out. That's not quite fair to Johnny Mac, who always gets his round in (and says that Yorkshiremen and Scots could learn a thing or two about parsimony from the Cornish), but let's just say today he opts for a coffee and a pastry. 'Something quick,' he says. 'We need to get there.'

But John and most of the rest of us ignore Macster's frugality and urgency. Chomping our way leisurely through full English fry-ups, we take our time as if an appointment with a Glastonbury stage in a few hours is the last thing on our minds.

Johnny Mac is smiling. 'What's funny,' he says, 'is you lot would rather spend time inside a little shack when all of Glastonbury is waiting out there.'

'That's right, Johnny,' says John Brown, a man who knows exactly what he likes and never wavers from it. John knows the words of just about every sea shanty that's ever been sung, but he has very little interest in other music, so he doesn't understand the significance of Glastonbury. He once went to an Elton John concert. When he got there he remembered he didn't like crowds, so he left after ten minutes. 'Seeing Elton John up on stage, just himself and his piano and his big square glasses and all those people,' he said. 'It was just so boring, so I went home.' No wonder John would rather finish his bacon and eggs in peace than be cooped up at a festival with hundreds of thousands of strangers.

The day is in full heat by the time we finish breakfast and it's a scorcher out there, the hottest, sunniest Glastonbury day for many years. We'd been told to expect torrential rains, floods and fields of mud. Instead, dust rises everywhere as we approach the festival.

All of us have seen Glastonbury on television but, even so, arriving at the festival is an eye-opener. The landscape, a long valley stretched between tree-topped hills, with the Tor at one end, looks like the site of a medieval battle. Flags, banners and the peaks of marquees jut into the sky. Fields of tents stretch as far as we can see. It's quite beautiful.

Bedraggled people are everywhere, filling the road along which we are driving. We're directed through them and on to a road for performers, then through a succession of high-security barriers like Checkpoint Charlie. At each barrier, someone with a clipboard climbs aboard the minibus to check our details or hand out armbands. At the final checkpoint, it's an actor who has worked in Port Isaac and has seen us sing on the Platt several times.

'Good luck, lads,' he yells as he gets off the bus. 'And give my best to Port Isaac.'

At last we pass through a final section of high metal fence into the festival. We drive along some metal trackways, Cleavey yapping all the time – he rarely shuts up – and then we're into what looks like a small city in the middle of the countryside. That's when the size of Glastonbury hits us. With more people than the population of York, it's overwhelming. And quite scary for ten old boys from Port Isaac. Terror and anticipation mix to make the adrenaline pump.

The site is like a vast maze and it takes us about half an hour to find our way to where we're meant to congregate before our gig. Flashing our wristbands at various officials, we're directed through a succession of fields towards the Acoustic Stage, a vast open-sided tent like a circus bigtop, but many times larger. A minder herds us into the backstage area, where we're delighted to find we're treated like proper musicians, not a bunch of part-time singers and footstampers.

For the first time in twenty years, we're not hauling our own equipment from the back of a van on to the stage. Instead of assembling our own microphone stands and connecting cables to monitors, we're ushered into a dressing room and shown a bar where we can share a few beers and relax.

'This . . .' says Jeremy Brown, 'I could get used to.'

If it was any other day, we'd be nervous about the impending gig. But today is different and we're distracted by a more pressing concern.

'We've got to get a telly,' says Peter Rowe. He's our oldest member and used to coach the Port Isaac football team when we were kids. 'We don't want to miss the match.'

England is playing Germany at the World Cup in South Africa. For many of us it's a bigger thing than playing Glastonbury.

As usual before a gig, we limit the beers to a maximum of two pints. One pint loosens us up and helps with the nerves. But any more than two pints and the performance suffers. While we're enjoying them, a few of us sidle over to the edge of the stage. Mayhew, the band before us on the bill, is still playing and we can see out into the auditorium.

'It's a bit quiet,' says Billy.

The tent is less than a quarter full with no more than a hundred people dotted around in front of the stage watching the band. Most of them are lying on the ground, reading the *Guardian* and sipping cold drinks. Some of them are asleep on blankets.

'Oh, that's all right then,' says Trevor, who is relieved by the small size of the crowd. Less pressure, maybe.

'This might not be so good . . .' says Billy.

Most of us agree. Coming all this way to sing to fewer people than turn out on a summer's evening on the Platt would be an anticlimax of unprecedented proportions. Glastonbury is a long way to come to sing to fifty or sixty people.

Mayhew finish their set and come off stage. Our Glastonbury debut is only half an hour away, enough time for the stagehands to strip Mayhew's kit off the stage and set up our simple line of ten microphones. In the meantime, we sip our pints and try to prepare for the gig.

'Can't relax,' says Trevor, putting down his beer and walking out of the bar towards the collection area at the side of the stage. A few minutes later, he returns.

'You won't believe this,' he says. 'I walked down to the collection area. There's a ramp there that leads up to the stage. I stood there, just thinking and listening. And then I noticed the noise – it's really loud. Just loads of people's voices. So I sneaked a little way up the ramp, holding on to the black railings and leaning out so that I could squint through these big black curtains. I peered out over the staging. And that's when I saw it. It's packed out there. And they're waiting for us to come on.'

The panic starts. The beers are put down, the joking and wisecracking stops, and we all go quiet. A couple of the lads go to have a look at the audience for themselves. All of them return just as awed as Trevor. It's suddenly hit us that we have to go out and sing in front of that audience and there's a hellish lot of them.

'We need to start taking this seriously,' says Billy. We all know what he means.

Cleavey disappears into a corner, puts on his reading glasses and studies his notes – he always needs a bit of peace and quiet to prepare what he's going to say when we get on stage – and then we gather in the collection area near the ramp.

We stand in a loose circle, like a rugby team in the dressing room before kickoff, and look each other in the eye. We're an anarchic ungovernable gang with no choirmaster or band leader – all Indians and no chief – so nobody takes a lead. Instead, what comes next just finds its own way.

'Right, come on,' says one voice. 'Let's go for it.'

'Just enjoy it,' says another. 'Give it your all.'

It's hard to keep Cleavey quiet at the best of times, so he says a few words too, and we all cheer and support each other in an all-for-one-and-one-for-all spirit. Then a stage manager dressed in black shorts and T-shirt appears.

'OK, you're up,' he says.

The moment of truth has arrived. Our biggest ever gig.

As we climb the ramp, the curtains are pulled apart and we can see on to the stage – it's vast and our ten microphones look lost on it – but we can't yet see the crowd. We wait in the wings for the announcement.

'Ladies and gentlemen, please welcome on to the Glastonbury Acoustic Stage Port Isaac's Fisherman's Friends.'

John Brown leads us out and even before we can see the audience, we hear them. A massive cheer goes up, deep, rich, guttural, unlike anything that has ever greeted us before.

We look at each other, half-smiling and half-shocked, thinking: *Can this be right? Do they think somebody else is coming out?* But from the response of the crowd and the many Cornish flags and fish kites flying, it's obvious it's us they're expecting, all right. Focusing on getting to our positions on stage and preparing for the first song, none of us studies the crowd too closely. It's just a vast sea of faces, stretching to the far edges of the tent, beyond which hundreds more people are jostling and pressing to get inside the big top.

As soon as we are all behind our microphones, Cleavey leans forward.

'Oh, hello,' he says. 'Fancy seeing you here.'

A big cheer.

'We are the Fisherman's Friends and we are going to sing you some rollocking, bollocking, saucy, bawdy, fruity, jolly-rogering songs of sailors from the days when Britannia r-r-r-ruled the waves.'

Cleavey takes a big breath, then launches into the first song. It's a rip-roaring sea shanty. No subtlety. He bangs it out full-on.

'*A drop of Nelson's blood wouldn't do us any harm.*'

Cleavey stamps twice on the ground.

'*A drop of Nelson's blood wouldn't do us any harm.*'
Another two stamps.
'*A drop of Nelson's blood wouldn't do us any harm. We'll all hang on behind.*'
The rest of us crash into the chorus:

> *So we'll roll the golden chariot along,*
> *An' we'll roll the golden chariot along,*
> *So we'll roll the golden chariot along,*
> *An' we'll all hang on behind!*

The lyrics are based on a legend that after Lord Nelson fell at Trafalgar, his body was preserved by sealing it in a cask filled with French brandy, ironically. When his body was removed from the cask to prepare for his state funeral, the sailors escorting it reputedly drank the brandy from the barrel in a toast to their great hero. Hence '*a drop of Nelson's blood wouldn't do us any harm*', meaning it would give the drinkers courage. The golden chariot refers to the carriage used to carry Nelson's coffin.

And from then on, sailors' grog became known as Nelson's Blood. It's as basic as sea shanties come, but it's catchy and effective. The crowd immediately responds, whooping, hollering and cheering, singing along and clapping.

We usually know from the first song if the audience is on our side. Sometimes it takes a couple of verses while Sam, our sound engineer, gets the levels right. But the kit is so good at Glastonbury that it all comes together in the first line of the chorus. We're firing on all cylinders and it feels great.

Cleavey continues with the second verse – '*A plate of Irish stew wouldn't do us any harm . . .*' – and we're away.

By the end of the third verse – '*A nice fat cook wouldn't do us any harm*' – we know it's going to be our day.

While Cleavey sings the verses, our job is to look happy then belt out the choruses with total commitment. But the verses leave time to think and thinking leads to nerves. Billy worries that by the time his turn to sing comes round, his nerves will have got the better of him and his mouth will be so dry he can't sing. It's happened to him twice before, once at the Albert Hall. Johnny Mac frets that he'll get halfway through his song and forget the words; it's happened to all of us at some time. Pete worries that he'll be distracted by someone in the audience; it happened to him on the Platt only a couple of weeks ago. He noticed someone asleep – too much beer, maybe, on a hot evening – and he lost his concentration. Meanwhile, the heat is starting to get to us. Under the lights, in a tent on one of the hottest June days for years, it's baking. Sweat streams down our faces and drips off our noses, but we couldn't be happier.

Glastonbury is all about having a good time, so maybe it's no surprise we're going down a storm. Our music is all about kicking back and enjoying ourselves. We're not preaching any messages or trying to prove anything. We're simply there to rattle it along and get people involved in the singing. And it appears to be working.

When the cheers and clapping subside a bit at the end of the song, Cleavey steps up to the microphone.

'Thank you very much. I can see we are among friends. It's lovely to see so many Cornish people here. I can see someone over there from Lanson . . .'

A big cheer goes up from the Launceston contingent – pronounced Lanson if you're Cornish.

'And somebody over there from Redruth . . .'

Another big cheer, then Cleavey directs his gaze towards the front of the crowd.

'And have you got any Cornish in you, madam?' he says with a cheeky smile. 'I don't suppose you'd like some, would you?'

Moving on quickly, Cleavey changes tack. 'And that first song, ladies and gentlemen, was called 'Drop of Nelson's Blood'. Now let us take you on a voyage through all your emotional seascapes. There will be laughter and tears. There will be joy and despair, bitterness and ferocity. Sweet, sweet sadness and heartbreak. Rudery, crudery and lewdery. And of course, it will all be completely spontaneous.'

The audience cheers.

'The songs we'll be singing this afternoon are all about sailors and the sea. They come from a time when sailors were clapped in irons, flogged from the highest yardarm, nailed to the mast, shanghaied, wanghaied, tattooed, marooned, buggered, muggered, rummed, bummed, crippled, blinded, deafened, drowned and blown to smithereens in battle, sometimes never to return to sweet, sweet Nancy. And that was all before they even set sail.'

After about forty minutes, we're nearing the end of our slot. We've all taken a turn in leading a song, so it's time for our finale: 'South Australia', a farewell song sung by wool and wheat traders as the clipper ships were leaving the docks in London for Australia. Jeremy Brown leads it.

'*In South Australia I was born.*'

And we all join in:

'*Heave away. Haul away!*'

Jeremy again:

'*South Australia round Cape Horn.*'

And the rest of us:

'*And we're bound for South Australia.*'

And so it continues.

> *Haul away you rolling king,*
> *Heave away! Haul away!*
> *All the way you'll hear me sing.*
> *And we're bound for South Australia.*

Again, it's a simple shanty and the crowd laps it up. They haven't stopped singing, hollering and cheering for the entire set.

Judging by the number of St Piran flags, we're playing to a largely Cornish crowd. It certainly has the feel of a home gig and we'd be happy to stay on stage for the rest of the day, but all good things must come to an end. The stage manager is waving from the wings to get us to come off. Wishing we could stay for ever, we leave the stage with cheers and shouts ringing in our ears.

As we walk down the ramp, one of the stage crew puts an ice-cold towel around each of our necks. On our dripping, sweaty skin, they feel fabulous. We all look at each other. Nothing needs saying because we're all thinking the same thing: *Bloody hell. We got through it!*

Johnny Mac is on the phone to his wife, Jill. His voice shaking as he tells her how well it went, he's close to tears as he describes the day so far. Jill is one of the many wives and partners who has been behind us every step of our journey, but she had other commitments that prevented her coming to Glastonbury.

A security guard appears beside us. 'There's people, lots of them,' he says, 'here to talk to you. Is there any chance you could come down and have a word?'

The guard leads us down to the side of the stage, where a large crowd is waiting, something entirely new to us. We're used to having a chat with the crowd after the Platt gigs, usually because we're hanging on to have a few pints outside the Golden Lion, but we've never been swamped like this at the end of a gig. They want us to talk to them or sign autographs. It's very gratifying. Billy meets a lad he hasn't seen since he was making pots in Gloucestershire fifteen years ago. Playing at Glastonbury has been such an overwhelmingly good experience that even John Brown is convinced it's been worthwhile.

'It's lovely when you're doing it and everything's working fine,' he says. 'I don't mind the doing-it bit. And there's something lovely in all going off together to do something. It's just the getting there I don't like. And the hanging around.' Maybe John Brown is our Charlie Watts, who grumbled that his first twenty-five years with the Rolling Stones was five years' work and twenty years' hanging around.

By the time we've finished speaking to the crowd, the next band is coming on and we have to move away from the stage.

As we chat quietly to one another backstage, the adrenaline rush that fired the performance and our initial post-gig excitement seeps away. Some of us seek a television to watch the World Cup football. Others drift off to look around the festival. Most of us are highly impressed. The atmosphere is fantastic, particularly at the Pyramid Stage, where tens of thousands of people congregate, all enjoying themselves harmoniously. Walking the length of the valley, some of us stop at small tents and bars to watch bands, sometimes finding just three musicians playing to two people, which makes us all realise how fortunate we've been to play to such a large crowd on the Acoustic Stage.

Billy and Johnny Mac take John Brown to see Jack Johnson, Ray Davies and Slash, but he is still unimpressed with Glastonbury's offerings. Celebrities and rock stars make no impression on John Brown, mainly because he doesn't recognise any of them. 'Point out anyone famous to me,' he asks Johnny Mac. Celebrity culture has really passed John by. When he and Johnny Mac shared a hotel room, Mac discovered that John didn't recognise any of the Rolling Stones in some photographs hanging on the wall. Mick Jagger and Keith Richard were complete strangers to him. So it's perhaps no surprise that John feels like a fish out of water at Glastonbury.

As the sun lowers in the sky, we return to the backstage area to get our bus home. No all-night parties or campfire conversations for us. Port Isaac beckons and we have to get home.

'Would you come back?' Billy asks John Brown as we wait to board the bus.

'I don't know, Bill,' says John. 'If we ever move up the bill, that's going to bugger us up. It would be nice – really nice – but there'd be a lot of hanging around, not having a drink until we've been on stage.'

Billy smiles. 'Yeah – and you're dropping into the realms of professionalism there.'

John looks apprehensive. 'That's right.'

'And I'm not sure any of us want that to happen, do we?'

'We want the recognition, don't we?' says John. 'But without the professionalism.'

They both laugh.

'But we do, don't we?' says John. 'After all, singing at Glastonbury's a nice thing to do.'

'Yeah,' says Billy.

'But we've done it now.'

It's been a long day. We left Port Isaac at the crack of dawn, travelled all day, performed, and now we're going to travel all the way back to arrive home at stupid o'clock. But at least it gives us a chance for a yarn in the back of the bus. And an opportunity to ponder the strange course we've taken in the last year. One of the biggest mysteries to us is how we managed to attract several thousand people to watch us at Glastonbury when there is so much else going on. There was only a handful of spectators for the band before us and a similar number watched the band that followed us.

Maybe, someone says, it's because sea shanties are timeless and not associated with any particular age group. Everybody can enjoy it.

Or perhaps there's something about our show. It's not particularly sophisticated, but it's different. It seems our mix of hearty shanties sung raw, a few risqué jokes, a bit of folklore and the sense that we are all lifelong mates appeals to our audiences.

Or maybe there's something in the songs' driving rhythm – after all, sea shanties have been helping sailors overcome the tedium of work for centuries. There's certainly something very basic and straightforward about shanties and, in the age of *X Factor* and manufactured bands, perhaps that honesty touches people.

But most of us suspect that the real reason lies in the fact that we're just a group of mates that got lucky. We're no different to any of the people in the audience at Glastonbury. Although we have a recording contract, when it's split ten ways none of us makes much money out of it, so we're all still amateurs who need to work for a living. The three Brown brothers still fish. Trevor and Johnny Mac are builders. Cleavey's a shopkeeper who writes kids' books. Billy's a potter. Nigel sells cakes, John Lethbridge is a farmer and Rowey, the lucky man, has retired and spends most of his time gardening.

Compared to the people who dedicate their lives to singing and making music, who have wonderful voices and great talents, we're a gang of middle-aged Cornish chancers. We're just normal folk singing songs that our ancestors would have sung and we're singing them because we don't want to lose our heritage. It means neither we nor our songs are particularly threatening. We might not be the best singers in the world, but we make a reasonable sound and have not the slightest interest in the trappings of celebrity culture. But above all, we're mates who were all born in the same village, or have lived there for a long time, and who, after living cheek by jowl for decades, have remained as close as we always were. In today's world, that's a relatively rare and precious thing.

By the time we've finished musing, we're nearly back in Port Isaac. Bodmin Moor has been skirted and we've turned off the Atlantic Highway to ride along the top of the hills before taking the turning after Pendoggett towards home.

It's a cloudless night. The stars and moon shine clearly above Lobber Point as we pull to a stop at the top of the village. Shoulders are patted and a good night's sleep wished before we all walk home weary, happy and full of thoughts about an extraordinary day.

By midnight we're all in our cottages, tucked up in bed, the way we like it. Back in Port Isaac. Ready for another day's fishing and working in the place we love.

Port Isaac Terms A–M

Agger Jagger – Very cold pocket of freezing fog.

Anythin' doin'? – Any fish being caught?

Awn – Local name for harbour, derived from the Cornish equivalent, *hean*.

Back – A string of (usually twenty-five) lobster pots lying on the seabed.

Biller – A wave caused by local wind.

Blow up and down – A southerly gale or gusting wind.

Bob lobster – Lobster without claws or commercial value.

Cast – Three herrings made one cast. Forty casts made a hundred herring. If it doesn't add up, that's because it was to the merchants' advantage.

Cripple – A lobster with one claw.

Cuttin' the 'am – To celebrate after the first good herring catch, a leg of ham would be cut.

Doubler – Two gull's eggs in a nest, probably OK for eating.

Dreckly – Any time, with no hurry.

Dummits – Dusk.

Eatin' up – When fish are biting voraciously on bait.

Egg scoffin' – Gull-egg-eating competition.

Emmetts – Outsiders, known in neighbouring counties as 'grockles' or 'blow-ins'. Original meaning: small and numerous crawling insect that infests a habitat (maybe like an ants' nest or woodlice under a stone).

Fairmaids – Smoked pilchards.

Frail – Shopping bag.

Goin' down chain – Going down to Tregardock Beach, which had a steep path with a safety chain.

Goin' down town – Walking down to the bottom of Port Isaac.

Ground sea – Large waves caused by Atlantic storms, often thousands of miles away (wave energy moves across the sea bed as well as the surface).

Gug – A large cave.

Haul, haul, haul! – Emergency call for help at the harbour.

Hoolie – A gale.

Horns! – Traditional Port Isaac superstition yelled when a lobster is spotted in a pot being hauled on to a boat.

Junk mooring – Largest mooring rope and chain in Port Isaac harbour, used to secure a boat fore and aft in a heavy ground sea.

Lake – Local name for the stream running through Port Isaac.

Lek – Mackerel strip used for bait.

Mizzen at half mast – Sign that something is wrong, derived from the wartime practice of fish boats putting their mizzen sail at half mast when returning with a body on board.

Mole – A blenny, or goby. A small fish.

CHAPTER TWO

PORT ISAAC

After the Glastonbury experience, life in Port Isaac returned immediately to the old routines of fishing, working and singing. Being early
July, that included the weekly ritual of singing on the Platt.

From May to September for twenty years, Friday evenings in the
village have followed the same procedure. First thing in the morning,
Peter Rowe loads the sign he first painted more than a dozen years
ago into his wheelbarrow and trundles it down to the Platt, where a
few fishermen are working and tourists are watching the world go by.
He sets it up on the Platt, outside the Mote Restaurant, beside the
lifeboat station, to let anyone who's interested know that Fisherman's
Friends will be singing at eight o'clock. Or as the sign says: *Sailing
Time: Eight Bells Me Hearties . . .*

On a busy Friday in the peak of the tourist season we'll get a few
visitors dropping in on our shops and businesses over the course of
the day, or asking at the Golden Lion, just to check that we really are
singing. And we have to tell them that if the sign's up, then it's happening come rain or shine. We've called it off at the last minute only
once or twice in all the years.

By about six-thirty in the evening, the Platt is starting to fill. By
seven-thirty it's getting tight and on busy nights the crowd will be

spilling on to the lanes up Fore Street and Roscarrock Hill, trying to get a clear view. At about quarter to eight, one of us – usually it's Trevor – will pick up the wheelbarrow to cart our microphones, stands and monitors on to the Platt and Billy will set up his guitar or any other instruments he's playing. If it's busy, we'll be fighting for space with the audience, but that's the nature of it. Sometimes we envy those groups who have roadies to help them set up their kit, but we'd have to pay whoever did it and we don't receive any money for Friday nights on the Platt. All the money we collect goes to charity.

While a few of us are setting up, the rest will be congregating in the Slipway, sipping a pint to steady the nerves. One by one we arrive, some more hurried than others. If the tide's been favourable, or work has been relatively quiet, then there will have been time to go home to eat and wash. But on some Fridays, Julian has turned up still in his fishing boots, having left his son or regular crewman Paul on his boat to deal with the day's catch and moor up while he downs a quick double espresso to kick-start his singing. On a good day, hellos will be exchanged and heads nodded as a greeting. But on a bad day, when the sea's rough or lobster pots have gone missing, it's a time of silence and you might not get a word out of Julian Brown or any of the other fishermen.

A few minutes before eight we drain our glasses and look to the door, often with a slight impatience. Nigel's got the shortest journey – his tea shop is only about fifteen yards from the Platt – but he's always last to turn up. There's a good reason for this and we can time his arrival to the second. The moment *Coronation Street* finishes, he'll be out of his front door and into the Slipway, a sheepish smile on his face.

All correct and present, we push out on to the Platt and line up behind our microphones. Then Cleavey steps forward.

As usual, he prefaces the first song with our promise of some rollocking, bollocking, saucy, bawdy songs, then kicks off proceedings with 'Drop of Nelson's Blood'. At the end of the song, he pauses to acknowledge the applause.

'Ladies and gentlemen,' Jon says as the clapping subsides. 'We are the Fisherman's Friends and we're very proud to be in front of you. We're all from this lovely fishing village that surrounds you.'

Cleavey sweeps his arm to point at the village around the harbour. 'Port Isaac.' He smiles. 'And we're very proud to announce that Port Isaac has just been declared a Unesco world heritage site for inbreeding. Mind you, I don't know what you're all laughing at. It looks a bit bib'n'brace and banjo out there to me. A little bit *Deliverance*, aren't you, eh? But we're wagging our tails with pride. Now, Captain John Brown of the *Winnie the Pooh* will sing this next song. It's called "Bully in the Alley".'

Fisherman's Friends is like a family. And like any family we have our ups and downs, our fighting and squabbling. Then, as Jon Cleave likes to think, 'they realise they're wrong and I'm right and we go on from there'. But really we just settle it over a few pints and a sing down at the pub and everything in our little world is restored.

Maybe we get on so well because actually there's an eleventh member of Fisherman's Friends who unites us and makes us realise that what we've got is something very special. That eleventh member, much older than our combined age of 561, is Port Isaac and it makes us what we are.

Living in such a small village cut into a narrow valley physically pushes us together and we can't help being involved in each other's lives on a daily basis. It's also spiritual. When Billy looks out of the window of his pottery, he can see nearly all our homes dotted along the east side of the valley, which creates a sense of always having your friends close by. People who grow up in Port Isaac might leave in search of work or to see the world, but most of them return. Roots are very important to us.

Eight of us were at school together in the village and our families go back for generations in a place that's been described as secluded from the rest of the world. That's not quite so true these days, particularly as Port Isaac has become known to millions of people through films and television series such as *Saving Grace*, *Poldark* and *Doc Martin*. However, the village hasn't always been quite as idyllic as it appears nowadays on screen. In the 1930s, many of the buildings in the heart of the village – the lanes of slate-roofed whitewashed cottages around the Platt – were in such a poor state they were going to be condemned. If the start of the Second World War hadn't distracted the attention of the authorities, much of the heart of Port Isaac would have been ripped out.

Life on the north coast of Cornwall has always been like the weather: harsh and wild. On average, we have the sunniest and mildest climate in Britain, but statistics only tell half the story and hide the extremes. Jutting into the Atlantic brings a lot of violent winter storms to our hardy, windswept peninsula, summed up in a story our grandparents used to tell.

It's late on the sixth day of Creation. God is admiring his handiwork and putting down his tools, when his eye falls on Cornwall. Standing back to take in a sight that he regards as among his best work, he is tapped on the shoulder by an angel.

'That's a fantastic place,' says the angel, pointing at Cornwall. 'You've given them one of the most spectacular coastlines in the world with rugged cliffs on the north and pretty coves on the south. You've given them inspiring moors and meadows dotted with wild flowers. The ground holds valuable minerals and ores, and the ocean is full of fish, lobster and crab. They're surrounded by beauty and the sun shines more often than not. But isn't Cornwall just a bit too good? Isn't it unfair on the rest of the world?'

God strokes his beard and considers what the angel has just said. 'You're right,' he says. 'You know what? I'll give them the wind.'

So it's perhaps no surprise that the land on the cliffs above Port Isaac bears the scars of hard winters in which gale-force winds pound the coastline for days on end as massive seas crash against jagged rocks below. In winter North Cornwall is a semi-barren place of high stone walls and thick hedges built to offer protection from the full force of the gales that blow in from the Atlantic Ocean. This is Britain's least-wooded county and, for several miles inland, the few shrunken, twisted trees that stand on the tops of hills, misshapen by wind and sea salt, are testament to the forces of nature and winter.

But when spring comes, everything softens. Coconut-scented gorse blossoms yellow on the cliffs. Orchids, cowslips and daffodils line deeply incised lanes. Wild flowers such as squinancywort, eyebright, milkwort, bluebell and thrift dot the fields. And if you trace the deep narrow valleys between the pillow-shaped hills, they lead to coves and bays in which calm, turquoise water sparkles in the sun. And on especially good days, the Atlantic rolls shoreward in corduroy lines that tumble and break into creamy, foaming surf.

Sometime before the fourteenth century, at the end of one of these valleys, in this case leading to the safest natural harbour on this particularly inhospitable stretch of coast, a fishing village was established. Two hundred years later, in the reign of Henry VIII, a landing stage was built (when the tide's low, a rough rectangle of large stones can still be seen just inside our breakwater).

By the seventeenth century, the place was called Porthissick or Portizick Haven or maybe Port Yzak (the names vary on different maps and documents). It's possible the name came from the nature of the village's main trade in those days, *yzak* being the Cornish word for corn. There's a ruin of an old mill about a third of a mile up Port Isaac valley, which adds credence to the theory. And within the village, several of the larger buildings used to be corn chandleries for storing imported wheat and local barley before it was exported.

Whatever the origins of the name, Port Isaac was a relatively prosperous place in the 1600s. Fishing and farming were the principal industries and the sea provided a valuable link to the outside world, making the village and its inhabitants less isolated and inward-looking than many inland Cornish communities. Coastal vessels plied a healthy trade in grain and other commodities to and from Port Isaac and our neighbouring village, Port Gaverne. Slates and ores from nearby tin mines were exported from the pier in our harbour, while timber, coal and stone were brought ashore from beached smacks and ketches. The boats' ballast of bricks was used to build the chimneys on many of the village's homes, which by 1834 comprised about 140 cottages, mostly inhabited by people who made their living from the sea.

By that time, Port Isaac was a jumble of cottages and larger houses, most of them built when the village was in its coastal trade heyday. Today, many of these dwellings have unusual dimensions; their interiors appear smaller than their exterior measurements. Concealed within many of the cottages are hidden rooms, connections to neighbouring properties and secret compartments for moving and storing contraband acquired through smuggling or wrecking, or for hiding young men from the press gangs that would suddenly appear in the village, seeking to seize the best sailors for service in the navy.

The buildings are linked to the Platt at the centre of the village by a network of tiny streets and alleys, or opes, as we call them (it's short for 'opening'). Anyone who visits Port Isaac for the first time is likely to be astounded at the narrowness of some of our pathways, and how they meander and twist. Built at a time when the only forms of transport were horse, donkey or human legs, our village had no need for wide, straight streets that might allow the wind to race off the ocean and between the houses. Among the narrow passageways is Shuggie's Ope, which leads from Rose Hill on to Fore Street (as the high street is called in many parts of Cornwall). Another called Bloody Bones Ope leads from the site of the Golden Lion pub to Bloody Bones Yard, where a dead body was apparently once found in a wheelbarrow. Also running off Fore Street is Squeeze-ee-belly Alley, only eighteen inches wide and deemed in 1978 to be the narrowest public thoroughfare in the world.

In contrast to Port Isaac's contemporary charm, anyone who visited the village in the mid-nineteenth century would have found somewhere that was far from the idyllic place in which we Fisherman's Friends now live and which attracts so many tourists today. The houses were run down, filthy and damp. Most families kept pigs and

ducks, which would wander the streets and beach, and which would
be slaughtered and cleaned in the lanes before being hung from hooks
in the cottage kitchens. And in the days before the breakwater was
built, the sea was a constant threat. A particularly large ground sea
would send waves over the Platt, flooding into cottages in the village.
So it's little wonder that John Watts Trevan, a customs official living
and working in the village, wrote in 1834 that Port Isaac was 'as
mean, dirty and tumultuous place as can well be conceived, a refuge
for all rag tag and bobtail from all quarters and without the least
control of government, the streets narrow and filthy as almost to
render them impassable in time of wet weather'.

Mr Trevan wrote in his memoir of the parish, 'Port Isaac is fast
going to decay, not being nearly so lovely as formerly.' He said that
most of the houses were occupied by 'poor families' as a result of 'the
slate trade being removed to Port Gaverne and the failure of the
pilchard fishing'. Trevan's description was accurate. Coastal vessels had
taken so much sand from the beach for use as ballast that they could
no longer beach in the harbour, tarnishing the jewel in Port Isaac's
crown by turning it into a morass of rocks. The trade on which Port
Isaac had relied for two centuries now passed it by. And to make matters worse, the generation of boats introduced on coastal routes in the
early nineteenth century were too large for small north Cornish
harbours. In the 1890s, the final nail was driven into the coffin of the
village's reliance on sea trade when a railway link to the wider world
arrived with the opening of nearby Port Isaac Road station.

So it is perhaps not too surprising that much of Port Isaac was fit
to be condemned by the 1930s, when our oldest member, Peter
Rowe, was born. Many of the properties were in a terrible state. Few
of them had bathrooms and none had mains water or electricity
supply. The streets were lit by oil lamps. In place of a toilet, most villagers had a pail with a wooden lid. The contents would be thrown
into the Leat, the stream that runs through the village. Bucket and
chuck it, they called it.

Pete grew up in a house that was relatively well appointed by Port

Isaac standards. Next door to the Golden Lion pub at the centre of the village, it had a toilet on the top floor, but the outlet wasn't connected to any kind of sewage processing system. Instead, everything plummeted down a pipe that exited halfway up a wall above the beach.

Ultimately, everything in the village made its way on to the beach. Much of it was carried there by the stream, which had a sluice to help it collect all the muck. Every day the roadman would put down a board across the sluice. Depending on the flow of water, he'd leave the board down all day, or when a big stream was running in winter, he'd leave it in place just for a few hours. When the pool in front of the sluice had filled, he'd knock a lever to release the bar holding the board, sending a tidal wave of the village's waste flowing beneath several buildings, under the road and the Platt, straight on to the beach. On a high spring tide, raw sewage would go straight into the water, but on a neap tide, the village's waste would be distributed across the sand. And in the days before the breakwater was built, the tides would sometimes send sewage rushing back up the stream and into the cottages, giving a nasty shock to anyone in their bathroom. What didn't arrive at the beach via the stream made its way in a series of pipes that emerged through the cliffs above the beach. Again, it all landed on the sand and rocks. The smell was unimaginable. In Pete's words: 'It was evil.'

By today's standards, Pete and the other villagers were living in a Third World slum. They had very little, they were hard-working and they kept their homes clean and tidy, but they would swim and fish in water that had all kinds of deposits floating in it. As for larger items of household rubbish and kitchen waste, a dustcart would do the rounds of the village about once a fortnight, but very few people had dustbins. Instead, they'd carry it all down to the beach and throw it on to the sand. Once or twice a week, someone would build a bonfire on the beach and burn it all. In the meantime, local dogs would roam wild across the beach and through the village, scavenging from the refuse and depositing their mess. It was very basic and remained that way for decades until a sewage farm was built in Port Isaac Valley in the 1970s.

A few years after Peter was born, electricity came to the village. Houses supplied with power were allowed two lights, so Peter's parents installed a light in two of the downstairs rooms, but the rest of the house remained dark at night and Pete took a candle to bed with him at night to read his comics.

Like his father, Peter was born in that candlelit house. He goes back at least three generations in Port Isaac – maybe more but, as he says, 'My grandfather was a bastard, so who knows what came before him?' His home, next door to the Golden Lion, was at the heart of the village. And when Pete blew out his candle, he'd be sent off to sleep by the sound of men singing outside the pub almost every Saturday night, so he grew up with song as the most natural thing to him.

In fact, singing was a very natural thing throughout the village and always has been. When money for the construction of the medieval breakwaters ran out, our fishermen raised funds by singing in concert. And when John Wesley, the founder of the Methodist Church, returned from preaching and singing in a Port Isaac chapel, part of which is now Peter's front room, he described the village as 'the liveliest place in the circuit'.

Compared with the Hickses and the Collinses, the Rowes were not an especially musical family. 'Boy,' Pete's father would say, 'I was a very good singer before tunes and melodies came into it.' But Pete's mother, Kate Symons, made up for her husband's lack of musical talent. She would sing and hum all day around the house. Her sister also sang and played the piano, and they would perform concerts at Bodmin, about fourteen miles away. Performing at Bodmin was part of a family tradition that had been started by their uncle, who as a youngster ran off to join Buffalo Bill's circus when it toured Britain. Having seen a photograph of all the Indians in Buffalo Bill's troupe lined up on horseback at Bodmin, Kate's uncle signed up to play the cornet in Buffalo Bill's band. When he returned a few years later, he formed a band to play concerts at Bodmin and Kate continued the tradition with her sister when Peter was a young lad.

At first, Peter followed his father's lead and had little interest in singing. Like most young tackers in the village, he was more interested in mischief and nonsense. Weekends and holidays would be spent on the beach, building dams, kicking balls about and climbing the cliffs. Inevitably time spent on the beach resulted in an upset stomach, so no summer holiday was complete without a visit to the doctor and maybe a day or two in bed.

Football was a universal obsession among the tackers. Pete and his pals would kick a tennis ball around in the playground of the school, which in those days was in the old school building on Fore Street, above the harbour. Inevitably the ball would get kicked over the wall on to the cliff, so one of Pete's mates would peer over the side and give an indication of how dangerous it would be to collect it. Sometimes it would fall as far as the cave at the bottom of the cliff. If that happened and the tide was in, they'd have to hope for an onshore wind. But more usually it would be stuck somewhere on the rocks.

'It's in second path!' the shout would come.

Of three tracks worn into the cliff, all but the first involved a tricky clamber and descent, more than 100 feet above the rocks. Only the best climbers went down to the bottom path.

'Joe, you'd better go down!' the shout would go out for the best climber when the ball was near the bottom path.

'OK, righto.' And then Joe would scrabble down the cliff while Pete and his mates held their breath.

At dinnertime, all schoolchildren were allowed out on to the beach to play, but only if they obeyed the strict rule of using the street to get there. The shorter route led directly down the cliff, but was strictly off limits. Woe betide anyone caught using the shortcut by Boz Richards, the head teacher. With his dark, slicked-back hair, a severe manner and a handy way with a cane, Boz instilled fear in the pupils. Fair to all, but merciless with anyone who crossed him, Boz had a selection of canes that included one specimen, about ten feet long, with which he could reach pupils at the back of class. It was said he was so strict he'd cane his own son if he misbehaved.

One lunchtime, Pete and four friends got talking to some of the old fishermen who were often down on the beach. Fascinated by the old boys' tales, they didn't notice that the school bell had rung until ten minutes after the end of break.

'You boys, the bell's gone,' one of the fishermen said. 'Get up to school or I'll smack your arse. And you better not let Boz Richards see you.'

Knowing they'd be spotted from the school if they returned via the road, Pete and his mates had no choice but to clamber up the cliff. When they got to the top, Boz was waiting, a tight smile on his face. Pete and his mates were in double trouble – late and using the forbidden cliff path route back to school. That evening, Pete returned home with three cane welts on each hand, an experience he vowed never to repeat.

The Second World War broke out shortly after Peter started his second year at school and the village, like many parts of Cornwall, emptied suddenly of young men. Thousands of vital positions immediately became vacant across the county, so when Peter's thirteen-year-old brother, Jack, announced he was fed up with school, no one persuaded him to stay. The day after leaving school, Jack started at the post office in Bodmin, delivering telegrams. Even in a time of war, child labour was illegal, but in this time of need, nobody took notice of the rules.

One day early in the war, Jack was delivering a telegram in the centre of Bodmin when a German fighter-bomber appeared out of nowhere, skimming the tops of buildings as it flew down Fore Street, the main thoroughfare, machine-gunning all the way. Shocked, he froze to the spot, unable to move as the plane banked towards the railway station and gas works. He gazed open-mouthed as he watched two bombs leave the underside of the aircraft. If it hadn't been for a sailor grabbing him and pulling him beneath a shelter, Jack would almost certainly have been killed by the blast of the bombs, which missed both their intended targets, landing instead on a house in which a very large family was eating lunch, killing the lot.

A few months later, a German plane appeared in the sky above Port Isaac. When it turned inland to follow the line of the valley, the target seemed obvious: Port Isaac Road station, less than four miles away. But the plane continued for about three-quarters of a mile past the station, towards the opening of a railway tunnel, before it dropped its bomb into a field.

The moment Pete and his mates heard a German bomber had attempted to bomb the railway, they started hatching their plan. The next Sunday, Pete, his brother Jack, Pete's friend Billy Brown (an older cousin of John, Julian and Jeremy Brown) and four or five other Port Isaac friends set off to investigate. Pete was only seven, the other tackers weren't much older, and only Jack was in his teens. Parents, they'd decided, should not be informed.

Equipped with nothing but ambition, this motley crew set off to find some shrapnel from the bomb. On their little legs, it was a long journey, but by lunchtime they'd got to the field. An hour or so later, they'd scanned the entire field for souvenirs and had found precisely nothing. Hungry, weary and thirsty, they set off for home. Near Port Isaac Road station, they came down a hill, passed through a valley and then found themselves passing the house of one of Pete's school-mates. In those days, if you lived outside Port Isaac you saw no one from school at weekends, so you can imagine the kid's excitement when Pete and the other tackers appeared on a Sunday afternoon. When his mother invited them all for tea, the poor lad was so excited, he was sick.

It was getting late by the time their school friend had calmed down and they'd all eaten their sandwiches, so Pete and his fellow explorers set off for home. The sky was darkening as they walked down a lane towards Port Isaac. Then they saw a car approaching. It was one of their fathers and he was furious. Ten minutes later, they were in their homes and Pete and Jack were clutching recently smacked arses.

'I got the police out, the coastguard out, everybody out!' Pete's father yelled. 'All looking for you boys. We'd thought you'd fallen off a cliff. I don't want to ever see you leave the village again.'

But Peter's father's threats fell on deaf ears. With all the young men called up to the war, the women did most of the jobs, leaving only children and the old folk in the village. No adult supervision and many children at a loose end made a lethal combination that turned the village into one big playground. And when they tired of the village, the tackers would roam the countryside. They'd go around the cliff edge to Port Gaverne, where Pete's aunts used to work in the net lofts, making nets for the fishermen. There they would play in the chimney stacks and tunnels of the disused copper and tin mines, getting up to the kind of mischief that's possible only when no adults are around. Like the time that Pete went rabbit hunting with his best friend, Brian Orchard.

With a container of nearly a dozen green crabs caught in rock pools and kept lively with some wet seaweed, Pete and Brian set off up Port Isaac valley in search of rabbit holes. Stopping at the first batch of holes, they prepared their ingenious rabbit catcher: a candle was cut into short lengths, one of the stubs was lit and wax dripped on to a crab's back so the stub could be stuck to it. Then the crab and its burning candle was pushed as far down the rabbit hole as Pete or Brian could reach. As soon as the candlelight disappeared into the depths of the warren, Pete and Brian nipped over the bank to wait at one of the holes, their homemade bows and arrows at full stretch, poised to strike. But their ambush was fruitless, so they moved slowly up the valley, releasing crabs and candles into hole after hole. None of them elicited a rabbit. Nothing at all, until they checked the first hole they'd sent a crab down. Faint at first, a light appeared from the darkness. It was the first crab with the lit candle still on its back. Pete and Brian were so impressed, they decided the crab had earned its freedom, so it was returned to the rock pools and released.

The war brought many changes to our village, some of which

seemed faintly ridiculous to villagers in a remote, strategically incon-
sequential corner of the country. Peter's father had spent the First
World War serving on coastal sailing vessels, but he was too old to
serve this time. Instead, he was enlisted into the maritime equivalent
of Dad's Army, the auxiliary coastguard. He already had a car, an
Austin 10 bought in 1933, so he was given a petrol allowance and
an Enfield rifle, and instructed to use his Austin to get to the coastal
lookouts, which were manned day and night.

One fine day some workmen turned up in Port Isaac and started
digging holes in the road directly outside the newsagent's shop that
Peter's mother ran on the days when her husband was fishing. An
official came into the shop, asking for Pete's dad in his capacity as an
auxiliary coastguard. Pete's father was about to go to sea, but first the
official insisted on showing him some concrete-lined holes his workmen had dug in the road outside the shop.

'In the event of an invasion of the north coast of Cornwall,' said the
official, 'your job is to run out and put girders in those holes.'

'You are having me on,' said Pete's father.

'No. These are your orders.'

'But what's to stop them taking the girders out and just driving up
the road?'

'It's not your job to question orders. If panzers come ashore in Port
Isaac, your job is to follow orders and put the girders in the holes.'

'But the houses are made of cob, plaster and lath. The panzers could
just drive straight through them.'

'We can have your orders sent down from London – and they'll still
be your orders.'

The idea that Port Isaac might be of strategic importance kept all the
village amused for weeks, but not as much as the events that occurred
after an American liberty ship carrying cargo across the Atlantic was
sunk by a German U-boat about three miles off Port Isaac. For three
months the ship's barrage balloon flew over the wreck as the villagers
eagerly watched and waited, hoping the cargo would drift towards the
harbour and wondering what helpful items it might bring.

The first container to come ashore split open as it cracked against the rocks, spilling its contents on to the beach. Some small packets with silver paper and American labels looked promising. At a time of severe rationing, the chocolate they contained was a very rare luxury. Unfortunately it had been ruined by sea water, although that didn't stop it melting all over the rocks and attracting the hungry tongues of the dozen or so dogs that in those days ran freely through Port Isaac. Fortunately, the remaining cargo in the container arrived on the beach undamaged. It was immediately seized upon by the kids, thrilled that the American ship had deposited a shipment of what appeared to be party decorations – although these inflatables were an unfamiliar shape. They spent the afternoon blowing up hundreds of the little pink balloons and playing with them on the beach. By that evening, the beach was in a sorry state, the rocks splattered with piles of chocolate-laced dog vomit, while puffed-up condoms bobbed on the water and dotted the beach.

Such amusements were a rarity in the war years. With the men at war, incomes were low and the village neglected. For tackers like Pete, winters were the worst time. All street lights were extinguished and by late afternoon it was too dark for them to do anything out-doors. They tried to play chase, or hide and seek, but soon got fed up, particularly as it was almost impossible to find anyone once they disappeared up a dark alley.

When spring came and the days lengthened, they could get out in the evenings and Pete and his pals would go egging. Pete's pride and joy was his collection of birds' eggs. The thought of it now horrifies him (collecting wild birds' eggs has been illegal since 1954), but in those days there seemed to be millions of birds about and no one knew better. Villagers would often take a boat out to The Mouls, a rocky island about four miles west of Port Isaac, and land a dinghy. With a bucket in hand, they'd collect all sorts of eggs from the nests of birds including puffins, shags, cormorants, razorbills, guillemots and gulls, but they all tasted very fishy. At home, the eggs would be scrambled, fried or boiled, providing a welcome alternative to the standard diet of herring and potatoes.

Pete's dad told him there used to be competitions to see who could eat the most gull eggs for a sixpence prize. The rules were fluid. Before the head-to-head competition started, the participants would decide the rules for the contest, often centred on the question of 'chick or no chick'. If the latter was chosen, they wouldn't eat any eggs that contained foetuses or chicks, but in an infamous bout before Pete's time involving Jimmy Vickery, a larger-than-life character with permanently unwashed hair and greasy, shiny clothes, the contest was neck and neck until it culminated in two eggs both containing chicks. Vickery, who had a reputation for a healthy and fearless appetite (he once ate twelve mackerel at a sitting, then drank the water in which they were boiled), promptly swallowed the entire contents of both eggs. His opponent was immediately sick and Vickery walked off triumphantly with the sixpence prize.

Peter, however, was more interested in the eggs as trophies of his hunting skills. When they got the eggs home, Pete and his mates would carefully make a hole in each end, then blow out the contents. The hollowed egg would be placed carefully in a display box filled with cotton wool. He even had a peregrine falcon's egg, now an endangered species, and one from a reed warbler, which was rare for this area.

In late spring and early summer, Pete's attention turned from his egg collection to fishing for moles, the local name for gobies and blennies. These tiny fish made good bait for larger fish, such as sea bass. To catch moles, Pete would use a slocker – a limpet – attached to a tin hook. With this contraption he'd 'slock' moles out of their hiding holes in the rock pools that lined the beach.

Eventually the days of playing on the beach or cliffs had to come to an end. Secondary school was looming and Pete was identified as a potential grammar school candidate. Mrs Hicks, wife of Port Isaac's singing butcher, spotted his talent and offered extra tuition at home, but Pete was a reluctant academic. He'd sit in the window of his parents' shop, doing his homework, wishing he was somewhere else. Too often, there would be a tapping on the window.

'Pete, come on.' It would be one of his friends.

'All right.'

As Pete headed towards the back door, his father would raise an eyebrow.

'Remember, boy,' his father would say, 'if you can't schemy, you must louster.'

Schemy was working your brain, as in scheming. And louster was working hard with a pick and shovel or a hammer and chisel. The message was clear: use your brain or you'll spend your life doing hard physical work, so Pete ignored his friends' distractions and signed up to Mrs Hicks's extra tuition.

A few months later, Pete passed his eleven plus and was admitted to Camelford Grammar School, about ten miles and half an hour by bus away every weekday morning. With the change in schools came a change in interests and the egg collection was soon swapped for a stamp collection. He also joined a singing class led by a German music teacher called Herr Kaiser, but it didn't last long. Herr Kaiser asked Peter to stop coming because he wasn't good enough. His singing career would have to wait.

Meanwhile the war had come to an end and the men who'd survived the conflict returned home. Among them was Pete's older cousin, Frank, who brought home tales of a very adventurous war. Stationed on tankers, Frank had been torpedoed three times. On the third sinking, he was shipwrecked off the East African coast. With several other sailors, he reached the shore and found himself in a long bay banked by vast cliffs up to 1,000 feet high.

The sailors attempted various escape routes, but after several days had to resign themselves to the fact that the cliffs were unclimbable. They had a few provisions, but only enough to last a few weeks.

Using driftwood and rocks, Frank and his mates laid out a huge SOS sign on the sand, pinning their hopes on the slim likelihood of being spotted from the air. A few days later, a South African mining plane passed overhead. The plane circled the bay several times, then descended low enough for Frank to see the pilot taking photographs. Then everything went quiet. Frank and the other sailors feared the worst. Maybe the pilot had not reported spotting them. Or maybe no one wanted them rescued.

A week or so later, a search party appeared at the top of the cliff. First they waved and shouted. Then they threw down ropes to Frank and his mates. When Frank had hauled himself to the top of the cliff, he learned the reason why they had waited so long to be rescued. The rescuers had come from a village about thirty miles away, cutting bamboo stakes and jabbing them in the ground to mark their route through the jungle to the coast. And, as they traced their steps back to the village, now accompanied by the sailors, they pulled out each bamboo stake until they got home.

It was an extraordinary story that was retold in dozens of Port Isaac homes over the next few months. Having seen Frank go through so much in the war, the Rowe family hoped he would be treated well when he returned to Port Isaac. Shortly before Frank was demobilised, his pregnant wife, Pauline, had applied for one of the prefabricated houses that were going to be built above the village.

As mentioned earlier, most of the houses in the old village were just as primitive as Port Isaac's sewerage system. Owned by a small number of landlords, some worse than others, they were small and damp, although many tenants kept them as clean and tidy as possible. With coal and wood fires for heat, and oil lamps for light, they were also ramshackle and dark, with little provision for the fixtures of twentieth-century life, even then. There was no place for installing a washing machine or parking a car. So when the council proposed building some prefabs at the top of the village, many villagers jumped at the opportunity to move up to larger, lighter, drier homes with toilets, bathrooms, gardens and sunlight streaming through large windows. Suddenly 'down below' emptied as everyone who could moved 'up top', turning the old village very quiet.

Demand was huge for the new prefabs and Pauline was only one of many who missed out. So many villagers were disappointed that the council called a public meeting.

In those days, even very ordinary council meetings were well attended. In the pre-television era, council meetings were considered an entertaining night out. They promised rows, arguments, drama. Sometimes there might even be fights.

On this occasion, with the prefabs at the top of the agenda, nearly everyone in Port Isaac turned up at the village hall, the adults in rows of chairs, the kids squeezed on to window sills at the back. Uncle Dick, twenty years older and much more outgoing than Pete's rather shy father, was nominated to speak on behalf of their cousin, Frank. Standing up to make the case for Frank and his wife to get one of the prefabs, he described Frank as a war hero who deserved a fitting home on his return. He began to make a rousing, impassioned speech, but his pleas fell on stubborn, unsympathetic ears.

'Mr Rowe,' said the parish council chairman, 'this is a council meeting and nothing to do with the war.'

'Wait a second,' the chairman of North Cornwall District Council interrupted. 'I think we should give Mr Rowe a chance. Let's hear his story.'

At the back of the hall, Pete and his mates listened spellbound as Dick related Frank's war stories. At the end of his speech, Dick held up his hand.

'This is what the *King* has given Frank Rowe,' said Dick, flourishing a long stream of medals. 'And *you* won't even give him a house to live in.'

'Mr Rowe,' said the chairman of the district council, 'see me after the meeting.'

At the back of the hall, the lads cheered as if Port Isaac village football club had just won the FA Cup. And, within a few days, Frank and Pauline had been allocated a house.

Pete was soon dropping in on Frank and Pauline to tell them about his newly discovered passion for the Methodist Church. It wasn't the teachings of John Wesley that attracted Pete. Nor was it a new-found spirituality. Pete had started going to chapel simply because the Methodists offered much better social activities than the Anglican church where he had been baptised.

The Methodists promised everything a teenage boy desired: girls, outings to the bright lights of Newquay and a youth club, none of which were offered by the Church of England. Also, the Methodists spent more time singing. Within weeks of joining the Methodist youth club, Pete was attending choir practices and discovering his voice for the first time.

The next step forward in Pete's singing career came when he left school and started his national service with the RAF in South Wales.

Like Spike Milligan, who famously described military service as long periods of boredom interspersed with moments of sheer terror, Pete found most of his national service extremely dull. One of the few interesting interludes occurred when he had the good luck to graduate from square-bashing only days after the death of George VI. Freshly turned out, Pete was among the airmen selected to line the King's funeral route in London and saw every head of state in the world pass by.

Pete was billeted with a group of airmen like the cast of a bad joke: a Cornishman (Pete), a fiery Scot, an Irishman who liked a drink, and a Welshman with a deep fondness for singing. Every Friday night the four of them went out to the pub. Afterwards, as they stumbled drunkenly back to their barracks, the Welshman taught Pete how to harmonise, a skill he never forgot.

When he'd finished his national service, Pete returned to Port Isaac to work in his mother's newsagent's shop. Wanting to settle down, he soon took over the business and set about finding a wife. After taking the advice of the old boys in the village, who warned him that 'you buy the cage first, boy; it's easy to find a bird to put in it', in 1955 he bought his first home. While in the RAF, he'd saved 10 shillings a week of his 24-shilling salary and, added to his other savings, he had accumulated enough money almost to buy outright a cottage in the old village for £550. Two years later, Pete put a bird in his cage, having met his wife Lesley when she came to Port Isaac on holiday from Essex. Married in 1957, they had three children before moving into a house beside one of Port Isaac's two Methodist chapels.

For the next twenty years, Pete grafted as the village newsagent, seeing off a potential competitor by opening a second shop at the top of the village and delivering to every farm and house in the area. The newspapers acted as fantastic slockers for other items in Peter's shop, drawing in customers to buy his sundry goods. Over those twenty years, Port Isaac changed beyond all recognition. The village had always attracted visitors, but in the mid-60s tourism started in earnest. Since many of the locals had moved out of the village to larger houses up the hill, outsiders started to buy up the empty properties to renovate and let them as holiday cottages.

In 1974, Pete split from his wife. Two years later, he was in the Bullers Arms, a pub in Marhamchurch, about twenty-five miles up the coast, on a trip with the Port Isaac ladies' choir. Standing in a back room, watching his pals dancing with their wives and girl-friends, Pete was feeling pretty sorry for himself while he waited for a mate, Mark Provis, to return from the bar.

'Rowey,' said Mark, as he handed Pete his drink, 'every time I've been to the bar, I've seen these two young girls and, do you know what, I think they might be interested in us.'

Pete needed no encouragement and was soon ambling with Mark over to where the two tidily dressed, pretty girls were standing, clearly out for the evening, looking relaxed and very attractive.

'I hope you don't think we are being too forward,' said Mark. 'I wouldn't want you to think we were trying to pick you up.'

'Oh yes we are,' said Pete.

Pete and Liz were married two years later in 1978. After the wedding, Pete and his brother decided to sell the newsagent's and succumb to their heart's desire by investing in a fishing boat. Called the *Francis Kate*, she was a locally built 38-foot fibreglass hull designed for lobsters and shellfish. For the next ten years, Pete devoted himself to fishing with his brother Jack until he retired in 1988. Now footloose, by day Pete devoted himself to his garden, while in the evenings he took his first tentative steps towards proper singing when he joined the Port Isaac mixed choir and, a year later, the Wadebridge Male Voice Choir. After years of making a din in the pub after fishing or gig rowing, getting louder as the pints went down, it was time to turn his talent towards something more harmonious.

Port Isaac Terms N–Z

Never sell before you catch – Harold Brown's superstitious warning, equivalent to counting chickens before they hatch.

Nothin' doin' – Very few fish being caught.

Pad – Round two-handled wicker basket used to carry fish, although we now use one to carry our beer on to the Platt when we sing.

Padstow Pride – Local name for red valerian, a plant that smells of cat's urine.

Parliament – Place in the village where the local fishermen would meet to yarn.

Patchy – Few fish being caught.

Port Isaac varnish – Tar.

Ravel – Waves coming in sets of eight to eleven.

Round turn – Circling the boat to catch mackerel.

Shoot – Put out pots or nets.

Skeggin – A moored boat thudding against the sand when hit by large swells.

Skerrick – Not a bean/complete blank/nothing. Port Isaac equivalent of 'nowt'.

Skiver – Wooden peg for keeping bait in lobster pots.

Slight – Few fish about.

Soldier, soldier! – Traditional local shout when spotting a lobster and crayfish in the same pot.

Spiteful hen – A lobster that has attacked and eaten other lobsters in its pot.

Spouts – Spray from an offshore gale. Fishermen would say that ''twas blowin' so 'ard ''twas comin' off in spouts'.

Tacker – A young lad, from toddler to pre-adolescent.

Thick – Plentiful fish.

Thin – Scarce fish.

Tides are cuttin' – Tides changing from spring to neap, so moving less.

Tides are makin' – Tides changing from neap to spring, so moving more each day.

Town Crows – Port Isaac name for Padstow people.

Town Platt – Flat stone and cement area above the beach and beside the slipway.

Trebler – Three gull's eggs in a nest, of which at least one would contain chicks, so none could be taken.

Weather dog – Large wide stumpy rainbow usually foretelling poor weather.

Weighter – Port Isaac name for a brown crab.

Wind's backin' – Wind direction changed from west to southwest.

Wind's gone out – Wind direction changed from west to north (onshore in Port Isaac harbour).

Yarnigoats – Padstow name for Port Isaac people.

CHAPTER THREE

FISHING

Every night on the Platt is different, but they all follow the same routine. After Cleavey kicks off proceedings with a tub-thumper such as 'Drop of Nelson's Blood', he tosses the lead from the far left of the line, where he stands, to the far right. That's where the three Brown brothers stand. We call them the Brothers Grim – they're fishermen, enough said – and they form a line, broad-shouldered and steady, like a row of statues hewn from Cornish granite. Maybe that's a bit of an exaggeration, but there is something solid and immovable about John, Jeremy and Julian when they're standing on the Platt, like they've grown up out of the ground around them. After all, Port Isaac has been home to their family for centuries. They're fifth-generation fishermen, so they're as much a part of the place as the Platt and the fishing boats.

John has just sung 'Bully in the Alley', a shanty about a group of paid-off sailors who stash their drunk mate – 'bully' – in an alley for safekeeping until they have to return to ship. It's a West Indian halyard shanty that John pinched from somewhere nearly twenty years ago. Although he can't remember where he first heard it, he likes it because the verses tell a story that's easy to remember and it brings back memories of his days at sea.

Cleavey steps up to the microphone to introduce the next song.

'That was Captain John Brown leading "Bully in the Alley",' says Jon. 'Now, ladies and gentlemen, we're very fortunate tonight to have three captains to sing to you, so it's a bit like buses really. You don't see one for years and then all of a sudden, three come along at once.

'Next up is John's brother, Captain Jeremy Brown of the *Free Spirit*, the nemesis of the lobster, ladies and gentlemen. With his hurricane-proof quiff, he's going to sing you one of his lovely songs. All these songs are round about two hundred years old. They date back to a time when maybe a quarter of the population was involved in seaborne activities, so these are *our* songs. These are songs of the people.

'If anyone out there is taking notes, this song that Jeremy is going to sing for you now is called "John Kanaka-naka". And John Kanaka was a name for a Hawaiian male that appeared in many crew lists on ships bound for the western seaboard of the United States during the Gold Rush, so this song has a bit of a feel of the *haka* about it.'

'*I thought I heard the old man say,*' sings Jeremy.

'*John Kanaka-naka too lie ay,*' we all respond.

'*Today, today is a holiday,*' Jeremy continues before we join him.

'*John Kanaka-naka too lie ay.*'

Then we all sing the chorus: '*Too lie ay, oh, too lie ay. John Kanaka-naka too lie ay.*'

Sometimes it takes a song or two for us to wake up to the fact that it's a Friday night and we're actually on the Platt again, singing. We all lead very busy lives, so we don't have a lot of time to think about it beforehand. The boys who are fishing will sometimes still smell of the sea when they're standing beside us. They'll have done little more than grab a bit of tea, have a shower and then they're straight back down again to the Platt. But by the end of the second song, at the latest, our attention is fully on the singing. Maybe that's why Cleavey starts to get fruity at this point.

'Now Captain Julian Brown of the *Helen Clare* is going to sing for you,' says Cleavey after we've finished 'John Kanaka-naka'. 'This next song is "Pay Me My Money Down". He's got a bit of a throat today, Julian. A few of us go down with these bugs and things over the year. He has had to consult his health-care professional, as they call doctors these days, who suggested he might like to suck on a well-known popular lozenge. Obviously I am not at liberty to say what sort because jokes about sucking Fisherman's Friends are obviously bad form and unworthy in this company. And jokes like that can easily leave a nasty taste in the mouth.'

Without further ado – and to spare the blushes – Julian cracks into 'Pay Me My Money Down', a work song that originated among the Negro stevedores working in the Sea Islands off the coast of Georgia and South Carolina. It came through Pete Seeger via Bruce Springsteen to Julian Brown, and we're not sure whether they're missing it yet. Julian likes to practise it when he's out at sea harassing lobsters and other innocent crustaceans, and then he sings it to the fish merchants he deals with. If Julian's had a particularly bad day at sea, these are the first words any of us will hear directly from him this evening.

> *I thought I heard the Captain say,*
> *Pay me my money down,*
> *Tomorrow is our sailing day,*
> *Pay me my money down.*
> *Oh pay me, oh pay me,*
> *Pay me my money down,*
> *Pay me or go to jail,*
> *Pay me my money down.*

Fishing has always been the heart and soul of the Fisherman's Friends. We all have the sea in our blood. Peter Rowe is a retired fisherman. Jeremy and Julian Brown fished with their father when they were lads and they now fish with their sons as crew. John Brown used to fish with his brothers and he now runs mackerel-fishing trips in the tourist season. Trevor fishes part time (but don't mention that to the Brown brothers). And the rest of us have all crewed or helped out on fishing boats.

Everyone in Port Isaac respects the fact that the village is still a working harbour. It is not a museum piece and the work of the fishermen always comes first. Visit Port Isaac in the early morning or late afternoon and it's likely you'll see fishermen standing over the stern of their small punts, motoring them or sculling them by twisting a blade to and fro in the water.

In the morning the fishermen use the punts to carry themselves and their baits from the beach to their fishing boats moored near the breakwater. At the end of the day they use the punts to carry their catch ashore. It's a scene that appears not to have changed for centuries, but in fact Port Isaac's fishing industry is now tiny in comparison to its eighteenth-century heyday, when most of the able-bodied men in the village were called upon to assist when the fishing was good. Nowadays only a handful of families fish full time. The biggest change, however, is in the type of catch. Port Isaac's fishermen now spend most of the year potting for crab and lobster, but the village grew up around pilchard and herring fishing, in part because of our unique position at the northern limit of pilchard-fishing waters and the southern extreme of the herring fishery.

Cornish pilchards have recently gone through a renaissance on the menus of some of the classiest fish restaurants in the country, but for decades they were regarded as little better than cat food. The turning point came about fifteen years ago, when sufficient people had visited Mediterranean countries to discover the pleasures of fresh sardines. In 1997, some bright spark had the idea of rebranding pilchards as Cornish sardines – sardines are the same as pilchards, but younger and smaller – and sales took off. Now, Cornish sardines are a recognised regional food, protected by European Union legislation, like Parma ham, Roquefort cheese or champagne.

Although the Cornish fishery dates back to around 1200, it didn't become significant until Tudor times. Elizabeth I was the first

monarch to regulate it. In her reign nearly 2,000 fishermen were reg-
istered as working out of Cornish harbours and the southwest
fisheries of Cornwall and Devon outclassed those of eastern England.
From around 1750 until about 1880, pilchard fishing was the largest
source of income for most Cornish coastal communities, even though
the main season ran for only eight weeks from mid-July to mid-
September. Providing food, income and oil for lamps, it wasn't for
nothing that Cornish villagers described pilchard fishing as 'food,
money, light, and all in one night'.

In the 1750s, the four principal Cornish ports of Falmouth, Fowey,
Penzance and St Ives caught an average of 900 million pilchards a year,
although in those days it was recorded as 30,000 hogsheads (the
hogshead was a standardised measure of volume equivalent to nearly 53
gallons). Most of the fish were preserved in salt to keep at least a year
and exported to Italy, which offered a better market for pilchards, particularly during Lent, when the Church forbade the eating of meat. The
irony that fishermen from predominantly Protestant Cornwall, which
had little time for Catholicism, supplied vast quantities of pilchards to
Catholic Italy was remarked upon in a poem that was traditionally
recited in a toast to the Pope at the end of the pilchard season.

> *Here's a health to the Pope,*
> *And may he repent,*
> *And lengthen by six months*
> *The term of his Lent.*
> *It's always declared*
> *Betwixt the two poles,*
> *There's nothing like pilchards*
> *For saving of souls.*

Even larger catches were recorded at the end of the eighteenth
century, by which time St Ives, about forty miles down the coast from
Port Isaac, was landing more pilchards than all the other Cornish ports
put together. These days of plenty came to an abrupt end in 1830,

when the bounty, a tax rebate on the salt used for curing pilchards, was abolished. Many fish merchants immediately pulled out of pilchards and by 1847 Cornish exports had declined by nearly 90 per cent, most of it still bound for Italy.

It might seem ludicrous that an island nation such as Britain had such a low appreciation of the food freely available around its own shores, but it's no different from the present day. Almost all the shell-fish now caught in Cornish waters is exported to Spain and France. Every Tuesday, Port Isaac fishermen haul their crabs and lobsters to the top of the hill above the harbour, where large seawater container trucks wait to ferry them to the Continent. If it seems ridiculous that few of these riches of the sea end up on British tables, there's a simple explanation: we are often happy to eat seafood when on holiday abroad – much of it, ironically, from Cornwall – but we don't buy it when at home.

The old pilchard fishery was quite different from any type of fishing now practised in fishing villages such as Port Isaac. The biggest difference was that the fishermen were not self-employed operators who shared the profit they made from their catch with their crews. Instead, a few wealthy businessmen paid a wage to the men of Port Isaac to fish for pilchards and then kept most of the profits.

The only local resident to gain a share of the profits was the huer, an eagle-eyed character employed solely to spot approaching pilchard shoals from the cliffs and alert the fishermen. In the seventeenth and eighteenth centuries the Cornish coast was dotted with huts, in which huers sat from dawn to dusk for four months of the season (a month either side of the main season). Although huers' huts have survived at other parts of the North Cornwall coast, such as at Newquay, there's no sign of a hut at Port Isaac, so it's more likely that the huer positioned himself on the cliff path above the harbour.

Strictly forbidden from indulging in anything that distracted his attention from watching the sea, such as playing cards or reading, the huer scanned the sea for the telltale purple oily patch on the water that heralded a bountiful pilchard shoal.

'Hevva! Hevva!' – or 'Here they are! Here they are!' – the huer would shout through a long trumpet as soon as he spotted a shoal. At the sound of the huer's cry, the leading fisherman, called the master seiner, rushed to sea with his crew in the main seine boat, a low-gunnelled wooden vessel up to forty feet long. Powered by up to eight oarsmen and pursued by two to four other boats, known as followers, they went in search of pilchards, as described in a traditional rhyme.

> *The Pilchards are come, and hevva is heard,*
> *And the town from the top to the bottom is stirred.*
> *Anxious faces are hurrying in every direction.*
> *To take a fine shoal they have no objection.*
> *The women now gathered before the White Hart,*
> *Their hopes and their fears to each other impart,*
> *'What stem have you got?' 'A first to the lea',*
> *'And look! Our men are now going to sea.'*
> *We see the huer with bushes in hand,*
> *Upon the white rock he now takes his stand.*
> *While 'Right off', 'Win tow boat', 'Hurray' and 'Cowl rooze'*
> *Are signals no seiner will ever refuse.*

The last lines of the rhyme describe how the huer typically stood in front of his hut or on the bare cliff, feverishly waving two small cloth-covered bushes to direct the master seiner towards the shoal. The nineteenth-century novelist Wilkie Collins, who wrote about pilchard fishing in a collection of travel essays, described the huer as 'a man standing on the extreme edge of a precipice, just over the sea, gesticulating in a very remarkable manner, with a bush in his hand . . . in short, apparently acting the part of a maniac of the most dangerous character'.

Any astonishment at the huer's antics would only increase, Collins suggested, if it were known that this man was receiving on average a guinea a week (around £900 in current earnings) for his apparently bizarre behaviour. But there was a method in the madness. 'The man with the bush was an important agent in the Pilchard Fishery of Cornwall,' Collins wrote. 'And ... the men in the boat were guided by his gesticulations alone, in securing the fish on which they and all their countrymen on the coast depend for a livelihood.'

This maniacal, wealthy character held the fate and fortune of the village in his hands. Under his direction, the boats encircled the shoal in a gigantic seine net with a mesh sufficiently small to prevent any escaping. At least 1,000 feet long, this 'keep' net had a row of corks along its top edge and weights along its bottom edge to keep it anchored to the seabed. The follower boats carried a smaller stop net, which was used to seal the open end of the seine net. In combination, the two nets functioned like a vast prison. Huge numbers of pilchards were caught in this way. At St Ives in 1834, fishermen trapped more than 30 million in one such seine net.

Once the seine net had been secured, the men used huge wooden capstans to drag the entire mass closer to shore. Then a second net, called a tuck, was used to encircle a portion of the catch, sometimes by dragging it up from the bottom of the keep net. When drawn in, the tuck net, which might stretch to fifty feet in width, could trap so many pilchards that the water's surface would turn solid with fish. Wicker 'dipper' baskets were then dropped into the water to remove the fish, which were emptied into a 'dipper boat', often filled until its gunnels remained only inches above the sea surface. If the catch was strikingly large, several groups of fishermen employed by different merchants would work together to land and store the fish.

The huer's cry of 'Hevva!' lives on today in the Hevva Cake, a thick, sweet, sugar-encrusted currant bun baked with saffron that's sold in many Cornish bakeries. Traditionally it was baked when the fishermen went to sea; by the time the crews returned to land, it had cooled and was ready for eating. These days, Hevva Cakes are sold in bakeries all along the Cornish coast.

As for the pilchards, bringing them ashore was only the beginning of a long process of preparing them for export to Italy. One of the cellars used to prepare pilchards still remains at Port Isaac. Looking out to sea, it's to the left of the Platt and now houses a couple of seafood stalls as well as John Brown's fishing museum and some storage space used by Port Isaac's fishermen. It's one of the few old cellars anywhere in Britain still in use by fishermen; most have been converted to very desirable homes with a view of the harbour and sea. In the eighteenth century, the cellars in Cornish ports were sometimes referred to as pilchard palaces. Given their enviable locations, it's not difficult to see why.

In their day, the lofts above the Port Isaac cellars were stuffed with seine nets and the courtyard was a hive of activity as the village's women raced to preserve each day's haul from the tuck net. The oily fish did not keep long in captivity or after landing; any fish remaining in the keep net after five days were released because there was little chance that they would last long enough to be successfully cured.

For the first part of the curing process, the pilchards were stacked five feet high in blocks of alternating layers of salt and fish. Over the next five weeks, large amounts of oil oozed out of the fish, which was collected for burning in oil lamps in the village. At the end of this stage of the process, the fish were washed off and laid in barrels for pressing. After another week under heavy stone weights, they were ready for transportation to Italy.

All this busy industry came to a fairly sudden end in the 1840s. Positioned at the northernmost reach of the Cornish pilchard fishery, Port Isaac was among the first ports to suffer from the decline in stocks. Some blamed overfishing. The locals blamed steam-powered fishing boats for enabling drift nets to be used further out to sea, unsettling shoals and preventing them reaching shallower water. Whatever the actual cause, the combination of declining catches and the abolishment of the 'pilchard bounty' tax rebate on curing salt prompted the fish-cellar owners to sell off their entire businesses including the boats, seine nets, ropes and sails, curing equipment and salt. Fortunately there was another fish in Port Isaac waters to keep the village population from starvation and penury.

Silver herrings never matched the riches that pilchards brought, but they provided Port Isaac with a dependable income. The season was short, lasting from late October to December, but at least it came. Port Isaac families could buy provisions and coal on the promise that payment would follow 'when the 'errin's come', although on the few occasions when the herrings failed to show, their absence bankrupted local businesses as well as the fishermen.

With much of their annual income dependent on the short herring season, Port Isaac's fishermen went to sea in almost any conditions that allowed them to shoot their nets and haul in their catch. Dusk was the optimum time for catching herring as it relied on the fish swimming into a long drift net, and they always swam at the end of the day. Herring crews aimed to shoot their nets shortly before dusk, then waited for a few hours to haul in the nets under darkness.

The inevitable risks of fishing under the cover of darkness at a time of year when Atlantic storms could be at their fiercest always played on the minds of the crews, but they had no choice. Fishermen had to go to sea when the season was short and when so much of the village's livelihood relied upon it. Early every afternoon, as the sun approached the horizon on the short autumn and winter days, the alley-ways of Port Isaac reverberated to the clatter of the heavy wooden-soled thigh-high leather boots worn by the fishermen making their way to the Platt, carrying sou'westers, oilskins, stoneware water casks and snack tins. Punts carried them to heavily built wooden carvel boats painted inside and out with tar. Depending on their size, each boat had a crew of two to five and anything from two to fifteen nets. Mean-while, the retired fishermen climbed 'uptill' (up the hill), from where these 'watchers' would keep an eye on the fleet, identifying the boats solely by their single lights.

After shooting their nets, the boats waited at sea, then hauled in their nets. When particularly large amounts of herring were caught, only half the net might be hauled in. The remaining net was marked with a buoy and a flare lit to advertise the net's contents to any other crew with a poor catch.

Successful catches were brought into Port Isaac harbour, allowing the boat to go aground on the beach. Then, under bright flare lights and frequently the gaze of half the village, the fishermen would shake out the herring from the drift nets on to canvas sheets. In December, when darkness fell particularly early, the school day had often not finished by the time the herring boats returned to port and, if there was an especially magnificent catch, the boys would be allowed out of school early to stand in barrels beside the boat so they did not become entwined in the nets as they helped with the shake-out.

The catch would be split. Fresh herrings did not travel well in those days; by the time they were hauled to market under horse power, they wouldn't be worth selling. So a portion of the catch was sold to villagers at knockdown prices. Some was hawked to other villages and farms. And the rest was preserved, either salted or smoked to make kippers that would last the winter. In the winter months it was said nineteen out of twenty Port Isaac families ate salted herring and potatoes – errin'n'spuds, it was called – six nights a week.

The big change for the village's herring fishery came in 1895, when Port Isaac Road railway station opened. At last, Port Isaac had ready access to a wider market and the amount of fish that left the village bound for Britain's cities immediately quadrupled. Sadly, this upturn in Port Isaac's fortunes came to a sudden end in 1901, when the railway reached Padstow and the village's fishermen had to compete with their greatest rivals for the attention of fish merchants up country.

Although no more than ten miles apart, there has always been a fierce rivalry between Port Isaac and Padstow, so the extension of rail to Padstow did a fraught relationship no favours. No one really knows from where the enmity stems, but everyone knows it's there and that it goes back a long way. Maybe it's because press gangs used to operate out of Padstow. They were always coming over to our village to force our young men with seafaring experience into joining the navy. In around 1770, a press gang arrived in Port Isaac from Padstow and a local character called John Barrett ran up the valley to hide. He was

so terrified (and, admittedly, a bit simple) that he climbed through a
gorse bush to stick his head and shoulders in a badger hole. He was
spotted by a husbandman, as farmers were called then, who cracked
up laughing. Unsurprisingly, the press gang decided he wasn't suitable
material for a life in the navy and passed him by, but many other Port
Isaac lads were forcibly recruited into service.

Part of the rivalry with Padstow stems from it being the nearest
fishing port to Port Isaac. We've always thought our Padstow counter-
parts were a bit soft and spoiled because their estuary port is protected
from the worst of the weather. It allows beam trawlers to operate out
of Padstow, which lobster and crab fishermen blame for damaging
their pots and the seabed. The Padstow fishermen also have a reputation for boasting. We call them Town Crows because they crow
about how many fish they've caught. In return, they call us Yarnigoats
because getting to sea from Port Isaac is so difficult that our fishermen
spend most of their time telling yarns. It's a fair comment, but does
nothing for relations between us.

Of all of us, the Brown brothers have the longest and proudest
fishing heritage. Their father was a fisherman, as were their grandfather, great-grandfather and probably several generations before
that. Of the three brothers, Julian and Jeremy fish full time, while John
runs his mackerel-fishing trips for tourists in the summer. Jeremy says
he decides whether to go fishing by putting a candle on his window
ledge and 'if it blows out, there's too much wind; if it don't blow out,
there ain't enough', but actually he will be out at sea whenever the
weather allows, even if that's every day for a month.

A fishing day starts long before the sun rises and often finishes after
it sets. Weather forecasts are taken with a pinch of salt – the Browns'
father used to say 'forecasts will either drown you or starve you' – so the
only reliable indicator is to take a look for yourself. Julian's living room
has a splendid view of Port Isaac Bay, so he barely has to step out of
bed to assess whether it's worth putting on his yellow wellies and water-
proofs to go to sea (among Port Isaac sailors, green is considered unlucky
and strictly forbidden on board). But there's little likelihood that Julian

would pass on his assessment to Jeremy. Fishermen are a competitive lot at the best of times (although they'll always help a colleague in distress), but few are more competitive than two fisherman brothers. Jeremy also likes to take a look up the coast for himself. From Port Isaac, you can see Lundy Island on a clear day. But as Jeremy says, 'If you can see Lundy, it's going to rain. And if you can't see it, it's raining already.'

Fishing these days is very different from the way it was when the village relied on herrings and pilchards. Although our fishermen will shoot a net once in a while, most of their effort is concentrated on potting for crab and lobster – and it can be back-breaking work. Every day they can get to sea, Julian and Jeremy will check and bait 300 to 400 pots spread over more than 150 square miles of the North Atlantic. Each of those pots can weigh 25 kilograms or more. And each of them has to be hauled from waters up to 150 feet deep.

On a good day, Julian or Jeremy will return to Port Isaac with half a ton of crab and maybe fifty or sixty lobsters on board. On a bad day, they'll return with a fraction of that, not even enough to cover the cost of diesel (around £100 a day), let alone the six-figure loan on the boat. And on a really bad day, it doesn't bear thinking about what might have happened. 'Sometimes Davy Jones has too much time on his hands,' says Jeremy. 'That's when he likes to mess with our heads.'

There's plenty of opportunity for Davy Jones to wreak havoc on a fishing boat. Those heavy pots are not hauled entirely by hand. A winch and a pulley are used to drag the pots from the deep. 'If you get your fingers caught in the pulley, you'll be looking for your fingers in your gloves,' says Jeremy. 'And if you get your fingers in the winch you'll lose your hand.'

But the most dangerous moment in lobster-potting comes after all twenty-five pots in a line (we call it a back of pots) have been hauled on deck. After each pot is lifted on to a stainless-steel workbench, it's wrenched open and the contents examined. Any lobsters in the pot are greeted with a triumphant cry of 'Horns!' – a Port Isaac tradition – but at least half of them and a similar proportion of crabs will be unsuitable for keeping. Their shells might be too soft, or they might be smaller than the minimum size specified by fishery officials, so they are tossed unharmed back into the water.

Each pot is cleaned out, then baited with gurnard, salt herring, salt mackerel or ray, cut with a razor-sharp blade. They're then stacked sequentially on deck, the line of rope connecting the pots carefully laid out so that it won't tangle. When an entire back of pots has been cleaned, baited and stacked, the skipper returns to his wheelhouse to decide where to shoot this back of pots into the water. Years ago, when the Browns' father was potting, his decision was based on years of experience plus a large amount of intuition topped with an even bigger dollop of luck. These days, it's a much more exact science. Lobster fishermen have a wealth of technology at their fingertips, ranging from GPS plots, online databases and three-dimensional topographs of the ocean floor on a touchscreen computer. They even use iPhone apps to track the movement of French trawlers or to provide a better appraisal of the weather than the shipping forecast. But ultimately, nothing beats hands-on experience.

When the optimum location for shooting the back of pots has been fixed with the GPS, the skipper reaches out of his wheelhouse window to release a rope that sends the back of pots and two buoys shooting through a trapdoor at the stern of the boat. As each of the heavy pots shoots off the back of the boat, the line of rope coils and flicks violently across the deck.

'If you get caught in those ropes,' says Jeremy, 'you will be pulled down fifty metres to the ocean floor in no time.'

Jeremy should know. He's seen it happen to a mate, who survived with burst ear drums, snapped ankles and a desire never to step on a boat again. All the modern wonders of today's computer and satellite technology cannot compensate for the sheer physicality and inherent danger of fishing off the North Cornwall coast. It's no wonder that few Port Isaac villagers now make their living from fishing; it's something that needs to be in your blood.

'I remember a few years back a bloke came up from Falmouth on the south coast to look at fishing here,' says Jeremy. 'But he took one look and turned back. He said: "To be honest, you have to be born here to fish here. No one would ever choose to fish out of Port Isaac. It's not an easy port.'"

All of the Brown brothers were born in Port Isaac, so they certainly have fishing in their blood. However, even though their father and grandfather fished, none of the Brown brothers took it for granted that they'd grow up to be fishermen. Fishing was strictly a working-class pursuit and their mother, Joanna, was very much a middle-class lady whose arrival in Port Isaac in the 1950s caused quite a stir.

Born in Pakistan to a 10th Gurkha Rifles colonel who had been wounded at Gallipoli in the First World War, Joanna grew up in Quetta, near the Afghan border. One of her earliest memories was being woken up by the crash of a clock falling off her bedside table when she was about four years old. As the house shook around her, Joanna's father grabbed her out of her bed and ran outside with her in his arms. The 1935 Balochistan earthquake, one of the largest ever to hit South Asia, was tearing Quetta apart. Up to 60,000 people died, but fortunately the local battalion was away on manoeuvres and escaped unharmed. It immediately returned to Quetta to take control of the situation. Within hours of the earthquake, soldiers were rescuing people from the wreckage of buildings and attending to the wounded. Put in charge of dealing with huge numbers of dead bodies, Joanna's father spotted a young woman's hand moving in the middle of a pile of corpses on the back of a bullock cart that was passing him. He grabbed the hand and pulled the young woman out from among the dead, probably saving her life.

When Joanna reached school age, she was packed on to a liner bound for Southampton so she could be educated in Britain. From then on, most of each year was spent at an English boarding school. Summers were spent in Pakistan or India, where she learned to drive, running over a local woman in the process (fortunately not seriously hurting her). When she returned to England, Joanna met an Oxford-educated man called James Pallister. When she reached her mid-twenties, she moved with Pallister to Port Isaac to take over the landlordship of the Golden Lion. One winter's evening not long after they arrived, Joanna's eye fell on a handsome young fisherman who had come into the pub in his white sea boots. Maybe Pallister noticed his wife's burgeoning new friendship with the fisherman in the white boots, but decided to turn a blind eye. Or maybe he never thought a Cornish fisherman, less wealthy and less educated than himself, could turn the head of his thoroughly middle-class colonial wife. Whatever Pallister's thoughts, his attention was soon distracted by the birth of his first child, a boy, at Queen Charlotte's Hospital in London. When Joanna returned to Port Isaac, they baptised the newborn at St Endellion, a few miles inland. He was christened Julian Pallister.

For six months, the three of them lived above the Golden Lion in Port Isaac. Meanwhile, the fisherman in the white boots moved to Bristol, where he had found a job working on the river. One day, Joanna took her young baby to Port Isaac Road station to board a train via Bristol to London, where the two of them were meant to meet Pallister. As the steam train puffed up country towards the capital, Joanna realised that she had to make a choice: she could stay on the train and meet her husband at Paddington station; or she could follow her heart and get off the train at Bristol.

The decision was not straightforward. Divorce was not an easy option in the 1950s, particularly in a small, isolated village like Port Isaac. But by the time the train pulled into Temple Meads station at Bristol, she'd made up her mind and the train continued to London without Joanna and her young son, Julian. Eighteen months later Joanna returned to Port Isaac, having divorced James. Her son, now approaching his second birthday, had taken on the surname of his true father, the fisherman in the white boots, Harold Brown.

Harold Brown was a Port Isaac man through and through. His father and grandfather had both worked the trading ships that plied the North Cornwall coast and the English Channel in the early part of the twentieth century. In common with the maternal side of the family, both of them saw action in the wars. In the Second World War, Harold's father was stationed on a barrage balloon boat in Plymouth Sound, while his great-grandfather, Carveth (Pa Brown), was lucky to survive a close encounter with the enemy in the First World War. Pa was working on a merchant ship off St Ives called the *Isabella* when a German submarine surfaced nearby. The U-boat captain ordered Pa and the rest of the crew off the ship. Rather than waste a torpedo, the captain sank their ship with gunfire while Pa and his mates looked on as they rowed towards St Ives. A relatively civilised way to conduct a war.

Joanna, Harold and Julian moved into a small chalet belonging to Harold's father at the top of the village. When they had saved enough money for a deposit, they rented Brook Cottage, a tiny property at the bottom of the village. By then, a second son, John, had joined them. Another two years and Jeremy came along, making four J. Browns under the same roof, causing no end of complications when the post arrived.

When he was three, Julian picked up a kidney complaint that was misdiagnosed. A course of antibiotics would have cleared it up, but by the time the infection was noticed, one of his kidneys had failed. His other kidney gradually became worse until at the age of twenty-one it had almost stopped working, and Julian would travel with his mother down to Plymouth twice a week for dialysis. The dialysis needles seemed like they were the thickness of knitting needles, but the procedure soon became such a routine that Julian would hook himself up to the machine. Eventually, he had his own machine in a hut in the Browns' garden, where he would sit for six hours twice a week to have his blood cleaned, a regimen he was told he'd have to follow for the rest of his life. While he was growing up, Julian didn't let it stop him indulging in the favourite pastimes of all young Port Isaac lads, such as looking after the fishermen's punts when the tide was too low – 'Will 'ee keep me punt for a while?' the fishermen would ask – or swimming among the condoms and 'sausages' in the harbour, fishing for moles with a bent pin and a length of cotton thread, or crabbing in the rock pools. Catching eels from the stream as it passed under Fore Street bridge was a favourite. The eels were caught only for sport, not for eating or selling, although Julian managed to use them to earn a few pennies from some tourists one day. Sitting out in the sunshine, eating at the Slipway Restaurant, the tourists felt their pleasant lunch was being spoiled by the sight of Julian's eels writhing in a glass tank beside the restaurant's tables, so they paid him to release them. Never one to turn down an easy buck, Julian happily obliged.

Like most young lads growing up in Port Isaac in the 1960s, the Brown boys had plenty of close scrapes with danger, such as the time Julian was swimming in the harbour when he was about ten years old. He had never been a good swimmer and this time he simply ran out of strokes. Thinking it was all over for him, Julian was fighting for his life, but lacking the strength he needed to keep afloat. Just as he was about to sink beneath the surface and drown, a hand appeared beneath his elbow. It was Mark Provis, one of his best mates and a lovely, polite, easy-going lad who Joanna Brown held up as an example to her three sons. Without Mark's support all the way back to the beach, Julian would probably have drowned.

On another occasion, he was on the cliffs, hoping to add to his sizeable collection of wren, swallow and gull eggs. He'd previously been attacked by a rook when climbing a tree to steal one of her eggs, but the pride of his collection was a fulmer's egg, which was considered especially hard to get. On this day, Julian was inching along the cliff beneath the coastguard station to climb on to a dangerously high and slippery section of cliff above a sewage pipe that ran out over the rocks. Beneath him, a friend was paddling a boat in the bay, keeping it off the rocks that lay directly beneath the part of the cliff on to which Julian had climbed. Julian had already found a few gulls' eggs, but they were relatively unprized among egg collectors, so he decided to throw them at his friend in the boat. The first couple of eggs fell short, so Julian abandoned caution, released his one-handed hold of the cliff and threw his third egg as hard as he could. Thrown off his feet by the momentum of his throw, he skidded down the cliff, desperately trying to get a hold as he slid and bumped down the slope. At the last moment, shortly before he was about to fall to certain death on the rocks below, Julian regained his balance and grabbed hold of a tufted bush to stop him falling off the cliff. It was the last time he went egging on the cliffs.

Growing up in a small village in which everyone lived on top of each other meant that there was always an older person around to keep an eye on us little tackers – either to tell us off if we were doing something we shouldn't, or to come to our aid if we'd fallen over, hurt ourselves or found ourselves in difficulty. Knowing that there was always a watchful adult nearby meant our parents had no worries if, from the age of five, we were out of the door straight after breakfast to play in the streets and around the harbour. We'd come home for lunch, then go out again until teatime. In the summer, we'd be outdoors again immediately after tea until the sun set and the village was dark.

That combination of freedom to roam coupled with almost constant adult supervision by other villagers was a good thing, as growing up in Port Isaac involved much more rough-and-tumble than today. Like all of us, Julian and his mates used to have stone fights, throwing rocks and pebbles at each other until someone got their head cut open or picked up a particularly nasty bruise. We'd stop, but do it all again a week later when the injuries had healed. Throwing stones at each other might sound extreme but it was just boys having a good time, doing what boys have always done. However, we were probably the last generation brought up in that way, a generation that had respect for its elders, but also knew how to fight and how to defend ourselves. The village had one of the best boxing clubs in the country and, even at school, we were often left to sort out our differences with our fists. When Julian joined the infant class at the village school, Boz Richards, the feared headmaster who had ruled over Peter Rowe's generation with a cane and an iron will, was still in place. Julian remembers a frightened hush descending on all the pupils when Boz appeared at the door that led into the dining room. But Boz's response to the sight of two boys fighting, and maybe some blood on the floor, was to walk away and let them get on with it. His attitude was that boys were like dogs; if you stopped dogs fighting, they'd do it again. But if you let them have a good scrap, they'd sort out some sort of pecking order.

Another favourite childhood pastime was to annoy the brass bands that used to visit Port Isaac in the summer. On Tuesdays, the Bodmin brass band would march through the village; on Thursdays it was the band from St Breward. They started on the Platt, then they would walk through the streets and alleys, playing marching tunes as they made their way up to the top of the village. Villagers and tourists would follow them, dancing all the way up to The Terrace, a street at the top of Port Isaac, and all the way back down again when the band returned. As they passed along the route, one of the band members would shake a tin to collect donations for charity. They would collect a small fortune. Without the drinking culture of today, there was little else in the 1960s for holidaymakers to do in the evenings, so they would come out and dance. At the peak of the season, there would be so many onlookers and dancers that Port Isaac needed two special constables to keep the traffic flowing and the crowds in line.

Of course, us young lads couldn't simply join in with the festivities. Not when there was potential for mischief. We would stretch a rubber band around an old wooden clothes peg, then jam half a match into it. When the clothes peg was opened, it propelled the match a long distance. On a good evening, we could get matches into the top of the tuba as the band walked past and we'd yelp with delight as we saw our little projectiles disappear down the big horn.

It was an intense, idyllic childhood, but back at home, times were hard for the Brown family. Julian remembers how his parents spent weeks deciding whether they could afford to buy him a pair of new shoes for his fifth birthday. And like many Port Isaac families, they didn't have enough money for a car, so the Brown brothers didn't venture far from Port Isaac until Julian was ten, John was eight and

Jeremy was five years old. Julian remembers going on a school trip to Rough Tor on Bodmin Moor, less than nine miles away, when he was nine years old, and being astonished that a lot of the other children knew about Bodmin Moor and had visited it before.

Money was tight for the Browns primarily because the price of fish plummeted in the early 1960s, when the fishing season lasted only from May to September. And although Port Isaac's fishermen had started to catch more lobsters, the demand for them was much lower than today, mainly because few lobsters were exported.

To make ends meet, in the spring and summer Harold would go mackereling in the evenings after he'd returned from potting with his uncle, Nibs. When Julian was only five or six years old, he joined his father for the first time, and so the love of the sea was passed on from father to son. A few years later, Julian's younger brothers took his place, first John and then Jeremy. Harold taught his sons the behaviour of the tides, the vagaries of the back eddies, the position of the rocks and the best marks for fishing. Using a hand-line, they'd reel out twenty fathoms of twine with about a dozen hooks, each a hand's span apart from the next. They would keep the boat moving until they found a shoal, then they'd circle the shoal, pulling up the line and flicking it against the inside of the boat to shake the mackerel off the hooks.

After Nibs gave John his first boat, an eleven-foot clinker rowing boat, when he was about eleven years old, John would go out with his mates, fishing for mackerel to sell on bits of string to tourists and to hawk around the village. A few years later, John got himself a small petrol engine, called a Seagull. John Mills, a neighbour, taught him how to start it using a piece of rope, how to replace the spark plugs, and how to service it. John could then venture further afield to fish for bass as well as mackerel and to haul pots for crab and lobster.

When he wasn't fishing for mackerel, Harold would spend evenings digging his vast vegetable garden. It was fortunate he was such a strong man, but eventually even the pots, the mackerel and the vegetable garden were not enough to keep the wolf from the door, particularly after the potting season ended in late October. Julian, Jeremy and John can remember how one year, their father, faced with a winter with no income, decided to join the men who left Port Isaac every winter morning on a minibus to the clay pits at St Austell, about twenty-five miles away. It was a filthy job and it paid a pittance, but at least it was steady money. Every evening, Harold would return covered in white dust after a day spent in part of the largest china clay pits in the world. His work involved using huge monitor jets to blast the clay out of the quarry with water. It was then pumped into settling pits. When the water had drained off, Harold and his workmates shovelled the clay into lorries that would take it to a plant where it would be dried and shipped off to customers. It was mind-numbing and demoralising work for someone who was used to fishing, out on the sea by themselves. After one winter at the clay pits, Harold decided he'd had enough. 'Let's put the trawl back on board,' he said. 'Let's have a go at that. Because I'm never going down that clay pit again.'

Trawling for dabs and plaice during the winter season was a less reliable way to make a living, but it was exciting and fun, and most important of all for a man who lived for the sea, it was on a boat. Harold left the harbour just as dawn was breaking and usually trawled twice in a day. By the time he and the other trawling fishermen returned, it was always dark and cold and none of us tackers waiting at the Platt knew what they had on board. The catch, in boxes, was brought up the beach, lugged into the fish cellars, washed off, then gutted properly. Then, when the catch had been assessed, Harold would get some of the boys in the village – among them a young Billy Hawkins, about fourteen at the time – and give them a few boxes of the fish that were too small to go to market.

'Here,' Harold Brown would say, 'take these, go up round the houses, knock on doors and bring me back the money.'

A few years later, Julian and John took over the rounds, but by then their father allowed them to keep everything they earned as pocket money. The fish they sold were so small they weren't worth gutting.

But they were so fresh, some of them were still moving when the customers rifled through the boxes looking for the best. Selling fish at
thruppence each (one and a quarter pence in today's money) wasn't
a fast route to riches, but on particularly good nights they would be
running back to the fish cellars for a second wooden box. On one
occasion, Julian made thirty bob (£1.50) from his round. More
importantly, he'd taken his fate into his own hands. The fishermen
earned a few extra pounds from their fish; John, Julian, and some of
the Port Isaac lads before them, earned a few bob for delivering the
fish; and the villagers got to buy cheap fish straight off the boat.
Everyone benefited. Good times for all.

The Brown brothers grew up thinking that only one future awaited
them: a fisherman's life. But when each of them finished school, Harold,
in spite of his passion for fishing, tried to dissuade them from staking
their future on such a precarious and potentially dangerous way of
making a living.

'Fishing will always be here,' Harold Brown told each of his sons.
'You want to get out and see a bit of the world. When you've got
your fill there, you can come back and go fishing – if you must.'

Fishing was a relentless pursuit, Harold Brown reminded his sons.
With all the days lost to rough weather and mechanical breakdowns,
no fisherman could afford to take time off when the weather was fine
and there was an opportunity to go to sea. In all their years together,
Harold and Joanna had tried only once to take a holiday with the
children. A chalet had been booked at Butlin's in Minehead, but at
the last minute Harold had told the family to go without him. Like
any fisherman, he couldn't make plans to be away from home, just in
case he missed favourable fishing weather.

Julian's mother, who never shook herself entirely free of her
middle-class roots, also wanted her sons to make something of their
lives. Her eldest son should be an accountant, she decided. Her
younger sons should train to do something other than fish. So the
lads surrendered to their parents' demands, but the concession only
went so far. The sea, they made sure, would still figure in their lives.

Julian went to university to study biological sciences, specialising in fish and taking his degree while still on a dialysis machine. John wanted to join the army, but was dissuaded by his parents, so he went to Wadebridge to serve an apprenticeship as a marine engineer. You can lead a Brown brother away from the sea, but you can't make him ignore it.

Cornish Fishing Facts

Some forty species of fish can be caught in the waters around Cornwall, more than off the coast of anywhere else in Britain. Of these, twelve – cod, Dover sole, haddock, hake, ling, mackerel, megrim sole, monkfish, plaice, pollack, saithe and whiting – are subject to quotas that restrict the amount we can land. Non-quota fish include bream, brill, conger, crab, cuttlefish, dogfish, grey mullet, gurnard, John Dory, lemon sole, lobster, octopus, ray, red mullet, scallops, sea bass, shark, spider crab, squid, tope, turbot and wrasse. In the Fal Estuary, we've also got oyster beds that date back to Roman times.

More than £26 million worth of fish are landed by Cornish fishermen each year. It might sound a lot, but with 4,000 people employed across the Cornish fishing industry (of which relatively few are fishermen), it equates to just £6,500 per person each year. Nevertheless, Newlyn on the south coast is Britain's largest fishing port by value of fish landed.

Less than one-third of all fish caught by Cornish fishermen is consumed in Britain (i.e. more than two-thirds is exported), but fish landed in a Cornish port at dusk will arrive at Billingsgate market by 3 a.m., to be sold by 6 a.m. and arrive on tables in London restaurants by midday.

CHAPTER FOUR

GROWING UP

After opening with some tub-thumping shanties, it's time for Trevor Grills – we call him Toastie – to change the mood. If we were in a concert hall, and if we were in any way professional and organised about our stage act, the lights would dim moodily at this point. But instead we're the anarchic Fisherman's Friends and we're on the Platt, so we just have to rely on Trevor's voice. But first Cleavey butts in.

'Ladies and gentlemen, at the end of the day, when the sailors had worked up a sweat splicing the main brace, heaving and hauling and jolly-rogering the ubiquitous cabin boy, the sailors would gather around the foredeck of the boat and cuddle up together.'

Cleavey grins. 'They'd plump up the Cath Kidston nautical scatter cushions. They'd light seaweed-scented joss sticks. And then they would sing one another sad songs and laments of home. Quite frankly, bloody miserable songs. And Trevor is a leading exponent of these songs. He's not miserable himself, just a little touchy-feely.'

On cue, Toastie launches into 'The Last Leviathan' and, to be frank, it's heartstring-tugging stuff.

My soul has been torn from me and I am bleeding,
My heart it has been rent and I am crying,

All the beauty around me fades and I am screaming,
I am the last of the great whales,
And I am dying.

But it's not just the words that put lumps into everyone's throats. It's Trevor's voice. Our wives, partners and girlfriends – we call them the FFWAGS – call Trevor the housewife's choice, and with good reason. If you came to Port Isaac by day, you'd probably spot Toastie in his overalls with a hammer in his hand, looking very macho. But when he's not repairing or building houses, he's the quietest and shyest of our group. And maybe that's what gives him the most emotive voice of any of us.

For years, Trevor sat in the pub, joining in the songs we were singing but never leading them. Then, one day, he sang a solo for the first time. Hairs on all our necks stood up, even on Cleavey's, and he's as bald as a coot. The rest of us have the kind of voices you'd expect from male shanty singers – loud, passionate and a bit bawdy – but not Trevor. Toastie's voice is like a bell. It rings clear and it drips with melancholic heartache. His high tenor makes grown women melt.

When Trevor finishes singing about the last great whale, Cleavey steps up to the microphone. 'Not a dry eye in the house,' he says. Then Cleavey shakes his head. 'Ladies and gentlemen, come on! Get over it. It's just a large lump of sushi.'

By now we've reached the centre of the line-up. It's also the naughty corner, where the trouble happens. First up is John Lethbridge. We call him Jubbers or Lefty. With Billy Hawkins, who's standing next to him, he's the butt of most of our mickey-taking. In fact, taking the mickey is what the Fisherman's Friends is all about. Lefty and Billy are both a bit older than some of us (and younger than others, no names mentioned). They're also a bit smaller, which is why we put them at the middle, a valley between two hills. Cleavey introduces Lefty.

'Now we come to the nasty little bit in the middle, ladies and gentlemen,' says Cleavey. 'Lefty's particularly proud of himself as he's just been approached by Matey bath foam. He's been asked to be the model for the next bottle of bubble bath.'

It's maybe a cruel joke, but Lefty really does look a bit like the Matey bottle, so we all break out in song. '*He's a bottle of fun. You'll always find him in the bath. He's always hanging around. He's always good for a laugh.*'

Lefty smiles weakly; he doesn't take it to heart, particularly as he's heard a lot worse. Then he opens his lungs to lead his song.

> *Well, me father often told me, when I was just a lad,*
> *A sailor's life was very hard, the food was always bad.*
> *But now I've joined the Navy, aboard a Man o' War*
> *And now I find a sailor ain't a sailor any more.*

Although it sounds like a centuries-old sea ballad, this shanty, called 'A Sailor Ain't a Sailor', is one of the few we sing by a contemporary songwriter. It's the first song ever written by Tom Lewis, a lovely man from Northern Ireland who served seventeen years as a Royal Navy submariner before becoming one of the folk world's leading shanty singer-songwriters. The rest of us join in the chorus.

> *Don't haul on the rope, don't climb up the mast,*
> *If you see a sailing ship it might be your last,*
> *Get your civvies ready for another run ashore,*
> *A sailor ain't a sailor, ain't a sailor any more.*

These days, you'll often find Trevor up a drainpipe or hanging from a gutter, renovating one of Port Isaac's old cottages or houses. He's worked in the village all his life, spending most of the last forty years repairing some of our finest buildings, which seems quite appropriate given that Trevor is one of only two in the group that were actually born in Port Isaac. Most of the other Fisherman's Friends were born in nearby hospitals, but Trevor was born in a house on Church Hill and his father was born in Middle Street, so Trev's Port Isaac to the core. Toastie is also one hundred per cent Celt. His paternal grandfather, Tom, emigrated from Ireland to Wales, where he met Trevor's grandmother, who was Welsh, and joined the Coastguard Service. In the 1900s, Tom was posted to Port Isaac, where Trevor's father, Fred, was born. After the war, Fred moved to Southampton to do building work on bomb-damage sites. While he was in Southampton, Fred met a young lass from Plymouth called Frances, who had spent the war interned in the Channel Islands. A few years later, Frances moved to Port Isaac to work for our local GP and bumped into Fred again. They soon got together and early in 1959, Trevor was born.

The Grills lived in the house in which Trevor was born until he was seven, when like many other villagers they seized the chance to move into a larger, brighter, drier council house at the top of Port Isaac. At that time, Trevor's dad was offered one of the old cottages for all of £50 (about £1,200 in today's money), but even that was too much for a cold, dark, damp cottage without heating or electricity, especially when modern comforts were being touted at the top of the hill. Nowadays a similar property wouldn't leave much change from half a million pounds, which is why few Port Isaac youngsters can afford to live in the village in which they grew up.

The exodus of locals from around the Platt opened up the traditional slate-roofed cottages to outsiders, who bought them as second homes. It changed the nature of the village, although it provided plenty of work for Trevor's father, a carpenter and builder. Trevor trained with him and took over the family business when his dad retired, most of their work coming from outsiders wanting to renovate and maintain the old cottages. As a result, the cottages are in a better state now than ever, but it has turned the centre of the village into a much quieter place outside the peak holiday times. In the summer, Port Isaac is completely lit up, but in November or December, you can look across the valley and hardly see a light on anywhere. The exodus of locals and the closing of the school halfway up Fore Street changed the feel of the place for ever. When a new school was built in the mid-70s, the final chapter was sealed. The closure of the old school moved the heart and soul out of the village. Until then, people would congregate around the school twice a day to drop off and pick up their children, keeping the old centre alive. When Trevor and his dad were working at the bottom of the village, they'd hear the school bell and they knew exactly what time it was. After the old school closed, they'd only hear it when the wind was in the right direction to blow the sound from the new school 'up top'. Same bell but in a different place.

With the closure of the school and the selling of the old cottages to holidaymakers and second-homers, many of the shops and businesses also disappeared from the village. We used to have a small supermarket, four banks, a post office, two butchers and a grocer in the streets around the Platt. We've got none of that now. Instead, it's all gift shops, galleries, cafés and restaurants. Nice places, for sure – and some of us run those shops, cafés and galleries – but it makes the village a different place from when we were tackers.

Now in his early fifties, Trevor's age puts him at the younger end of the Fisherman's Friends. He always says he had a perfect childhood with wonderful parents. These were happy times, playing on the beach, sailing home-made tin boats, sculling punts in the harbour, exploring the valley and building camps. On Sundays his mother would dress him up in his best gear, then take him up to chapel, where Trevor would go to Sunday school. Afterwards, they'd go home for Sunday dinner and then the family would go for a walk in the afternoon. It was the same routine every Sunday and Trevor loved it.

Trevor also loved school, not so much for the work and lessons, but for the fun to be had at break times. There were only around fifty pupils, divided into three classes in one large school room separated by screens, so everyone knew everyone else. Boz Richards was still the headmaster then, but he'd mellowed a bit and when the lifeboat came to Port Isaac in 1967, he joined the crew. Whenever a shout went out, he would let all his class run out to watch the lifeboat leave the harbour. At lunch break, a lady called Mrs Gilbert looked after us.

A real proper old dear with grey hair in a bun with a needle through it, she'd bring out old-fashioned games for us to play and teach us playground games like Tim Tom Tammy, which was a bit like hide and seek crossed with catch.

While Trevor was at primary school, the council built a sewage processing works up the valley and, at last, Port Isaac's harbour became a much cleaner place. In those days, treated sewage was pumped out to sea, a long way beyond the breakwater. In order to sink the discharge pipe beneath the beach, a trench was blasted out of the rock, leaving piles of stones all over the bay. Trevor and his mates built huge columns, about five or six feet high, from the stones. Then, as the tide came in, they would climb on to them and see who could remain standing the longest. Most would bail out when the water neared the tops of their thighs and their shorts were about to get wet, but one of Trevor's mates, a lad called Nicky Hicks who got into some real squeaks, would stick it out for much longer. Trevor and his pals would shout at him – 'I bet you can't stay there that long, Nick'– and Nick would just smile as the water rose around him. Eventually, when the water was up to his neck, he'd give in and swim up to the beach. His clothes were soaked, but he had won the bet.

One of Trevor's earliest memories is of hanging around the main gate at the primary school, playing with an orange in his hand. Behind Trevor's back, John Brown crept up on him from behind and pinched his orange. He taunted Trevor for a short while, then let the orange roll off down the road. It was all an innocent laugh. That is until a car appeared, coming up the hill, and ran over Toastie's orange. Trevor's never forgotten – or forgiven – John for it. In fact, he says, he doesn't think he ever will.

Trevor would always have us round to his house as a kid for his birthday parties. John Brown would be there and maybe Julian, too, although he was slightly older. One year, when he was old enough, Jeremy Brown was invited. Always a shy tacker, he arrived, took one look at Toastie, gave him his present, said nothing, burst into tears and rushed out the door. His mum took him straight home. Again, Trevor's never forgotten it.

If you ask Trevor how long he's known the Brown brothers, he'll say he doesn't know. It's not that he's forgotten; it's just that he can't remember a time when he didn't know them. They all played together in the alleys and opes and on the beach. When they were older, they were all members of the Port Isaac football team, managed by Peter Rowe. Being fast, Trevor was on the wing, although we called it wide left or wide right. John Brown was at centre-half (although he later moved to full back) and several other future Fisherman's Friends also played. Cleavey was intermittently in the team because he spent some of his childhood living in Wadebridge. When he was twelve he moved to the village, but he was still in and out all the time, even though he was by then a permanent resident. That's when we realised the true cause of his on–off attendance. Cleavey was afraid of getting his hair messed up. Ironic, maybe, considering how little he has nowadays.

Jeremy Brown was also always keen to play but, being a few years younger, didn't always get a game. And when he did get to play, sometimes it didn't last long. On one occasion, we played out at St Kew, about three miles from Port Isaac.

'Come on, Pete,' said Jeremy, jumping up and down on the line, desperate as ever to get stuck in. 'Put me on. Put me on.'

But Pete was a very tactical manager. That's to say, he had tactics, even if they didn't always make much sense to any of us. On this occasion, as on almost every other previous occurrence, he wasn't going to let on to us, his players, just what he had in mind.

'Hang on a minute, Jeremy,' said Peter. 'I've got a plan.'

Eventually, when Jeremy was looking like he'd burst if he didn't get a run-out, Peter turned to him and nodded. 'Get warmed up, then, Jer,' he said.

Jeremy needed no encouragement. Like a bull suddenly unleashed, he ran on to the pitch, full of enthusiasm and vigour.

The ref immediately blew his whistle.

'Oi you!' he said. 'Over here. Now.'

Jeremy ran over to the referee. Seconds later, he was headed back towards where he'd just come from, his head lowered. The ref had booked him for running on the pitch without permission. Jeremy was gutted. Sent off and he hadn't even touched the ball.

We'd all train once a week on the football field above the village. Pete had a Triumph Herald with a soft top in those days and somehow he managed to get the whole team in it every week to give us a lift up the hill. Two of us would sit in the front, one on the passenger seat, the other on his lap. Pete would put the roof down and open the boot. Four of us sat on the back seat. Three of us sat on the collapsed roof, above the back seat, our knees between each of the lads sitting in the back of the car. And two of the team would be in the boot, facing backwards, our legs dangling over the bumper.

Even when we went to away matches, Pete would transport all of us, squashed into his Triumph Herald, legs dangling over the sides for the ten or so miles to Wadebridge or Camelford, and fifteen miles to Bodmin. And when we arrived, we'd promptly get hammered. Always.

In those days, there was only one junior football league in our part of Cornwall. It was ideal for under-sixteens teams, but not so good if you were under-elevens or under-twelves. Like us. Wadebridge beat us 17–0. It sounds bad, but that was nothing. Bodmin beat us 19–0.

Week in, week out, we got stuffed. It went on for years. Returning home after a match every week, we didn't need to tell our families the result. They knew before we walked in the door that we'd been beaten. Thinking back on it, it seems crazy to have put up with it for so long, but we just liked playing together, so we endured the weekly ritual of defeat, actually enjoying it and consoling ourselves that we weren't being beaten because we were rubbish, but because we were often half the size of our opponents. And then, when we were about to run out of youthful optimism and enthusiasm, we came good. Sometime before we reached eighteen, we gelled as a team. We'd been playing together for so long, we instinctively knew what to do. And after years of defeat, we learned how to win. From then on, we were one of the best teams in the league. We carried on playing for years after that, Pete still managing us, involved in all our lives through football. The only downside, as far as Trevor was concerned, came when we reached the cup final one year. He'd played in every round, including a crucial role in winning the semifinal, but when final day came, he chose to work instead. He needed the money and reasoned that he'd already done his bit. Well, we only went and won the bloody cup. And Trevor, through his own actions, missed out. Of course, we still tease him about it today.

Of all the Fisherman's Friends, only one of us that grew up in Port Isaac didn't play football regularly. That was Billy, who stands with Trevor and John Lethbridge at the heart of the line-up on the Platt. Billy's among the older members of the group, so he was leaving Port Isaac for art college just as the rest of us were starting to play in the team. Although there's nine years between them, Billy and Trevor knew each other as kids. In those days there were so many kids knocking around the village that none of us needed to mix with anyone older or younger, but Port Isaac was so small and contained that you couldn't help knowing just about everyone else. Billy's mother was particularly close to the Brown brothers' mother, so he was always round at John, Julian and Jeremy's house, playing or killing time while their mothers drank tea or whatever else came to hand, gossiping, laughing and putting the world to rights.

Both from military backgrounds, Joanna Brown and Billy's mother, Di Hawkins, were really thick with each other. Boxing Days and other family celebrations were always spent in each other's houses, partying and yarning. Brought together by their similar backgrounds, they were a well-to-do, larger-than-life, fearsome and formidable duo. Woe betide anyone who got caught in their radar. If any of us kids were causing trouble or making too much noise, just a glance or a few words from Di or Joanna would be enough to silence us. We respected them and would never think of giving them any cheek. It just didn't happen; there was no talking back.

Di was born in Plymouth, where her father ran several grocer's shops. In the 1920s, her father put her in charge of collecting the rents every Friday from his shops and various other properties he owned in Plymouth. But Di was a wild thing and one week she disappeared after collecting the rent money, blowing it all on fur coats, having a good time and making the most of the Roaring Twenties. Eventually she met Billy's dad, a pilot from Staffordshire, and they married. For the next twenty-five years they hopped between air-force bases around the world and what remained of the British Empire. Billy spent three years in Egypt until, at the age of six, he and his parents had to make a sharp exit because of the Suez crisis. A few days after they left, Billy's older brother was among the pilots who flew bombing raids on Egypt from Malta. Just over a year later, this same brother was involved in the British nuclear weapons tests at Christmas Island, flying close to the detonated hydrogen bomb's mushroom cloud. He died six years later of ill-health that Billy's family believes was related to the extreme doses of radiation that he suffered.

Meanwhile, Billy's father progressed up the ranks to squadron leader before retiring. Like several other ex-military people who headed west, they wound up in Port Isaac, simply because if you had a forces pension to support you, it was an idyllic place to live. The baby of his family, Billy also had an older sister. He came to Port Isaac when he was ten years old. It was the first place he'd lived in for more than two years.

Billy's parents settled in very quickly, Di frequently setting up camp in the bar of the Golden Lion for drinking sessions with Joanna Brown and a bunch of ex-officers. And when Di got together with Joanna, mayhem ensued. Boy, those two could party. Wearing big hats, dressed to the nines and with gin'n'tonics in hand, they'd put the world to rights. You could hear them giggling and yapping from down the street. Meanwhile, Billy and John were left sitting outside, knowing there was no chance of tea that night.

Billy found settling in to Port Isaac slightly more difficult than his mother. With his background, he found it quite a hostile place. To him, we seemed a big group of local lads who didn't speak like him. Billy found us intimidating, but within six months he had slotted in. You might say he learned how to stick up for himself, but it was more than that. From the moment he arrived, Billy took Port Isaac into his heart. To him, the village was all about fishing and he loved it, so it wasn't long before he felt at home. And when we noticed that, he immediately became one of us.

Shortly after arriving, Billy found himself a Saturday job as a butcher's boy, delivering meat all over the village for Mr Carling, grandfather of Will Carling, the future England rugby captain. It was a good job, paying 7s 6d (37.5 pence) for a day's work, but the best time was Christmas, when Billy would pick up a five-bob (25 pence) tip from every house he visited.

Billy was also a dab hand at making skivers, the wooden skewers that went on the side of lobster pots to hold the mackerel bait in place. With a reputation as the best skiver maker in the village, he'd get half a crown (12.5 pence) for fifty of them, which would take him all day to make. Sitting in the fish cellars, whittling at wood, Billy would sell them to three or four fishermen in the village. It was important to find the right wood with very slight grain. Old pine pit props from the coal mines, found at sea or washed up on the shore, were ideal. They had to be chopped to a certain length, then split.

Billy was taught how to make skivers by Chingy, one of the old retired fishermen who would congregate in the village to tell yarns and watch the world go by. When we were tackers, there would be little gangs of ten or twelve old boys dotted around the village whenever the weather was at least half-good. Some of them would be down on the beach, a few would be around the Platt and a couple would sit on the benches halfway up Fore Street, outside the old lifeboat station that is now Cleavey's shop. That seat was particularly popular because it's a sunny little spot. It's warm and the wall offers protection from the cold wind, so you could always find an old fisherman there, sitting and watching the goings-on in the harbour.

These old boys didn't do much. Most of the time, they would

congregate in lines, waiting their turn to walk up and down the street, three or four or more abreast. Having spent a lot of time at sea, they'd got used to a life in which their main form of recreational exercise was walking across the deck, again and again. Now on dry land, they continued the habit, so we would see groups of them striding back and forth. Sometimes they talked, sometimes they didn't talk and sometimes they just smoked their pipes. For hours on end, they just walked up and down in companionable silence. And when they weren't walking, they sat on the edge of the Platt, yarning, smoking their pipes and, occasionally, arguing. Some would get up and walk away when politics entered the conversation, but most of the time, they reminisced about their lives at sea and kept an eye on us tackers, making sure we didn't cause too much trouble.

All the old boys dressed the same: a peaked cap, big boots, a navy-blue thick serge suit so dark it was almost black, and a white wool guernsey jumper often embroidered on the back with the name of a famous racing yacht in navy-blue lettering. They were tough men who had seen a lot, so we all respected them highly and they had a big influence on all of us growing up in the village.

One of the best things about living in Port Isaac is that no one sticks only to their own generation. It's such a small population that we all have to mix well with each other. When we were growing up, everyone knew their friends' siblings and their parents and grandparents by their first names. And the old boys were part of that. We saw them as friends, but we never thought of being cheeky to them or disobeying their instructions. And if we crossed them, they'd grab hold of us and shake us like rats. Even making a couple of skivers badly was enough to get a shake out of them, usually with a barked telling-off: 'No, not like that. I showed you once!'

Of all the old boys, Norman 'Chingy' Short was the most respected by some of us and probably the most mischievous. All of them had a twinkle in their eye – if a visitor was to come down and act rudely or arrogantly while asking directions, they might send them off in the wrong direction – but Chingy was the cheekiest of them all. He taught Billy to roll cigarettes and smoke when he was thirteen.

About six foot six and thin as a bean stem, Chingy had fished in the winters, but in the summer, like many of the fishermen of his generation, he crewed big yachts in the Mediterranean. Nearly every Port Isaac fisherman working in the first half of the twentieth century would shoot off in the summer to crew on yachts. Port Isaac sailors had a good reputation and were highly sought after. Without much ado they could find berths on the best boats in the Mediterranean and North America. One of them, Dan Mutton, even crewed on an Americas Cup yacht. After competing at Newport on the east coast of America, Dan's crew sailed their boat back across the Atlantic. Somewhere in the mid-Atlantic, they were hit by a fierce storm. A few days later, back in the village the locals heard that the yacht had not arrived as scheduled after passing through the storm. Believing Dan had drowned, no one in the village expected ever to see him again. But three weeks later, the yacht arrived in a British port. Although she had lost her mast, the crew had retrieved half of it, rigged up a smaller jury mast, cut the sails to fit and limped back home.

The Brown brothers' father, Harold, also occasionally went yachting in the summer. He crewed a millionaire's boat in the Mediterranean, spending most of his time polishing the brass, moving the boat from port to port and looking smart.

Having lived through two world wars, experienced countless adventures at sea and seen things that most of us in Port Isaac couldn't even imagine, the old boys were extremely capable men. But the thing that impressed us most about Chingy was his ability to gurn. Somehow (none of us could work out quite how) Chingy could bring his lower lip right up over his nose, so that it almost touched the bottom of his eyes.

In some villages, gurning is a competition sport, a rural English tradition that we haven't adopted in Cornwall, where we've got better things to do, like eating pasties. There's even a world gurning championship at which contestants traditionally frame their faces through

a horse collar – known as gurnin' through a braffin'. Some of the best
gurners are those with no teeth, which allows them to squeeze their
jaws tighter together, but Chingy had all his teeth; he could just do it
anyway and we loved to watch it.

Chingy was an all-round entertainer for young tackers and we never
tired of listening to him holding court or teaching us things. One day
it would be knots. Another day he'd teach us to make skivers. But he
was a hard taskmaster. 'That's a good boy,' he'd say, looking at one of
our skivers. Then he'd break it and chuck it away. It was good, but not
good enough.

In the summer, Billy often rowed Chingy down on a spring tide
towards Port Quin, west along the coast from Port Isaac. Chingy
knew the whereabouts of a rock near Port Quin that was particularly
good for large mussels that were only exposed at spring tide. It was
about three miles – hard work for Billy, so he often took another lad,
Mark Townsend, with him to share the load and the reward of ten
Senior Service cigarettes each. Then, while Chingy collected buck-
ets of mussels, Billy and Mark would wait in the boat before rowing
him the three miles back to Port Isaac. Chingy always collected more
mussels than he could possibly eat, but he never offered any of them
to Billy or Mark. Nor did he ever appear to sell them, leaving Billy
and Mark wondering what he did with them. The mystery was never
solved; it was just another one of those things.

When the conditions were right, Billy and his mates also rowed
Chingy down to The Mouls, the rock on which there were particularly rich pickings of gulls' eggs. The sea had to be absolutely flat,
not only to land a rowing boat on the rocky island but also to
accommodate a row of more than ten miles, not including the effect
of the tide. When Chingy got back, he chucked the eggs in a bucket
of water to make sure they weren't addled. If they floated, they were
no good. But being Chingy, he was often more pleased by addled
eggs than non-floaters. Addled eggs could be thrown at someone or
something.

All of us regularly ate gulls' eggs. They made the best cakes, so we'd happily collect them from cliffs or rocks at sea. But when egg collecting was outlawed, we had to stop. Ironically, we wouldn't need to raid the cliffs or rocks nowadays because there are so many eggs on the roofs. Gulls are apparently endangered and protected, but there are so many of these airborne menaces around the village that their eggs are found all over the place. Unfortunately the same cannot be said of the old boys who used to sit and stroll around the harbour. By the 1970s, the last of them had moved into the council houses or prefabs at the top of the village and they no longer congregated around the Platt. They had swapped damp cottages for homes with central heating and inside loos, and a Port Isaac tradition had been driven into extinction. These days there are no old boys padding up and down Fore Street or the Platt to teach Port Isaac's youngsters the vital skills of life, like how to make a skiver or how to tie a rolling hitch, and Port Isaac is poorer for it.

The money Billy earned making skivers was saved for bonfire night when he spent it all on bangers. Dressed in a huge military greatcoat, Billy would stagger up to the bonfire at the top of Roscarrock Hill, his pockets bulging with fireworks. Under the coat, he had rows of bangers strapped around his body, a bit like a suicide bomber. Then, as the fire was lit, battle commenced as Billy and the other lads went bananas, lighting their fireworks and slinging them at each other. Those with the most money to spend had Roman candles, considered to be the best weapons in the young pyrotechnician's armoury. To any outsider, the sight of gangs of tackers flinging bangers and Roman candles at each other must have appeared to be complete madness. It was a tradition, in a way, that no one in the village ever questioned, but how nobody was ever seriously injured or killed as a direct result of the firework battles on bonfire night is still a mystery.

Nevertheless, the village had its share of tragedies in those days. When Billy was eleven, the brother of Nigel Sherratt, one of the Fisherman's Friends, slipped off the cliffs. It happened before Nigel was born, but Billy remembers it well. Nigel's brother was believed to have been playing with fireworks when he slipped off at Gees Gug, a point on the cliffs between Port Isaac and Port Gaverne on which we all played as tackers. The slippery grass along those cliffs made a perfect slide, but we still managed to control our descent. However, Nigel's brother lost his footing somehow and fell off the cliff. The accident devastated Nigel's family and shook the village, but it wasn't the only tragedy. Two or three years later, there was another unfortunate accident. A lad called Alec Shay had, like many of us, built a tin boat from old oil cans. He used his home-made boat as a tender for rowing out to his fishing boat, but one day it started to take on water. As the boat sank, Alec tried to swim to shore, wearing sea boots that went up to his thighs. The water immediately filled his boots, acting like a vacuum to prevent him from removing them. And very quickly, the weight of the water in his boots pulled him under the surface. He drowned.

The effect of such tragedies on Port Isaac was extraordinary. We'd all pull together and the village would be silent as everyone turned out for the funeral. In later years, the Fisherman's Friends often had the privilege of being asked to sing at funerals, a task that was particularly difficult when the service involved someone close to us. At Harold Brown's funeral we sang 'The White Rose', an emotional song at the best of times, but particularly tough on that day for Julian, Jeremy and John.

When Harold died, the Browns' mother, Joanna, said she didn't want to carry on living. Five years later, we all thought her intention had come true when her bowel burst and peritonitis set in. Several of us visited her in Bodmin hospital and when we saw her lying on her bed, weak and emaciated, we all thought she was close to the end, as the surgeon made clear.

'If I don't operate, you'll die,' the surgeon said.

'That's fine,' said Joanna.

'What do you think?' the surgeon asked the Brown brothers, who were standing around her bed.

'If that's what mother wants,' they said.

Joanna was given antibiotics and painkillers and moved to a hospice. A few days later, she looked better. The recovery continued. Somehow the antibiotics were enough; Joanna's bowel healed and she returned home. Everyone who knows Joanna says she's got the constitution of an ox.

Now eighty-seven years old, Joanna still gets together with the gang that used to meet at the Golden Lion. Her primary partner in crime, Billy's mother, Di Hawkins, died shortly before Harold – 'a candle that burns twice as bright only lasts half as long', is how Billy described it – but some of Joanna and Di's former colonial friends from the postwar years are still around. These days their tipple of choice is Bailey's rather than gin'n'tonic, but they still like nothing more than getting together for a good yarn and a session.

Such tight, long-standing friendships hold Port Isaac together when tragedy strikes our little community. In spite of the accidents that have occurred, few people in Port Isaac would want to see any restrictions placed on our access to the coast. We now live in a culture that tries to remove anything from our lives that has any form of danger to it, but that is such a stifling way to live. It's the opposite of the way in which we Fisherman's Friends all grew up. It sounds callous and cold-hearted, but death is one of the things that anyone who lives on a harsh coast has to face. Many of the Fisherman's Friends have had to bring in dead bodies from the sea, encountered either while fishing or serving in the lifeboat. It's just part of life in a small coastal community. Tragedy happens in places like this and we have to remind ourselves that it's just what it is.

At times of tragedy, Port Isaac's church and chapels played a central role, but they weren't only there for the bad times. Many of us first started singing at Sunday school or in church choirs. The first time Billy heard harmony music, he was ten years old and was passing the Methodist chapel (which now houses his pottery) when he heard a fabulous sound seeping out of the door. Sneaking inside, he discovered the Treviscoe Male Voice Choir in full voice. For a

boy raised on The Shadows and rock'n'roll, it was quite a revela-
tion. The sound of the harmonies sent a shiver down his back that
Billy remembers to this day.

Those harmonies clearly made a lasting impression on Billy. As well as
playing the guitar, Billy's job in the Fisherman's Friends is to harmonise
with the tenors and bass singers, a task he shares with Trevor Grills and
John Lethbridge. Little John stands at the centre of the line-up. We like
to tell Lefty, as we call him, that he's an outsider. That's because he grew
up in St Kew, all of three miles inland, and didn't get close to any of us
until he was an adult. Three miles doesn't sound like much, but it
meant Lefty had quite a different childhood from the rest of us.

Lefty grew up on a farm, sharing a room above the kitchen with a
cowman called Harry Sampson, or Sampy. The farm came from his
mother's side of the family while Lefty's father spent most of his
working life as a highly skilled fitter and turner at a ship repair works
down at Falmouth docks. Employment was sketchy, so his dad would
help out on the farm when he was out of work. He hated farming;
fortunately Lefty loved it.

His younger brother wasn't born until Lefty was five years old and,
living on a farm, he rarely saw other children. From a very young age,
Lefty helped around the farm as much as he could. One hot summer
afternoon, when he was four, he was watching Sampy bring in the
harvest. Thinking the time for bringing in the cows was approaching
and they might be getting hot, Lefty decided he'd bring them in
himself to take the pressure off Sampy. Barely tall enough to reach
halfway up a cow, he opened the gates, brought in the entire herd
from the fields and led them into the shed, then climbed on to the
trough to tie them up to the steel rings on chains, which we call stit-
tles. Task completed, he went to get his mother. Initially, she
panicked when she saw the field was empty of cows. Then, when she
saw the cows tied up in the shed, a big smile creased her face.

The Platt in the early days (circa 2003).

The Platt more recently, in 2010. Since June 2011, crowds of two thousand people have been a regular event when the FFs sing on summer Fridays.

The Platt in the late 1800s. Jon Cleave's Great Granfer Oaten (the large man with a beard and floppy hat) is at the head of the *Richard and Sarah*, the Port Isaac lifeboat. The Brown's great-great-uncle is also in the photo.

On the left is the Browns' great-great-grandpa, known as Granfer Pink, who retired in Port Isaac. His daughter married Pa Brown.

From left: Peter's cousin Frank, Peter's uncle Will Rowe and the Brown's neighbour John Mills, sitting in the fishing boat *Hope*, in the post-war years.

Pa Brown, the Brown brothers' great-grandfather, is on the far right. He is thought to be the first fisherman in the family.

An edited version of this photo was used on The FF's album cover 'Another Mouthful From . . .'. Jon Cleave's great-uncle Walter Mitchell (the man with his hand on his hip) later drowned with his cousins when their fishing boat was overladen with herring.

Another of Cleave's great uncles, Captain Tabb, wearing a traditional gainsay embroidered with the name of the yacht *Sona*. Circa 1920s.

Leading aircraftsman Peter Rowe during his RAF National Service in 1952-1953, St Athans, South Wales.

Peter Rowe and his brother Jack bringing aboard a store pot in the 1980s.

From left: Neville Andrews (with his back to the camera), Peter Rowe (seated), his brother Jack Rowe, their cousin Francis Thomas, and Bryan Nicolls; all fishermen.

Postcard from 1965 showing Jeremy Brown as a boy (in a blue jumper and shorts) with his father.

John Brown sitting inside the engine on the *Big End* taking 'leads'.

Port Isaac FC – in the late 1980s it featured numerous FFs including the team's manager Peter (back row, far right), Nigel (back row, second from left), John Brown (middle row, third from the left) and Trevor (front row, far right).

Launching the gig. John Brown (front left), Johnnie Mac (back left with beard), Trevor (second from front right with moustache) and Mark Provis (right).

Billy helping to set up a pottery when living in France in 1975.

Billy & Barbara Hawkins' wedding photo in 1975.

Billy Hawkins (or Rod Stewart?!) at St Albans Art College circa 1970.

St Philip's cricket team 1960–61. Johnnie Mac (back row, third left) with his mate he phoned from Abbey Road, Tony (back row, centre). We couldn't afford whites!

Johnnie Mac and Peter Rowe getting ready to sing, 2010.

Johnnie Mac with his wife Jill raffling 'The Barrow of Booze' for the RNLI Lifeboat fundraiser, 2005.

A few years later, Lefty was allowed to help milk the cows. Their herd was beef, not dairy, so they weren't easy to milk. Getting the cows to let down their milk involved driving their calves into a little room at the end of the shed, then leading the cows into the milking parlour. When the cows were tied up, Lefty would get a milking bucket and squeeze what he could out of them. These first squirts of milk were usually kept for the farm's own use. Then, when the cows stopped releasing their milk, Lefty unleashed the calves. The calves rushed into the parlour and made for their mother cows, who immediately let down their milk. Lefty started milking like fury, the froth flying and the milk squishing into the bucket as he battled against the calves lunging for access to the cows' udders. If the calf was large, the battle for its mother's teats could be intense and, as Lefty says, 'Her bloody teats would go flying out of your hand.' That was one of the many joys of farming.

Another challenge was to introduce new calves to the herd. These calves would have been bought at market for fattening, but they needed a cow's milk so Lefty and Sampy would try to introduce the new calves to a cow already with calf. They'd let the cow's calf have the first dibs at its mother's udders. Then they'd push in one of the newly bought calves. The first few times, hell would break loose. The cow would kick and struggle, and the calf would recoil. One cow's kick was deadly because she was so accurate; she got Sampy right in the leg and he was hobbling for days. But most of the cows would, after a few attempts, let the new arrivals sup from them and within a few days a cow would be supporting two bought-in calves as well as her own.

When he wasn't helping out on the farm, Lefty would spend weekends fishing with his father on an old fishing boat his uncle had bought from a Port Isaac fisherman. With his father away working from Monday to Friday at Falmouth docks, these fishing trips were one of the few opportunities they had to spend time together. Early on Saturday mornings they'd drive to Rock, across the Camel Estuary from Padstow, and dig up a bucket of sand eels. If the weather was good, they'd head out of the estuary to fish for mackerel with feathers. If the water was choppy, they'd stay within the cover of the estuary and fish for sea bass on lines baited with their sand eels. Lefty enjoyed every minute, but it never made him want to become a fisherman. Compared to farming, fishing was a gamble.

In spite of his healthy country life, Lefty was frequently ill as a young kid. Whatever was going around, he seemed to get it. Glandular fever, scarlet fever, chickenpox. He had them all. As a consequence, he missed quite a lot of school. And school wasn't his strong point, anyway, particularly as he later found out he was dyslexic. His primary schools at St Kew and Delabole were fine, but when he went up to the secondary school at Camelford, the trouble started. He hated the place from the day he went until the day he left.

Lefty had plenty of good friends at school. His problem was that he was always getting into trouble, mainly because he was bright but not academic, so teachers assumed he was lazy. The only member of staff Lefty respected was the woodwork teacher, a strict old boy but a very talented ex-cabinetmaker. When he showed Lefty and his classmates how to make a mortice-and-tenon joint, they watched in awed silence, aware that they were being taught by a master craftsman they genuinely respected. But when Lefty was less taken with a teacher, trouble happened.

Always good with his hands, Lefty once fancied having a go at a bit of pottery. To him, art was pointless. He couldn't draw or paint, but pottery seemed different. He'd have something practical to show for his efforts, like a jug or a bowl. Convinced pottery was something he could do, Lefty waited his turn on one of the potter's wheels in the art department. Eventually, after waiting for several weeks, it was Lefty's turn. He positioned his clay carefully on the wheel, then set it spinning. He felt it was going well as he trimmed away the centre of the clay and shaped the sides while it span on the wheel. It was starting to look like a proper pot, something of which he could be proud, when another pupil, known in those days as Piss Arse, walked past. This lad is now a respectable member of the community, a local councillor and chairman of a sports club, but in those days he was a thorn in everyone's side. Without a glance at Lefty, Piss Arse slammed his fist into his pot. It was flattened.

Lefty's red mist went up. Instead of simply telling Piss Arse to 'bugger off', he smacked him one. Not a clever response, particularly with someone like Piss Arse. Seconds later, Lefty and Piss Arse were on the floor, scrapping, clay flying everywhere. Next stop: the head-master's office.

'You again, Lethbridge?' said Mr Sprayson, the head teacher.

'Yes, sir. That's right.'

'Go and stand under the clock.'

Lefty spent many hours of his secondary school days under that clock, waiting to receive his punishment, which was usually a caning. At times it seemed like it was his permanent home.

A few months later, Lefty went into Camelford one lunchtime and bought a few bottles of beer. Intending to drink them on the bus on the way home after school, he had hidden the bottles for the after-noon in one of the cupboards in the sewing room. Somehow his stash had been found and Lefty found himself on the familiar path to the headmaster's office.

'You again?' said Mr Sprayson. Fortunately for Lefty, Mr Sprayson had other things on his mind. 'This is my last day of teaching,' he sighed. 'I'm retiring tomorrow and thanks to you, on my last day I'm here wasting precious time having to tell you off.'

Lefty still got a full-on bollocking, but that was all. No threat of suspension or expulsion, just a handshake and a weary request to change his ways. Another lucky escape, not that it stopped his mischief-making misbehaviour.

Always good at practical tasks, Lefty was handy at engineering things. When Phil Hunt, a mate, borrowed the caretaker's master key, Lefty took a print of it. At the very least, he thought, it might give him access to the treasures hidden inside the school chocolate machine. Having pushed the key into a lump of putty, Lefty found a piece of metal of an appropriate depth and filed it down to the right size. Using his dad's tools, he cut notches and filed grooves into the metal slice until it fitted perfectly into the imprint of the key on the putty. The final touch was a washer on the end so that he could grip and turn his makeshift skeleton key.

With his home-made key complete, Lefty could open any door in the school. During lunch hour, he'd open a classroom, enter and lock himself inside it, chuffed to be inside on his own when everyone else had to be outside. As long as he cleared out of the classroom five minutes before lessons started, no one would ever know. But after a while, Lefty got bored with creeping around empty classrooms, so he lent his key to his mate, Keith. That was a big mistake.

Keith was much less cautious than Lefty and before long, he was unlocking doors all over the school. One lunchtime Keith was caught red-handed opening a locked classroom and promptly paraded in front of the headmaster. Keith squealed. A few minutes later, the call went out.

'Lethbridge! Headmaster's study. *Now!*'

Mr Sprayson had been a fairly kind old boy, who wanted a quiet finale to his years in education. The new headmaster was what we called a Bible puncher. With a very clear idea of what constituted acceptable behaviour, he saw the world only in terms of right and wrong. No shades of grey in his world-view, and Lefty was very much in the wrong. Walking into the headmaster's study, Lefty realised his future was at risk. 'Here we go,' he thought. 'I'm going to get kicked out of school here.'

Then he had a brainwave. He knew there were about a dozen copies of the master key in circulation. And he knew that a couple of the best-behaved boys, Danny and Satch, the goody-two-shoes who always sat at the front of class, had a copy each. With a triumphant sense of realisation, Lefty saw that Satch might be his saviour. 'I ain't one for grassing nobody up,' thought Lefty, 'but I'm in deep shit here.'

Satch's father was a school governor and Satch was never caught doing anything wrong. He came from a wealthy family and always had the latest gadget. It used to be a slide rule; now it was a digital watch and a pocket calculator with a fancy red LED display. Butter wouldn't melt in Satch's mouth, making him just what Lefty needed. 'That's all right,' thought Lefty. 'I'm gonna have to drop you in it.'

So Lefty dropped Satch in the smelly stuff from a great height. Of course, Satch squealed like a pig and everyone who had a key was up in front of the headmaster. The only one who didn't get collared was Phil Hunt. He escaped the punishment of having to return to school for two days in the school holidays to do cleaning work.

Lefty survived to see another day at school. Sometimes we wonder if he's semi-feline, he's had so many close brushes with disaster. And when he gets together with Billy, trouble is almost guaranteed, which is why we put them at the centre of the line-up, where we can keep a close eye on their incident-prone ways.

Cornish Bun Recipes

We like our buns, cakes and scones in Cornwall. One of the best is the Hevva Cake, which was baked by pilchard huers on their return to their homes, so it would be ready for the fishing crews coming in to harbour.

Hevva Cake

125g self-raising flour
Pinch of salt
140g butter and lard mixed
100g mixed dried fruit
50g sugar
Milk to mix

Rub fat into sifted flour and salt until it resembles breadcrumbs. Mix in sugar and fruit. Add milk to make a soft dough, but not too wet. Spread out evenly until about three-quarters of an inch thick with a rough top. Bake at 200°C (gas mark 6) for about 20 to 30 minutes (until the top has browned). Sprinkle with granulated sugar and cut into squares while hot. Lovely with a cup of tea.

Figgy 'obbin

250g suet
450g self-raising flour
1 teaspoon salt
450g raisins (in Cornwall we call them figs)
Milk
Sugar

Rub suet, flour and salt together. Add water gradually to make a dry elastic dough. Knead lightly, then roll out to about an inch thick. Sprinkle on raisins and roll in lightly with a rolling pin. Fold up, like a jam suet pudding, sealing the ends. Crisscross the top with a knife, brush with milk and sprinkle with sugar. Bake at 180°C (gas mark 4) for about 30 minutes. Serve hot with Cornish clotted cream.

CHAPTER FIVE

GOING AWAY

On the Platt, after incident-prone Lefty has led us through 'A Sailor Ain't a Sailor', somehow it seems appropriate that next up is Billy, our potter and resident clown. If something daft is going to happen to someone, that someone will be second tenor Billy. He attracts trouble and mishaps like iron filings to a magnet.

Since we introduced more instrumentation last year, Billy's also become the linchpin of the group. He plays guitar and mandocello, so quite a few of us rely on him to give us an indication of the key of the song we're about to sing. In fact, it's only recently that we've had any idea at all which song is coming up next. Until we recorded our first album with Universal Records, the concept of a set list was far too organised for us. We preferred to fly by the seat of our pants. For years, nobody knew what song anyone was going to sing until that person opened their mouth and sang it. No idea at all. Which could be quite fun. But it could also be totally disastrous, particularly if it was a song we hadn't sung for two years. In those instances, we could see the look on everyone's face and know exactly what they were thinking: 'Oh shit, how does this one go?'

That anarchy has always been part of the Fisherman's Friends ethos. And even with set lists nowadays, there's always an element of surprise to our gigs. We're not trained singers, so we can never be sure in which key the next song will be sung. The more nervous we are, the higher we often pitch the song. The trickiest customer is Julian. Often he doesn't know himself which key he's going to choose. He'll even change key halfway through a song. When that happens, Trevor, Billy and Lefty will look at each other wide-eyed with surprise. While everyone else just sings the tunes, the three of them at the middle of the line-up have to harmonise with us. And if the lead singer starts too high, the central trio know there's no chance of them reaching the high notes of a harmony.

Our ramshackle, casual approach to set lists is a bit of a macho thing. Avoiding anything that smacks of professionalism, we just want to get on with our singing without fuss or fanfare. But sometimes we come unstuck. Asked to sing at the carnival at Delabole, we were caught short when Nigel decided to sing 'Huckleberry Hunting'. Not only was it an awful choice – the song had nothing to do with the sea – but none of us had ever sung it before. As Nigel struck up, Billy looked at Jeremy and they both collapsed with laughter. That finished us all off. We all giggled for five minutes. And from then on, none of us dared look around until we finished the gig when, leaving the church, Jeremy turned to Nigel: 'What kind of bloody song is that?' Nigel just shrugged.

Meanwhile, Cleavey is about to introduce Billy's song. 'Most of these songs we're singing are traditional songs,' he says. 'Maybe two hundred years old. And there are dozens and dozens of them.'

Cleavey's voice softens. 'They've inspired Bill and me to try and compose a few songs of our own. In the course of our research, we've come across a very rare, small Cornish document. It's the Cornish book of lovemaking, the *Farmer Sutra*.

'In particular we were inspired by the chapter on foreplay. Well, it wasn't a chapter so much as a paragraph. Actually it wasn't a paragraph; it was a sentence. To be honest with you, it's not even a sentence, it's just a word. Frankly, it wasn't even a word. It was just an exclamation . . . duh?

'So Billy and I have composed this tender, yet erotic, love lament from the words of the *Farmer Sutra*.'

Billy immediately cracks into 'Johnny Gone Down to Hilo', singing as loudly and rumbustiously as he can, ensuring that this loud, hearty shanty will never be confused with a tender love song.

> *Well, never seen the like since I been born,*
> *A great big sailor with his sea boots on . . .*

Port Isaac has always been a place of traditions. And leaving the village to find work and to see the world is as much a local tradition as smuggling or wrecking. Generations of fishermen spent summers working on yachts in the summer. Like them, many of us Fisherman's Friends left to find adventure and seek experiences, knowing that one day we would return and that Port Isaac would be waiting for us, the same as ever.

We've often asked ourselves why so many young Yarnigoats leave Port Isaac to seek wider experiences. Julian thinks we have an appetite for exploration that stems from our childhoods, which were very secure and loving. He thinks it creates a self-confidence that we'd always be safe wherever we might venture. Another factor is Port Isaac's trading history, which meant that seafarers were always coming and going, so we were always adept at integrating with incomers and hearing their stories about the world beyond the valley. It gives a certain quality to Port Isaac, a curiosity and an easy-going outlook, because we've experienced more of life and seen different things.

Of the ten Fisherman's Friends, half of us left the village in our late teens or early twenties. And for the sake of our story, it would be romantic to say that those who stayed smuggled and wrecked – or free-traded, as we call it. But that's something that's now firmly in the past. Well, almost.

Our rocky coves, sheltered bays, tumultuous waves, and wild and untenanted landscapes are often said to have turned Cornwall into a haven of smugglers, although that might be slightly overstated in the case of the north coast. Rugged and facing Ireland or Pembrokeshire in Wales, the north coast of Cornwall and Devon was less ideally suited to smuggling than the south coast, which provided relatively easy access to Brittany and the Channel Islands. And compared to the southeast of England, which was close to France, which had a much larger and wealthier market for contraband, and which offered relatively benign landing spots, anywhere in the southwest was a hard smuggle. But that's not to say it didn't happen.

In spite of penalties including death, imprisonment and heavy fines, smuggling was rife in Cornwall until it peaked in the mid-nineteenth century. Widespread poverty, a lack of law enforcement and the uncertainties of seasonal work in the tin mines, plus the prospect of 'something for nothing', provided the impetus. While not as glamorous and romantic as we like to imagine, smuggling was certainly a recognised, even respected, profession through which the majority of the population gained a better standard of living. Though illegal, they did not consider it a criminal act to evade the customs duties. In some areas smuggling was the principal source of income and the Scilly Isles were almost bankrupted when customs officers cracked down on smugglers. A committee appointed by the government to investigate smuggling found in 1783 that vessels of up to 300 tons manned by as many as 100 men were regularly smuggling goods across the Channel. In the local economies surrounding the inlets along the south coast and ports such as Falmouth, Fowey and Polperro, almost every member of the community from sailors, fishermen and merchants to farmers, miners and magistrates profited in some way from smuggling.

Closer to home, smugglers sometimes chose to use harbours along the north coast simply because customs officials kept less of a close watch here on the movement of vessels than on the south coast. Julian Brown remembers seeing steps leading up from a cave on the western side of the harbour into Halwyn House, a large whitewashed building perched above the beach. And according to local legend, a tunnel leads out from beneath the Golden Lion pub to the beach so that contraband could be dragged into the village without having to pass over the Platt.

Intercepting shipments of tobacco, tea or West Indian rum on ships bound for Bristol was a local speciality. In 1765, a Padstow resident called William Rawlings wrote to the Earl of Dartmouth to warn him that up to a hundred horses were waiting almost daily on a beach two miles west of the town to unload smuggled goods. Wool was surreptitiously exported to France and in return brandy, tea, rum and gin were imported. When pepper was heavily taxed, smugglers ran boatloads of spices into a tiny cove about four miles from Padstow, known now as Pepper Cove. With a sandy, rockless beach and enclosed by cliffs and rocks, it was ideal for unloading boats out of the gaze of the Revenue. Within Padstow itself, a smuggling vessel from Ireland once chased an excise ship into the harbour, hanging out its flags and firing its guns as a victory taunt before sailing on to Newquay, where the customs authorities were known to be very happy (as Kipling described it in 'A Smuggler's Song') to 'watch the wall, my darling, while the Gentlemen go by'.

Although not an ideal harbour for smuggling, Port Isaac was at the heart of a network of smugglers' haunts on the north coast. Jamaica Inn, the mist-entombed public house on Bodmin Moor made famous as a smugglers' stopping point by Daphne du Maurier's novel, was less than twenty miles away. It was favoured by smugglers running booze from Boscastle, about twelve miles up the coast. When a farmhouse on the edge of Bodmin Moor close to the London main road was demolished, a large hidden chamber was found behind the great hall chimney. Accessible through a hole in the floor of a bedroom above the hidden chamber or via a low door concealed behind a kitchen dresser, the room was used to hide kegs of smuggled spirits and tobacco. From the house, a network of rough lanes led to Boscastle. These lanes, cut deep into the surrounding fields and flanked by high hedges, were ideal for obscuring any view of smugglers moving their contraband.

In contrast to the usual image of smugglers creeping ashore with their booty under the cover of night, many Cornish smugglers were for a considerable time engaged in exporting goods, particularly Cornish tin. Only when duty tariffs were increased in the mid-eighteenth century did the balance of smuggling trade switch towards imports from continental Europe. At about this time, a swashbuckling sailor became Cornwall's most celebrated and daring smuggler and pirate.

Cruel Coppinger was a smuggler straight out of Central Casting. In 1792, he arrived on the north coast when his ship was blown on-shore at Welcombe Mouth, an inappropriately named cove of jagged rocks at the heart of the wreckers' coast. While a crowd braved howl-ing winds on the surrounding cliffs, watching in hope of looting the wreck, a single figure at the wheel of the boat was spotted being swept into the waves and disappearing beneath the water's surface. Minutes later, this figure emerged Herculean from the pounding surf. Staggering up the valley, he grabbed a coat from an old woman in passing, then fought his way through the onlookers to where a young damsel was sitting on a horse. Without uttering a word, this huge, muscular man promptly vaulted into the saddle and galloped away, whisking the woman, Miss Dinah Hamlyn, to her home. There he carried her across the hearth, announced to her father that he was Jan Coppinger from Denmark and ensconced himself at Mr Hamlyn's table.

When Dinah's father died, Coppinger married Dinah and took over the house, turning it into a refuge for his band of smugglers, wreckers, poachers and other lawless characters in North Cornwall. Eager to force his widowed mother-in-law to hand over her hus-band's estate, Coppinger regularly tied Dinah to the post of their oak bed and threatened to whip her with a cat-o'-nine-tails until his mother-in-law relented and paid him some of the inheritance. He repeated this at intervals until he had squeezed every last penny from her, adding it to the considerable fortune he was amassing as the southwest's most ruthless smuggler and pirate.

Unidentified ships soon became a regular sight off our coast and would be led into safe coves by signals flashed from headlands. Their cargoes would be smuggled inland along a network of bridlepaths called Coppinger's Tracks, over which the tyrant had total control, forbidding any stranger from using them by night. These paths converged at Steeple Brink, a 300-foot-high headland. Some 100 feet below the brow and accessible only by rope ladder was a vast cave said to be as large as the parish church at Kilkhampton, a village about thirty miles north of Port Isaac. Known as Coppinger's Cave, it was stacked with kegs of French brandy and Dutch gin, and iron-banded sea chests containing tea and other contraband. Outside the cave, sheep were tethered and fed on stolen hay until ready for slaughter.

Cruel Coppinger's ferocious reputation kept revenue officers away. Few would venture west of the Tamar into Cornwall and those that did often met a nasty end. One was beheaded and his body taken out to sea. Others were left tied to rocks on a rising tide. Revenue cutters that dared to follow his ships were led into dangerous waters, from which Coppinger's vessel emerged unscathed while the revenue vessel would crash into rocks and sink with all on board. And any local who crossed him would be taken away to sea and forced to work on his boats.

Coppinger's methods soon turned him into a wealthy man. He bought a freehold farm bordering on the sea, paying for it entirely in gold coins of various currencies. But eventually his luck ran out. His only child with Dinah, a son, was born deaf and dumb and was exceptionally spiteful. The locals said of him that he was born without a soul, a reputation he confirmed at the age of six, when he was found laughing after having murdered a neighbour's child by pushing it off a high cliff.

As in most tales of criminal capers, eventually the authorities caught up with the villain. A constant presence of several armed customs vessels off the north coast hampered Cruel Coppinger's trade and Cornwall's most feared pirate left in much the same way as he'd arrived. Coppinger was last seen boarding a ship heading into a fierce storm. Whether he survived or not isn't known.

Some people question whether Coppinger existed in quite the way he's often described. Certainly, a man called Coppinger lived in North Cornwall at the time of the stories of a ferocious pirate. The parish register at Hartland records his marriage to a Dinah Hamlyn and there is further evidence that a man called Coppinger was given refuge in 1792 by a Hartland farmer after his ship was wrecked nearby at Welcombe Mouth. There are also records of the purchase of a farm near Liskeard by someone called Coppinger. However, the most detailed account of Cruel Coppinger's smuggling was written by the Reverend Robert Hawker of Morwenstow, an eccentric vicar who liked to dress as a mermaid and smoke opium in a hut he built into the side of a cliff near his church. Hawker, a respected historian and writer of the lyrics to 'Trelawny', the Cornish national anthem, possibly based his account on an amalgamation of several smugglers operating on the north Cornish coast in the late eighteenth century. Whatever its veracity, it's a great story and that's what matters.

The closest any of us Fisherman's Friends have been to getting involved in smuggling was when Harold Brown – Julian, Jeremy and John's father – came ashore one day with three bottles of wine, a bottle of rum and some cigarettes. Harold had been out at sea, working some ground off Port Isaac with his pots, when a couple of French trawlers turned up. Harold went alongside and jumped aboard, then showed the skipper on a chart where his pots were positioned. In return, the French crew gave Harold a basket of gurnards for bait and some booze and fags. Harold had given up smoking at the time, so his crewman had the cigarettes and a bottle of wine. The other two bottles of wine and the rum were taken home, where Julian drank most of it. As smuggling escapades go, it's unlikely to concern customs and excise, but it's a start.

We don't do much smuggling in Port Isaac any more, but one thing we did do was to smuggle Johnny Mac – a Yorkshireman, no less – into the Fisherman's Friends.

Although he's a Yorkie through and through, Macster fits right in with us. It might be because his father came from County Mayo in

Ireland, giving John a Celtic heritage he shares with the Welsh, the Bretons, the Basques and, of course, us Cornishmen. Or maybe it's because Macster grew up on a council estate in Leeds that, like Port Isaac, was a tight little community. At Christmas, they'd put on a pantomime. In the summer, there would be a fête, and other communal events happened throughout the year. Most of the residents on the estate were Irish or had an Irish background, but it was predominantly Protestant, which set a Catholic like Macster slightly apart – not that it led to anything more serious than being called names in the street, which was handy as it made Johnny Mac familiar with being called names in the Fisherman's Friends.

Although we like to think it was fate that brought Johnny Mac to us, in fact it was nothing more than chance. When he left grammar school, John did an apprenticeship in mechanical engineering, but then decided a factory life was not for him. So he started travelling and worked as an industrial roofer, on oil-rig constructions, picking grapes, as a chef, bus conductor, tiler and builder. Eventually he got a position at one of the hotels in the Channel Islands. That's where he met his wife, Jill, who's from Birmingham. They hit it off immediately and, for a few years, concentrated on enjoying themselves, working and travelling all over the place. One day Jill announced she was going to Cornwall. It was nothing more than curiosity, but she fancied somewhere new. John thought it sounded a good idea and he had nothing else lined up, so he went along as well. In the summer of 1977, when punk rock was ripping through the airwaves and the Queen was celebrating her Silver Jubilee, they arrived in Port Isaac. Jill got a job at the Golden Lion and John found work at a hotel. With them both working in the catering and hospitality trade, they soon got to know a lot of locals. They found Port Isaac was a great community with a lively social life. And having planned to stay only for the summer, they decided to hang around for another year or two. That was thirty-four years ago. John and Jill loved Port Isaac so much they never left.

John was twenty-seven years old when he arrived, but he's about a

decade older than most of us (Peter Rowe excepted), so just as he was
slipping into Port Isaac life, a bunch of the rest of us were reaching
our late teens and getting ready to leave.

Billy had already left Port Isaac when Johnny Mac turned up. By the
time he finished school at Camelford Comprehensive, Billy had
amassed a grand total of one qualification. That was in art, so his
careers teacher sensibly advised him to apply for art school. Billy was
sceptical, but he went down to the Redruth School of Art to investigate. Walking into the school, Billy immediately thought he had
entered a different world. Beautiful girls were draped everywhere,
smoking cigarettes. There was an anarchic air. Billy knew it was just
the place for him, a paradise of freedom and no authority.

Three years later, Billy had completed a one-year art foundation
course and two years of ceramics. His formal education finished, he
moved to St Albans to work as a ceramics technician at an art college,
where he met his wife, the beautiful Barbara.

Billy and Barbara stayed for a while in St Albans, but all the time
they were there, Billy was scheming to return to Port Isaac. He hadn't
wanted to leave in the first place, but he knew he didn't want to
return empty-handed to chance his luck in Port Isaac's fragile economy. Over the next few months, he hatched a plan to set up a pottery
back home, but he knew he would need a lot of capital to pull it off.
The first step in the plan was to save some cash.

In 1974, Barbara and Billy moved to France to help a friend start a
pottery. The next year they returned and Billy found work with a furniture restoration shop in Bristol, where his boss spotted his talent with
ceramics and suggested they go into business together with a pottery in
the centre of Bristol. The pottery was immediately successful and Billy
saved every penny he could spare, working in his spare time as a
labourer in an iron foundry and as a bouncer in a Bristol ballroom to
supplement his savings. Four years after arriving in Bristol, Barbara gave

birth to their first daughter, Faye. By the time Barbara was pregnant with their second daughter, Jo, a year later, Billy and Barbara were moving their young family to Gloucestershire to open their own pottery for the first time. Their new pottery was even more successful than its predecessor in Bristol and Billy was soon flying across the Atlantic with the Craft Council to exhibit his work in New York. Soon thereafter, he started selling his pots in America.

Billy and Barbara stayed in Gloucestershire for eighteen years, but they would return to Port Isaac whenever they could, keeping in touch with all Billy's childhood friends. Then one day, Billy was in an amusement arcade in Bristol, killing time playing the slot machines, when he felt a firm hand on his shoulder. Gingerly, he looked at the hand and noticed it was poking out of the cuff of a policeman's uniform.

'You're nicked' said the voice attached to the hand.

Slowly, Billy turned around. As far as he was aware, he'd done nothing wrong. At least nothing that could warrant arrest. And as he turned, his face lit up. The hand was attached to an arm belonging to a uniformed copper with a very familiar face. None other than Jon Cleave. The last time Billy had seen Jon he'd been about to leave Port Isaac for art school and Jon had been a little squirt causing mischief and trouble in the alleys around the Platt. Now Jon was a strapping six-foot-plus plod with a beaming smile.

Cleavey's journey to that Bristol amusement arcade began shortly before Billy left Port Isaac. That's when Cleavey first moved to the village, just as Billy was off to art college. Born less than nine miles away, Jon first came to Port Isaac when he was three days old. In those days, his parents lived in Wadebridge, where his father ran a garage and car showroom that had been in the family for many years. Cleavey's dad was from Rock, across the estuary from our old foe, Padstow, but his mother was a Port Isaac girl, one of four sisters born in the village. She brought Cleavey to see Port Isaac as soon as possible after his birth. Her side of the family goes back in the village for generations, so Cleavey is Cornish through and through on both sides, a noble heritage that his family carefully maintained until Cleavey met his wife Caroline, an up-country lass, and spoiled the thoroughbred bloodline.

Jon was an only child, which might explain why he's such an attention-seeker these days. He's always been an absolute nutcase – quick-witted, a real good laugh and a nice chap – and without those attributes we'd all be a bit lost as they make him the perfect choice for the Fisherman's Friends' master of ceremonies, introducing our songs.

Cleavey's mother always dreamed of returning to Port Isaac, even though it was so close they'd come to the village every Wednesday and Saturday. When he was thirteen, his mother fulfilled her dream, and her little boy could now grow up surrounded by his grand-parents, aunts, uncles and other relatives. They moved into their cottage in the village that they used to let, so it took several months for Cleavey to twig that the move was permanent. It was only when he realised his mother had joined the choir, the ladies' social group and the young mums' group, even though he was nearly fourteen, that Cleavey became aware that they hadn't moved back to Wadebridge after the school holidays.

Even before he moved full time to Port Isaac, Cleavey knew many of us. He was in the same year as Trevor at school. And he knew the Brown brothers, simply because everyone did. Like most of us, Cleavey joined the football team under the management of Peter Rowe, playing in the under-16 team with a lad called Adrian Williams. Wills, as we called him, matured very quickly. He started shaving when he was nine and was always able to kick a ball a very long distance, so Pete put him at full back. But one day, when the under-16s were playing Camelford, a good team compared to us, Pete decided it was time to change tactics.

'Wills,' he said, 'today you're centre-forward.'

Pete's management methods were always unorthodox, to say the least. But this time Cleavey was really baffled. 'Peter?' he said. 'Why have you put Wills at centre-forward?'

'Erm, we won't get into their half very much. So I just figured that Wills has got a big hard kick on him and he might just crash one in from the halfway line.'

Those were the days before we learned how to win, so Pete's argument was convincing. Cleavey walked away, shaking his head in wonder. Fair enough, he thought.

When he wasn't playing football, Cleavey spent any spare time on the beach, although he was never really a keen waterman. His Uncle Bill gave him his old fishing punt, the *Yvonne*. It was named after Cleavey's mother, but Cleavey was never much for going to sea. He'd fish for mackerel a bit, but he said he always felt a bit inadequate against the rest of us as we'd been in boats since we were six or seven years old. Having come to it at the age of thirteen, he used to wonder what he was doing in a boat. Even today, he's the same. He'll happily go out fishing, but only if someone else will do all the work. 'It's nice,' he says, 'but as regards flopping around and trying to catch fish, I really can't be arsed.'

Like all of us, Jon spent his early years collecting gulls' eggs, fishing for mullet, dam-building on the beach and larking around. One prank was to put some of the younger boys in one of the fishermen's lobster storage pots and then poke them with sticks. The little tackers would jerk around, trying to dodge the sticks. On one occasion, two of them even started fighting one another in the pot. That amused Cleavey and his mates no end, so they rolled them into town in the pot and left them there.

Jon arrived in the village in the last years of the old sewage system, so he was very familiar with always swimming breaststroke to push the turds out of the way. Even though he always kept his gob firmly shut, Cleavey was ill the first couple of summers he lived with us. Maybe that's how long it took an unexposed immune system to develop a resistance to the old Port Isaac water quality. In those days, a less than happy old boy called Sid used to run the beach car park, where cars could park on the sand when the tide was low. Sid spent hours every day raking channels for the stream to flow down the beach. Sometimes he'd look up and wonder why the stream had dwindled to a trickle, not knowing that further up the stream, Cleavey and his mates had dammed it up. They'd wait until there was a hell of a backlog, then hit the sluice with a sledgehammer and run down the street shouting, 'Flush! Flush!' Down on the beach, Sid would be waiting, scratching his head at the lack of water flow, when suddenly a tsunami of turds would flush all his handiwork away. Happy times.

Billy Hawkins was about ten years older than Cleavey, but he was always very friendly to the younger ones when he returned to the village on one of his frequent visits. He'd jump off the breakwaters with Cleavey and John Brown and their mates, joining them when they graduated to Tag's Pit in Port Gaverne, a pool beside a big triangular cave that had an overhang with various levels from which we jumped. They call it tombstoning these days and most of us leaped from a ledge about thirty feet up, high enough to know about it and to feel the acceleration towards the water as you dropped. If you got it wrong, you could hurt yourself badly, which made Bill's frequent dives off the very top ledge very impressive to us youngsters. We also jumped into the Gut, a narrow strip of water between Castle Rock and the Main at Port Gaverne. But the ultimate challenge was a little inlet called Pigeon Gug. Here we had to jump out quite a distance to clear the rocks below before dropping into the water. But if we jumped too far, we'd clatter on to rocks beyond the inlet, so it was all a bit dodgy.

John would jump with Peter Rowe's nephew and son, Johnny and Mark Rowe, and his best mate Nicky Hicks, who had lost his arm in a mincing machine at his father's butcher's shop when he was three. Nicky didn't let his injury hamper his daring escapades. He learned to do everything with his left hand and became the most enthusiastic cliff jumper of us all. Nicky was big and incredibly strong; if he'd had two arms he could have been a heavyweight contender. Just before Cleavey left Port Isaac to go to college, Nicky was found washed up on the beach at Port Gaverne. He'd gone missing after leaving home for a walk during a winter storm. We assumed he'd slipped off a cliff, but no one knew what had actually happened. It was a horrid time for everyone, another reminder of the dangers of our coastal environment and yet another tragic event that reverberated through the village, pulling it together at a time of crisis. Nick had a great singing voice, and if he'd lived beyond his teens he would surely have become a Fisherman's Friend.

As he approached his A levels, Cleavey started harbouring an ambition to follow in Billy's footsteps to art school, but he messed up his exams. So, in October 1977, that fateful year of punk rock, the Queen's Silver Jubilee and Johnny Mac's arrival in Port Isaac, Cleavey left the village for Bristol Polytechnic to train as a teacher. It was a strange choice for someone who wasn't that interested in children or teaching, but these were the days of no tuition fees and full maintenance grants, and Cleavey wasn't going to miss the opportunity to misspend his youth at the taxpayers' expense.

The next four years were spent nominally studying how to teach history and physical education, but the bulk of Cleavey's effort was spent having a good time, establishing a network of friends that he's kept to this day. Some of them have even moved down to Cornwall after Cleavey showed them its wonderful assets. At every opportunity, Jon would come back to the village, working in the old chemist's shop or the Headlands Hotel in his holidays. At the end of his second year, he was working in a café, flogging ice creams and making the working day pass faster by devising imaginary exotic flavours of ice cream with the boss's son, Sean. Each day they'd think up a new outlandish flavour, such as squirrel shit or seagull sick, then post a note on the fridge, offering it as the daily special.

On 21 August 1979 – a date etched into Cleavey's memory – a bunch of young girls walked into Port Isaac. Having taken their A levels in June, they were off to college that autumn, and they were spending a last few weeks together camping at Daymer Bay, on the Camel Estuary between Polzeath and Rock. Among them was a pretty, willowy brunette called Caroline. She walked into the café, spotted Cleavey's weird daily-special ice cream flavour and burst out laughing. Thinking she was lovely, Cleavey struck up a conversation, then served her an ice cream. They chatted some more, then Caroline left and Cleavey thought he'd probably never see her again.

That October, Jon returned to Bristol for his third year of teacher training. In his first week back at college he bumped into a young first-year student who seemed strangely familiar. They spent a while chatting, then the girl said she'd been to Port Isaac that summer.

'I was served by some bloke who couldn't scoop an ice cream without breaking the cone,' she said, 'and who devised really weird flavours.'

Jon instantly knew it was the girl who'd giggled at everything he said in the café that summer. Caroline has been putting up with Cleavey ever since that day they met at Bristol Polytechnic. It led to a marriage, three sons and (so far) over thirty years together.

At the end of the following academic year, Cleavey graduated. Caroline still had two years to complete at college, so Cleavey found himself a job at a local psychiatric hospital, an old Victorian pile on the edge of Bristol. Officially he was a nursing assistant, which usually amounted to being an arse-wiper on the wards, but as a graduate he was assigned to a new project to convert the old Victorian farm within the hospital compound into an occupational-therapy market garden. Neither Cleavey nor the other two graduates allotted to the task had ever planted anything, but they took to it like expert horticulturalists and were soon selling the produce twice a week in the hospital, aided by a dozen patients. Among them was a lovely lad with Down's Syndrome called Lloyd. He played the drums and was a brilliant dancer. Another of the lads had hydrocephalus, manifested as an abnormally large head, and he had a filthy temper, brought on by the pressure of fluid pressing on his brain. A third patient had macrocephalus and the others suffered from several severe problems. Cleavey still talks of them fondly and often says they were the most memorable group of people he has ever known – more memorable, even, than any of us in the Fisherman's Friends – simply because they were all so different. He even took them all down to Cornwall, bringing them to Port Isaac one day to meet his mum.

Cleavey would have been happy to keep working at the hospital, but this was the height of Thatcherism, when most psychiatric hospitals were closed down and their highly institutionalised patients turned out, supposedly to be cared for by the community. It was

1983, Britain was emerging from a crippling recession, industrial strife was widespread, the miners were about to strike and Cleavey found himself without a job. He'd already decided that teaching wasn't his bag – his college mates were applying for forty jobs and not getting any interviews – so he looked around for a secure, reliable job. After a short search and a brief tussle with his conscience, Cleavey fell upon the solution: he would join the police force.

With unemployment and dissatisfaction rising, it was a tough time to be a policeman, particularly on Cleavey's beat of pubs, clubs and breaking up fights in Bristol city centre. He was a good copper, passing his sergeant's exam after two years in the force, but as someone always inclined to laugh at the absurdities of life, he knew he was a square peg in a round hole. During one interview at a police training centre in Somerset, Cleavey's superintendent told him he had an overdeveloped sense of humour. His instinctive response was to suggest that maybe the superintendent had an underdeveloped one. Fortunately he resisted it.

For a Cornish lad, whose path through life had taken him from a sheltered fishing village to a cushy four years at university on a full grant, the police force was a rude awakening. Cleavey was never a shirker. If he takes on a challenge, he makes sure he does it properly, but the police force didn't sit well with him. His beat took him to countless flats in and around Bristol where dog shit covered the floor and the only furniture was a brand-new hi-fi system, television and video recorder. Inner-city violence, usually related to drink, drugs or racial strife, was a daily occurrence, particularly in the St Pauls area.

In 1985, some of St Pauls' most disaffected residents, inspired by rioters in the Soweto township of Johannesburg, announced they were going to necklace a policeman. This involved putting a tyre doused in petrol around a copper's neck and setting it alight. A few weeks later, PC Keith Blakelock was murdered at a riot at the Broadwater Farm Estate in north London. The authorities feared a summer of trouble and, as riots spread to Bristol and other English cities, Jon found himself spending weeks at a time in the back of police vans with a shield on his knees, playing chase the lady with other coppers. Knowing Cleavey would happily yarn away to anyone in the van and keep the other constables happy, his inspector had always picked him for riot duty. He'd already served stints at miners' protests in Nottinghamshire, with the peace convoy at Glastonbury festival and at the perimeter of the nuclear missile base at Greenham Common.

For Cleavey, these were tough times. With a keen sense of right and wrong, he became disillusioned by the way in which the police force was being politicised by a radical and, at times, extreme government.

Shaking with cold as he stood beside the perimeter fence at Greenham Common for a long succession of moonlit nights, wrapped in a greatcoat, scarves, long johns and a balaclava, Cleavey struggled with his conscience. One night, as he guarded the air-force base from a camp of peaceful protesters objecting to the presence of American nuclear cruise missiles on British soil, Cleavey voiced his thoughts. 'They're trying to save the world,' he said to a colleague as they stood beside the camp where the protesters were sleeping. 'And we're trying to stop them?'

It was about then that Cleavey decided to start growing his moustache as a small sign of his dissent. For a Cornish bloke in his mid-twenties, only just married and trying to make an honourable living, these were difficult dilemmas to face. As one of 'Maggie Thatcher's boot boys' he was well paid, but when he met up with his old student friends, he felt alienated by their attitudes towards the police and the sense that they had little idea what was actually going on.

Whenever he and Caroline could find the time, Cleavey would come home to Port Isaac. Caroline loved the village as much as Cleavey did and although they both enjoyed living in Bristol, Cleavey didn't feel a part of it, like he belonged. However, it was too early to think about moving back. Their lives were so busy that Cleavey and Caroline didn't have much time for thinking about anything at all beyond work. And when they could seize a rare chance to ponder, their thoughts usually turned to the prospect of starting a family. Thoughts of home would have to wait.

Many thousands of miles away, another Fisherman's Friend was entertaining similar thoughts. After he completed his marine engineering apprenticeship, John Brown left Port Isaac to join the merchant navy. At the age of twenty, he flew to Barcelona to join his first ship, a vast freighter with 2,000 containers. Next stop Canada, then New York. The voyage continued down the eastern seaboard of the United States to Havana, then Jamaica and across the Gulf of Mexico to pass through the Panama Canal into the Pacific for their next port of call, Los Angeles. From there, the ship took him to Japan, Hong Kong, Taiwan and all the way back to Spain and around the Mediterranean before docking again at Barcelona.

Quite some journey for a lad from Port Isaac, not that John got the chance to see much of the world when the ship was in port. On the day he started, he was shown the engine room. His first question was simple: Where's the engine? The answer was direct: You're standing on it. Beneath John's feet was the top of a cylinder head, a platform at the top of a cylinder so large you could climb into it. And that's exactly what John had to do every time the ship docked in port. One of the pistons would be lifted out and he would descend a ladder to scrape off all the burned carbon from the side of the cylinder. It was painstaking work and the scale was vast. When he'd finished, John would help the engineering crew rebuild the cylinder, install new rings and adjust them with millimetre accuracy. They would then clamp a tiny strip of lead to the crankshaft, start up the engine for a short while, stop it and dismantle the cylinder again so they could remove the strip of lead. From the width of the lead, the engineers determined the amount of slack in the big ends. Too much and the engine would wear more quickly. It was all preventative engineering, a time-consuming but vital job to ensure the engine didn't break down at sea.

Keeping the engines running took John all over the world. He enjoyed every moment and would do two trips back to back so he could come home for the entire summer to go fishing with his father or out in the dinghy, mackereling or pulling crab pots. But after eight years at sea, John was in his late twenties and had started to look at the older sailors on board. They were in their thirties or forties and had been on ships for so long they no longer bothered going ashore. Instead, they sat in the ship's bar and got wasted. When he looked at how hard-drinking these older sailors had become, John realised that he didn't want to end up like them. He set himself a target.

A few months later, John was on a ship docked in Southampton when he heard on the grapevine about a ship about to leave for Australia and New Zealand. He went straight to his cabin, wrote a letter and handed it to the chief engineer.

'What's this?' said John's boss.

'It's my resignation. I'm getting off after the next trip.'

'Why's that?'

'Once I've got down there and seen Australia and New Zealand, that's all I want to do before I'm finished with the merchant navy. After that, I'm going home to Port Isaac.'

John left immediately for the Antipodes. A few months later, he returned to Southampton. Thinking his seafaring days were over, he went for a drink in a dockside pub with a mate. As they sat drinking at the bar they heard news that the *QE2*, the famous Cunard passenger liner, was seeking crew. John and his mate had only ever worked on diesel-powered ships, but all the old engineers insisted that steam was the gold standard of marine engineering. A marine engineer couldn't call himself a proper marine engineer if he hadn't worked with steam, they said. And now, just when John was about to retire back to Port Isaac, the most prestigious of steam-powered ocean liners was seeking crew. It was too tantalising an opportunity to pass by. John signed up. Dreams of returning to Port Isaac would have to wait.

The Cornish National Anthem

Written by the Revd Robert Stephen Hawker of Morwenstow parish in North Cornwall, 'The Song of the Western Men' has become the unofficial Cornish national anthem. Sung at gatherings such as rugby matches, it's usually known as 'Trelawny' and commemorates a march on London by 20,000 Cornishmen seeking the liberty of Jonathan Trelawny, one of seven bishops imprisoned in the Tower of London by James II in 1688.

> *A good sword and a trusty hand,*
> *A faithful heart and true,*
> *King James's men shall understand*
> *What Cornish lads can do.*
>
> *And have they fixed the where and when?*
> *And shall Trelawny die?*
> *Here's twenty thousand Cornishmen*
> *Will know the reason why.*

114

And shall Trelawny live?
And shall Trelawny die?
Here's twenty thousand Cornishmen
Will know the reason why.

Out spake their Captain brave and bold,
A merry wight was he:
'Though London Tower were Michael's hold,
We'll set Trelawny free!

We'll cross the Tamar, land to land,
The Severn is no stay,
With "one and all", and hand in hand,
And who shall bid us nay?'

And shall Trelawny live?
And shall Trelawny die?
Here's twenty thousand Cornishmen
Will know the reason why.

And when we come to London Wall,
A pleasant sight to view,
Come forth! come forth! ye cowards all:
Here's men as good as you.

Trelawny he's in keep and hold;
Trelawny he may die:
Here's twenty thousand Cornish bold
Will know the reason why.

And shall Trelawny live?
And shall Trelawny die?
Here's twenty thousand Cornishmen
Will know the reason why.

CHAPTER SIX

COMING HOME

Concentration has never been our strongest suit, so we're always relieved when we've finished 'Johnny Gone Down to Hilo', the song that Billy has just led. Over the years, we've explored all the permutations between Johnny and Tommy, Jimmy and Timmy, as well as 'gone down' and 'go down' and 'come down' to Hilo, until Billy finally settled on 'Johnny Gone Down to Hilo'. Even now, we're never quite sure which one he might sing as it varies from week to week, depending on how the ale's flowing.

If there is one thing that unites us when we're singing on the Platt, it's the growing sense of nervousness as the songs progress down the line and our own turn to take the lead approaches.

Over the years, we've all had our nervousness-induced moments. Some of us have dried up completely, our anxious mouths too parched to lead our song. Others have forgotten the lyrics, sung them too quickly or in such a high key that the lads at the centre of the line – Lefty, Billy and Trevor – struggled to harmonise. Or we've struck up a song that few of us have heard before, let alone sung together.

But by the time it reaches the middle of the line, we've usually settled. We've had a couple of changes of pace. First the rollocking stompers delivered by Cleavey and the Brown brothers. Then a tearful lament or a simple ballad served up by our tried and trusted housewife's choice, Trevor. Another change of tempo when Lefty brings it right back up again with his cavorting around, backed up by Billy singing 'Hilo'. By the time it passes Billy, we know whether we've got the audience on board and Cleavey can start to have fun with the introductions.

'Ladies and gentlemen, we're the Fisherman's Friends,' says Cleavey when Billy has finished singing. 'The men who did for singing what Long John Silver did for tap-dancing before he fell into the sink and twisted his ankle.'

Before the audience stops laughing (hopefully), Cleavey continues. 'We are very privileged to be able to announce this next song as we have Port Isaac's crown jewels with us.'

By now, the audience knows the formula well, so all eyes fall on the next person in the line: Peter Rowe, who is standing in his own little dream world, staring into space and looking bewildered.

'We brought him all this way on a sedan chair with a velvet cushion: Mr Peter Rowe, ladies and gentlemen! Please be gentle on him. He's seventy-seven years old.'

Peter blinks at the audience, still looking like he's a bit lost.

'Seventy-seven ...' says Cleavey, craning around Nigel Sherratt and Johnny Mac to catch Peter's eye. 'I said seventy-seven ...'

Still no response from Peter, so Cleavey raises his voice. 'You're *seventy-seven*, you know.' But Peter stares vacantly ahead, apparently deaf to Cleavey, who is becoming impatient. 'I say ... there's an audience out there.'

Peter comes to his senses, albeit only slightly, so Cleavey addresses him directly. 'Yes, Peter. Seventy-seven. *You.*'

But still Peter doesn't realise Cleavey is talking about him.

'Oh for Chrissakes,' says Cleavey, losing his patience. 'Someone tell him he's seventy-seven.'

Either side of Peter, Billy and Macster nudge him. Peter looks startled. It's all an act and meant very affectionately, so Peter plays along with it.

'Oh no,' says Cleavey. 'Did you remember to put your teeth in, Peter? Hello?'

Macster and Billy nudge Peter again, who makes a great pretence of realising at last that he's on the Platt. And that he's here to sing. Playing panicked, he launches into song, but it's the wrong one. With much tutting and shaking of heads, we all tell him to shut up.

'This next one's called "The Mollymawk",' says Cleavey patiently. 'And *Peter* . . .' Cleavey glares at Peter. 'And Peter is going to sing it.'

'*Oh, the southern ocean is a lonely place,*' sings Peter.

'*Where the storms are many and the shelter's scarce . . .*'

Peter's fishing days are a long way behind him now. For the last twenty years he's been a house-husband to his wife, Liz, a radiologist at Truro hospital. But at the time that Cleavey, John Brown and Billy were seeing the world and dreaming of returning home, Peter was one of Port Isaac's busiest fishermen.

With his brother Jack, Pete used to run a 38-foot fibreglass cata-maran with twin Volvo diesels, the *Francis Kate*. In the late 1970s and early 1980s, the boats had less powerful engines than today, so instead of coming back to Port Isaac every evening, they would spend a week at a time away, fishing up at Lundy Island, a tiny lump of rock at the mouth of the Bristol Channel, and sleeping on the boat.

But the boat was without facilities for staying aboard and very cramped, so Jack and Pete made friends with the Lundy Islanders and eventually found accommodation with the island's boatman and the agent, two of Lundy's population of fewer than thirty souls. Evenings would be spent in the only pub, the Marisco Tavern, which never closed. It's named after Lundy's martyr, William de Marisco, who had his bowels burned by Henry III for offering the island as a refuge for pirates, smugglers and other enemies of the crown. Even before Pete and Jack holed up there, Lundy was a haven for outcasts, ne'er-do-wells and eccentrics. In the seventeenth century, it was used as a

Catholic gathering ground for a lunge at the English crown after the death of Elizabeth I. In 1834, it was bought by William Hudson Heaven, a former sugar baron who declared it a free island, beyond the remit of British law, which gained it the nickname the Kingdom of Heaven. Even when a resident shot a rowdy drunk, he escaped conviction for murder in the Devon courts because he lived on Lundy. Although Parliament eventually dragged Lundy into line with the mainland, its residents were still not liable for income tax in the days shortly before Pete and Jack spent weekday nights sleeping on the island. Had this fiscal anomaly not ended in 1974, the Rowe brothers might technically have been able to declare themselves tax exiles, as they would only return on Friday nights to Appledore on the north Devon coast, where they would moor the *Francis Kate* and drive back to Port Isaac for the weekend.

Compared to running his newsagent's shop, fishing was hard work for Peter, but it was much more satisfying. Pete loved being outdoors and at sea. From early spring to late autumn, they would fish. In winter, they'd haul the boat ashore for repairs and spend their spare time making lobster pots. Nowadays fishermen buy their pots ready-made, but in those days they would be cobbled together from strips of wire, plastic, rubber and tyre. It was a practice left over from the days when fishermen made their own withy pots from willow grown especially in a plantation at the top end of the valley, above the village.

Mooring off Lundy was a risky business. About three miles long and three-quarters of a mile wide, this reef of volcanic granite is shaped like a hook. A long, curved, rocky spit extends from its south-eastern corner to form a natural cove sheltered from the prevailing southwesterly, westerly and northwest winds. But the tides are some of the largest in the world and if the wind has anything east in it, any boats moored in the sheltered cove need to move quickly to avoid being swept on to the rocks. Pete discovered that his anchor didn't find much purchase on the soft, muddy seabed, so he and Jack developed their own anchor for Lundy. They filled three Land Rover tyres with concrete, linked them with long sections of heavy chain and then released them every twenty-five feet as they approached the bay. It worked.

Early on the morning of Monday, 14 August 1979, Peter, Jack and Pete's son, Mark, left Port Isaac bound for Lundy. Around 200 miles away, the Fastnet Race, one of the classic offshore yachting events, was in crisis. The flotilla had left Cowes on the Isle of Wight three days earlier to round the Fastnet Rock off the southwest coast of Ireland before passing south of the Isles of Scilly. If all had gone to plan, the 306 yachts participating in the 605-mile race would typically have reached the Plymouth finish line around 48 hours later on Sunday, 13 August. But the race had not gone to plan. When they set out, the BBC radio shipping forecast predicted 'southwesterly winds, force four to five increasing to force six to seven for a time'. Two days later, those winds changed to force eleven (violent storm) and twenty-five of the participating yachts had been sunk or disabled in high winds and mountainous seas between Land's End and Fastnet.

As they left Port Isaac behind them, the three of them listened to details of the rescue operation in progress in the Irish Sea. The winds had dropped to severe gale force nine and Royal Navy ships, RAF Nimrod jets, helicopters, lifeboats, a Dutch warship and other craft including tugs, trawlers and tankers were in the process of picking up 125 stranded yachtsmen. The news didn't stop Peter, Jack and Mark from leaving Port Isaac. The storm was more than one hundred miles away and, according to the forecast, the wind would be in decline.

But as they motored towards Lundy, the wind didn't decline. It increased substantially. By the time they arrived they were very relieved to be able to moor in the lee of the island. That's when they discovered they'd left their special Lundy anchor in Port Isaac. Pete cast out his conventional anchor, but it didn't hold very well.

The only option, they decided, would be to keep a 24-hour watch and to attempt to hold the *Francis Kate* in position by using her motor to supplement the inadequate anchor. After several thousand miles of open ocean, Lundy was the first landmass to encounter the wind. No more than 400 feet high and almost entirely barren, the island hardly slowed it down. Instead it generated a pressure differential that sucked the wind on to the surface of the sea. The southwesterly was coming over the island with such force that it pressed the *Francis Kate* down into the water. Feeling the pressure in the wheelhouse, they watched as the wind overturned half a dozen boxes of bait, each weighing about forty kilograms, and scuttled them over the deck. They'd never seen or experienced anything like it.

With the anchor slipping, Jack had to run the motor intermittently to force the *Francis Kate* back into the protection of the cove. But as they pushed into it, they could see that near the stony beach the wind was generating whirlpools and water spouts large enough to pick up a passing dinghy.

As darkness fell, they considered their options. If the wind direction changed suddenly there was no question that the *Francis Kate* would be blown on to the rocks. Their only option, they decided, would be to blast the engines full ahead and hope to beach the boat on to a narrow stretch of stony shore between large banks of rocks at either end of the cove. If they timed it right, they might be able to jump off the bow to safety as the *Francis Kate* ran aground. The boat would be wrecked, but their own survival was more important than protecting their marine hardware.

None of them slept. It was a night of listening to all their radios, monitoring the wind direction and force, scared it would fly out to the north or east, and periodically gunning the engine to keep themselves within the lee of the island. Shortly after the sun came up the next morning, Pete peered out of the wheelhouse window. From where they were moored, he could see through a gap between the end of Lundy Island and Rat Island, a small rock at the end of the cove (it's one of the few remaining homes of the aboriginal black rat, now almost exterminated by the brown rat). As he gazed through the gap between the rocks at the fierce ocean, a yacht came into view, tossing in the waves like a paper boat.

During the night, Pete had heard discussion on his radio between the coastguard and a large German vessel standing by, near Lundy.

The coastguard was unable to do anything for them and could only advise her captain to keep distance from Lundy's western shore. Now they could see a small English yacht as she went by. The size of the waves, some as tall as houses, and the speed of the tide dashed any hope that Pete might have had of lending assistance to the yacht. All he could do was watch as the waves lifted her so far up into the air, he could see her keel. And then when she came down, the waves around her were so high, Pete lost sight of the top of her mast. One thing was for sure: her English skipper was a hell of a sailor to have survived in those seas for so long.

The yacht disappeared out of view and then reappeared around the end of the long promontory at the southern end of the bay. Of the half-dozen vessels taking shelter in the cove, the *Francis Kate* had been dragged out the furthest because of the inadequacy of her anchor. The yacht came alongside the *Francis Kate* and the skipper yelled over to Pete.

'Where's the best place to drop an anchor?'

'God, you've had a journey,' shouted Pete over the wind.

'Yes, and we've got two children down below.'

Pete was astonished. The only way he could imagine the children surviving was if they had been strapped to their berths for the last forty-eight hours.

The yacht pulled in and anchored, lucky not to have become yet another statistic associated with the storm that had devastated the Fastnet Race. A day later, when the wind had subsided but not completely abated, Pete, Jack and Mark headed for home, leaving the yacht still anchored in the harbour. They soon wished they hadn't decided to bash away home because the wind went right back up, making the voyage back to Port Isaac a long and frightening ordeal.

All three made it back to port safely. Pete and Jack continued fishing together for another nine years before Pete retired to begin work on Port Isaac's most lovingly tended garden, while Mark joined the police force. That was about the time Cleavey, Billy and John Brown were starting to entertain thoughts of returning home.

At the time Peter was making his living from the sea, another member of the Fisherman's Friends was embarking on a fishing career that was much more clandestine. Trevor joined his father's building firm after leaving school and has worked as a builder and carpenter ever since, eventually taking over his father's firm on his retirement. But that's only the official story, because Trevor's a bit of a dark horse. Really he's a frustrated fisherman. Although he keeps it quiet, he's always had a boat of his own, even when he was a little tacker. And since the late 1970s, much to the displeasure of full-time fishermen like the Brown brothers, Trevor has even had a licence and has regularly fished for lobster.

Within the Fisherman's Friends, there's an unwritten rule that Trevor's fishing is never spoken about. Once in a while, though, one of the Browns will mutter a comment.

'Oh, I saw you buggered off out of the harbour again, then,' one of them will say.

Trevor will just nod and smile and say nothing.

'Bloody part-timers,' they'll say next.

If it's John Brown taking the mickey out of Trevor, he might respond with the quip that John's a fine one to talk, given that he's the only person who can have a bag of sweets in his pocket, unwrap one and put it in his mouth without anyone noticing.

If it's someone else, Trevor will point out that he's doing nothing wrong. 'You don't bloody worry about it when you're doing a bit of decorating,' he'll say. 'You don't worry about it when you're repairing your window or putting in a pane of glass. That's no different to what I'm doing.'

That usually stops the griping, but if it doesn't put the moaner back in line, Trevor pulls out his trump card. 'At least I was born in the village.'

Having grown up together, everyone knows exactly how far to push everyone else. We all know each other's past. What they've done and what they shouldn't have done. Who they've been with and who they really shouldn't have been with. And when fishermen are throwing their weight around, no one has more gravitas than a fisherman who was born and brought up in the village.

That doesn't stop some of us calling Trevor a part-timer, like he's not really dedicated to fishing. But we know when to stop. And he just lets us rib him. But if you asked Trevor for an honest answer to the question of how often he gets out in his boat, he'd tell you: 'As much as I can. But not as much as I'd like.' A typically evasive fisherman's answer. What it actually means is a few times a week between May and the end of September, when the ground seas get hillier and boats can be damaged in the harbour. And if he can't get out in the evenings or weekends, Trevor will take four or five hours off his building work to go and check half his lobster pots.

Part-time fishing is a sensitive issue. It has always rankled with full-time fishermen, especially when the part-timer has a profession like a solicitor or a doctor by day. Although part-timers are just as entitled to the fish in the sea as full-timers, their living doesn't depend on it, so it's perhaps not surprising that the full-timers regard every fish, lobster and crab caught by part-timers as one that they can't have. Full-time fishermen understand that part-timers might be repressed fishermen, but they moan nonetheless.

Potting for crab and lobster is a competitive business with many unwritten rules. In theory, anything is allowed, even shooting pots directly beside another fisherman's line, but in practice a fisherman won't make many friends if they get too close. And anyone who shoots their pots over another fisherman's line is liable to find their own line cut in half.

Although the full-timers think otherwise, part-timers like Trevor say they don't make any money from fishing. Maybe that's because no fisherman will ever talk about how many fish he's caught. They'll always skirt around the subject because they don't want their rivals on their patches. All Trevor will concede is that he catches enough to cover his fuel and insurance expenses, and that's all. He'll say Port Isaac is fished out along the shores where the part-timers fish, so his takings are small. It means he'll never cover the cost of buying his boat, which makes his fishing a costly hobby rather than a profitable enterprise (and Trevor's wife always tells him: 'If we get short of money, the first thing that's going is the boat.' His response? 'Yes dear.'). Ultimately, though, part-timers fish for exactly the same reason as the full-timers. They do it because they love being out at sea. It's the thrill of pulling up a pot and, when it's just below the surface, seeing something blue in it with claws. And what price can be put on that kind of enjoyment?

While Pete was fishing openly and Toastie was doing the same clandestinely, Lefty was getting ready to leave school. By the age of sixteen, he'd had enough of running the gauntlet of the school authorities, so he left school to start working on the family farm with his uncle and grandfather. Their 350-acre farm also provided a living for Sampy, the farm labourer with whom Lefty had shared a room since he was a little tacker, as well as another chap close to retirement called Bill, and two brothers, Tony and David Powell.

Tony and David were into motorbikes. Triumphs were their thing, but they also had an old 350cc AJS that they'd dumped in a hedge. Lefty's father had taught him how to ride an old BSA when he was twelve, so one day the Powell brothers dragged the AJS out of the brambles and gave it to him. Lefty disappeared into his father's shed and within a few weeks had it fixed and working.

When he wasn't working on the farm, Lefty would be up in the woods, riding around, hoping his repairs to the AJS wouldn't let him down. Quite often, after having kick-started the bike, he'd notice it was getting quite hot beneath him. The bike would be on fire, but it happened so often that Lefty learned to react quite calmly, simply turning off the petrol and laying the AJS on its side so the escaped petrol could run off, flame and burn. A quick soldering of the petrol pipe and Lefty would be back in the saddle.

The AJS taught Lefty more about mechanics and engineering than he would have learned through any apprenticeship, but he soon grew bored of the AJS, so he bought himself some BSA Bantams. These were lighter two-stroke road bikes, one of which had no front brake, but that didn't stop Lefty taking it up the steepest hill in the area, to the top of some woods where it broke down. Unfazed, Lefty decided he'd take it home to repair it, so he slipped it into gear to slow his descent down the very severe incline, but he missed the gear. Starting to panic as the bike rolled faster, Lefty put a foot on the rear brake, but a nut on the brake rod had come undone, so he now had no brakes at all. Swearing at himself, he searched for an escape plan. In the distance, at the bottom of the hill, he saw a truck pass by and turn right into a long, level road. Maybe he could swing the bike into that road, he thought. But with his speed increasing at a frightening pace as he approached the turning, Lefty realised he was going too fast to make it into his run-off road. The next thing he knew he was flying through the air before coming to a sudden stop in a bush. The bike was a long distance away, lying upside down a few yards from a stream. A lucky escape, maybe, but not the last.

Lefty was forever running into things. It didn't matter if it was moving or stationary, Lefty would collide with it, often with his mate Keith on the pillion. On one occasion, they were returning home late at night from seeing girlfriends. Passing through the very narrow single-lane high street of Camelford, they came around a bend to find a Mini directly in front of them. Evasive action was needed, so Lefty took the snap decision to overtake the Mini on its right-hand side. But he hadn't reckoned on the Mini shooting off up Back Street, a right turn. With no other option available, Lefty leaned hard right to take the corner into Back Street fast.

With Keith hanging on behind him, Lefty made it round the bend, overtaking the Mini in the process, but not noticing a huge block of granite at the side of the road. The front wheel slammed into the granite block, catapulting Lefty and Keith off the bike into a shop front. Somehow – they still don't quite know how – neither Lefty nor Keith went through the window. They came to their senses lying on the road with the bike nearby, a thick tyre mark leading up the wall of the shop showing where the bike had been. Lefty hurt his knee in that crash, but he lived to fight another day. The tyre mark across the shop front, however, didn't fade for years.

His appetite for carnage whetted, Lefty joined a local motorbike club and started competing in trials events. Riding an old Tiger Cub, he won Best Cornish Resident in his first enduro, a tough rain-sodden event in which only fifteen of more than a hundred starters completed the course. He also met Trevor Grills and Jeremy Brown, fellow motorcycle enthusiasts, for the first time. On Sundays, they'd go off on rides together, up to a dozen bikes threading through wind-ing lanes. And sometimes Lefty would have his girlfriend, Mary, on the back, digging him in the ribs to slow down.

Lefty met Mary one evening in Port Isaac. He'd ridden into the village looking for a pint and the first person he saw was Mary. He'd known her at school. Three years younger, but taller than Lefty (which wasn't difficult), Mary had fine curly hair and a wicked smile. Lefty had always liked her, winding her up on the school bus, where he'd dared her to give him a kiss and she'd kicked and scratched, threatened to bite or do anything to avoid a clinch with Lefty. That night in Port Isaac, Mary was off to babysit for the landlord of the Golden Lion, but Lefty wasn't going to let that stop him.

'Hey, Mary,' he said, 'how're you doing?'

By the time they'd finished chatting, Lefty had set up a date for Saturday night. They took it from there and courted for five years before marrying and settling in Port Isaac, in a house opposite the garage.

On leaving school in 1972, and encouraged by his father, Lefty sat an exam and applied for an engineering apprenticeship at Falmouth Docks. Out of more than thirty applicants, Lefty was one of the suc-cessful five to be offered employment. He was back on the farm when the phone rang.

'Would you like to come down next Monday to start?' said the voice on the phone.

Lefty paused to think. It was one of those moments, he realised, at which he was faced with a decision that could determine the course of the rest of his life.

'Thanks,' said Lefty, 'but no.'

When the crucial moment had arrived, Lefty couldn't pull himself away from his farm. Like those of us living in Port Isaac, he couldn't turn his back on his home.

Lefty continued working on the farm and participating in motocross club meetings. One day he was marshalling a trials event, standing in the middle of the track because it seemed safest, watching as several outfits (motorbike and sidecar combinations) practised their starts. The race hadn't even started when Lefty spotted an outfit coming directly towards him, clearly out of control. Having just moved off, the sidecar man was directly behind the driver, pushing all his weight down on the back wheel for extra traction. Unable to steer left because it would turn the outfit over, the driver had no option but to continue straight ahead on a collision course with Lefty.

If I run left, thought Lefty, I'll end up on the track, where I could be hit by one of several bikes or outfits. But if I remain stationary, he thought, the nose cone at the front of the outfit will strike me and I'll be a dead man. By now, the outfit was topping 70mph, and again Lefty was facing a decision that could alter his existence. This time he decided to run to the right. Shouting 'You prat!' at the outfit, he made his lurch for safety, but a section of heavy scaffolding pipe along the front of the sidecar slammed into his leg, hurling him through the air – again.

The collision snapped Lefty's tibia and fibula, the two bones beneath his knee. Unable to work for thirteen months, he spent nine months in plaster. The timing couldn't have been worse. Two weeks before the accident, Mary and Lefty had moved into a barely habitable cottage on the farm, intending to renovate it. And their first child had just been born. When he'd recovered, Lefty thought he was going to take over his part of the family farm from his uncle. Having completed an apprenticeship with a City & Guilds qualification, he had ideas about how he wanted to run the farm, which he thought was his inherited right. But his uncle refused to pay him the extra amount his qualification usually attracted and made it very clear there was going to be only one boss. Lefty's uncle wasn't a man for taking partners. In fact, he wasn't a man for paying Lefty a full day's pay, so Lefty, needing more stability in his working life than toiling on the farm, accepted Mary's father's offer of a permanent position at his garage in Port Isaac. For the next ten years, he worked as a mechanic and drove coaches for his father-in-law, Mark, dropping off and collecting schoolchildren from the outlying villages on the school bus run. He still reared a few calves at the farm and sold them on.

Mark was the fairest and kindest man Lefty had ever met. After Lefty handed in the job sheets, Mark would often call him into his office to tell him to cut down the billing hours and costs to a customer that Mark knew was struggling. 'Exactly how long did you take to do it?' he would ask.

When Lefty answered, Mark would say, 'Well, how much money are we making on it? Can't we do it a bit cheaper?'

Mark was so straight and so conscientious that he refused to reduce his price when he had to re-tender for a council contract after he'd been running school buses to Camelford and Wadebridge for decades. He said the only way to reduce his costs was to cut corners and he said that was inappropriate when he was transporting children. A few weeks later, an envelope arrived from the council. Mark, sixty-five years old by then, opened it gingerly and read the enclosed letter. From the look on his face, Lefty knew it was bad news before Mark said a word.

'I'm going to have to sell up,' he said. Lefty asked him if there was any other option, but Mark just shook his head. 'The school buses were my bread and butter,' he said. 'Anything else was cream on top, so I always knew it would be curtains if I lost it.'

Lefty found himself a new job as a mechanic at a boatyard in Wadebridge, where he went on to qualify as a crane driver. He still works there occasionally, but these days he runs his own milking-parlour fibreglass coatings business, alongside marine and commercial vehicle engineering. A jack of all trades, he says. And master of none, we reply.

While Lefty, Trevor and Peter were at home, the pull of Port Isaac was exerting itself on the lads who'd flown the village. First to return was Julian Brown, whose kidney condition forced him to come home (not that he needed much encouragement) as soon as he finished his degree. More than anything else, Julian wanted to follow in his father's and grandfather's wellie-booted footsteps, fishing from the harbour, but he was now so debilitated that he didn't have the strength to work a boat. Instead he picked up other jobs. For a while, he was a postman and helped out at the village school. Month by month Julian's energy levels declined and with them his spirit. By his mid-twenties, he was becoming seriously depressed by his listlessness. Then, just when he was about to abandon hope, Julian received a telephone call telling him that a matching kidney had become available.

The operation transformed Julian's life. Slowly but surely he regained his strength and eventually he felt ready to go to sea. However, his mother still harboured a dream of Julian pursuing a middle-class profession. As her eldest son, he felt obliged to indulge his mother's wishes and soon found himself enrolling for postgraduate teacher training at Plymouth. His hankering for the sea would have to wait.

To make it worse, Julian's brother, John, was about to return to the village. As soon as he joined the crew of the prestigious *QE2*, he realised he'd made a massive mistake. The *QE2*'s engine room was a mess. One of his shipmates took him aside for a terse warning. 'Be careful,' he said. 'Someone is going to die down here one day.'

When John looked around the engine room he immediately saw the reason for the dramatic words. High-pressure steam is extremely corrosive. It attacks any exposed steel or iron. And its corrosive effect could be seen all around the rusting engine room. It looked like a hospital case, with all the joints between the steam pipes bound together with bandages.

'Whatever you do,' said his colleague, 'don't take off any plates or nuts unless I'm there with you.'

It was a very different world from the slick, spotless engine rooms of diesel-powered ships and their regime of preventative maintenance.

John now spent most of each day fire-fighting, making emergency repairs needed solely to keep the ship running. One day, as the *QE2* steamed from Southampton to New York, her passengers oblivious to the chaos in the engine room, John was sitting out on the foredeck with some engineers when a colossal bang made them almost drop their mugs of tea. They all looked back at the funnel, expecting the boiler to have burst. Instead, the bang was Concorde passing through the sound barrier, many miles overhead, but it was a forewarning of what might happen. A year later, the *QE2* went into dock for a refurbishment and the steam engines were replaced by diesel, but by then John had long disembarked. He lasted only six weeks before jumping off at Southampton and putting his merchant navy days behind him.

When he returned to Port Isaac, John joined his father, Harold, fishing from the *Winnie the Pooh*. When Harold retired, John took over the boat, recruiting a crew from Johnny Rowe, a nephew of Peter Rowe, and a couple of young lads at the top of the village. The young lads were hard workers but John insisted on paying them on Mondays because he knew that if he paid them on a Friday, they'd spend it all on drink and he wouldn't see them again until Monday, which wasn't helpful on those weekends when conditions were ideal for fishing. Modern-day fishing has an early morning start and John needed lads who would turn up at 5 a.m. any day of the week to pump diesel, get the bait out and prepare the boat.

But the most significant addition to John's crew was Julian, who was teaching at a school at Saltash, leaving him free to fish in school holidays. After a year at Saltash, Julian transferred to a school at Bodmin, which was closer to home and allowed him to fish also at half-terms and weekends. Two years later, he was supply-teaching at Wadebridge School, teaching English one warm afternoon to a class of children who didn't want to be cooped up in a stuffy classroom any more than Julian did. At that moment, he realised that he really couldn't deny himself his true vocation any longer. The next morning, when the school secretary called to ask him to cover for an absent teacher, Julian spoke from the heart. 'I won't be coming in,' he said. 'Not now, or ever. I don't want to teach any more.' He never went back.

Julian joined John as a full-time crew member. Meanwhile, their brother Jeremy, who had been running a fish round in the village, also went to sea on a boat of his own. Now all three Brown brothers had followed their father to sea. Although Harold Brown was no longer fishing, his sons' choosing to follow him in the same trade created a special bond deeper than that usually between father and son. If any of them had a good day at sea, they could tell their dad, knowing he'd understand exactly what a good day at sea felt like. Julian felt his father was the only person he knew who would ever fully understand what he was talking about. More than a parent to the Brown brothers, Harold was a true friend, someone they could go and talk to about anything.

John and Julian concentrated on potting for lobster and crab, and shooting wreck nets for fish. Wreck-netting was a risky game, one that Julian perfected better than John. It exploited the behaviour of the fish, which would shelter on the down-tide side of the wreck when the tide was going out, then move over to the up-tide side when the tide came in. The wreck provided shelter and security, and harboured hundreds of different types of food that the fish would pick at, protected from the stream of the tide.

Shooting wreck nets was an art, and Julian was more the skilled artist than John. He would shoot his net parallel to his target, whereas John just shot it over the wreck. John's net would tangle in the wreck and he'd need a powerful winch to rip it out of the water. The net would be ruined, but as long as John netted more fish than the value of the net, it was worthwhile. If Julian shot his net just right, it would rest along the side of the wreck, just touching it but not stirring up the food attached to the wreck, and it could be lifted undamaged from the water.

About a year after Julian started fishing with John, Julian scraped together enough money to build a boat of his own, one almost exactly the same as John's new boat, the *LEJ*, named after the initials

of John's daughter, his wife and John himself. For a while, the brothers fished separately, but Julian was always more dedicated than John.
If John had a good day, he'd take the next day off and have a lie-in.
But if Julian had a good day, he'd get up even earlier the next morning to make sure he had an even better day. Eventually, John realised
that his heart was no longer in it. He was discovering that what his
father had told him was absolutely true: fishing was a hard way to
make a living and it wasn't good for a man with a young family.
Forced to calculate his earnings for a grant application, he worked out
that he caught on average one lobster in every eight pots. It meant
he was earning 87p for every pot he hauled, a meagre sum for the
amount of work involved. And fishing was taking him away from
his wife and child. When conditions were good, John once fished
for twenty-seven days in succession, putting a huge strain on his family.
He felt trapped.

One afternoon, John was sitting on the Platt with some of his crew,
watching the sea and debating whether to go out fishing, when
Johnny Rowe turned up. He'd crewed for John years earlier, then he'd
bought his own boat and gone fishing on his own. But more recently
he'd sold that boat and taken up window cleaning. Johnny sat down
with his ladder and bucket and had a chat.

'Are you still trying to make up your mind?' said Johnny. 'Still don't
know whether to go fishing or not?'

John nodded.

'In the last half an hour,' said Johnny Rowe, 'I've earned seven quid
and this is a bad day. It's cold and wet, the kind of day you wouldn't
even go to sea unless you really needed to. And while you've been sitting here, wondering what to do, I've got myself seven quid for easy
work on dry land.'

At last the penny dropped with John. The price of diesel had just
risen again. His wife and children rarely saw him. Fishing for lobster
was hard work for meagre returns. And his opportunities for earning
depended on the vagaries of the weather. His father was right: fishing was a very hard way to make a living.

'If you ever want to pack up your window cleaning,' said John, 'just give us a shout.'

Nothing happened for a while. John continued fishing. But a few years later, Johnny decided to leave the village. John immediately stepped in and took over his window-cleaning round. Not long after that, he sold his boat. These days, he runs fishing trips for tourists from his father's old boat, the *Winnie the Pooh*. Occasionally, he fishes part time for crabs and lobsters, but having been a full-time fisherman, he always feels guilty doing it against his brothers. Old habits die hard.

When the Brown brothers weren't fishing and Trevor wasn't building (we won't mention his part-time fishing) and Peter wasn't gardening, they'd often spend evenings in the Golden Lion. Years earlier, the Golden Lion had been a place of song. In the 1930s, Peter used to drift off to sleep in his bedroom at the top of his parents' house, next door to the pub, to the sound of singing in the street outside the saloon bar. After the war, Trevor's father and uncle used to play their accordions outside the pub and sing songs. Of course, there was no television then to distract people, but in Port Isaac singing went beyond a search for a way to pass the time of an evening. There was a sense that it was a part of our heritage and many people made an effort to keep the tradition of public singing alive. Somehow – no one knows why or exactly when – that tradition died out. By the late 1980s, hardly anyone sang outside or inside the pub any more. Occasionally one of the old boys would sing a few bars of a shanty or a Cornish folk song, but it didn't happen often.

Then, on a Christmas Eve in the late 1980s (none of us in the Fisherman's Friends is good on dates, but it was probably 1987 or 1988), a bunch of us went down to the Golden Lion. It was a Christmas Eve like countless others before. Cold outside, but warm indoors near the golden light of the fire. The Brothers Grim – Jeremy, Julian and John – were there. So was Trevor, with his brother Kevin. Of course, Trevor's close mate Mark Provis was with us, as was Peter Rowe's nephew, Johnny, and a few other locals. We'd never sung in the pub before, but that year, for some inexplicable reason, it seemed appropriate to sing Christmas carols. With pints in hand, leaning against the bar and the bare stone wall, we worked our way through all the carols we knew. It felt great.

As we sang, we all realised how much we were enjoying it and how much we missed hearing regular singing in the pub, that evocative sound of our childhoods. It was obvious that John, Jeremy and Julian had been doing a bit of practising; they've always been dark horses and we suspected they'd been singing a bit at home. Beside them, Johnny Rowe was singing his lungs out, clearly enjoying every second of it, but unfortunately, he was quite out of tune. He's a wonderful mate, a fantastic bloke who we love to bits, a great pal to many, but his singing is as flat as a dab, which is a bit of a tragedy really as we'd love to have him in the Fisherman's Friends with us, but it's not to be. And Trevor was his usual self: quietly singing along with the rest of us, but keeping out of the limelight.

Later that night – it might even have been early the next morning – we left the pub to go back to our families and prepare for Christmas Day. Full to the brim with beer, good company and the joy of song, we wished each other a Merry Christmas, then muttered a few words about how we should maybe sing together more regularly, maybe meet to try out a few old Cornish folk songs. Heads nodded, lips pursed. One of us might even have grunted approval. It was nothing momentous, but we all knew then that singing together was something we wanted to do again. And in that moment, the first seeds of the Fisherman's Friends were sown.

Cornish Comin's 'n' Goin's

We're always getting strangers arriving from up country and further afield – 'blow-ins', we call them. And like most Cornishmen, many of us Yarnigoats have been known to venture beyond the valley in search of work and adventure.

A few years ago, 50,000 of us left the duchy in search of rugby adventure at the County Championship final at Twickenham. Trelawny's Army, they called us. 'Last one across the Tamar turn out the lights and cancel the milk,' said the local papers. However, the biggest movement of our people took place in the Cornish diaspora of 1861 to 1901, when 250,000 Cornish (half today's population) emigrated in search of work and a better life. Coinciding with the decline of tin and copper mining, many were miners but there were also farmers, merchants and tradesmen. Most went to North America, the Antipodes, South Africa, Brazil and Chile, leading to the saying in Cornwall that 'a mine is a hole anywhere in the world with at least one Cornishman at the bottom of it'.

The Cornish diaspora introduced the first farmer to Australia, a John Ruse who settled in New South Wales. It also introduced the Cornish pasty to Mexico, where the *paste* is a speciality derived from the pasties eaten by Cornish miners working in silver mines in the central Mexican state of Hidalgo.

As for blow-ins, we're no strangers to famous names moving into our remote corner of the country. Madonna has apparently bought a pad on the south coast, but we're too discreet to let on about our celebrity neighbours in Port Isaac (if you're nosy, you can Google it).

However, the most famous blow-in to visit the county was apparently a chap from Nazareth called Jesus. According to local legend, the Son of God was brought to us as a young man by Joseph of Arimathea, a tin trader, to visit Ding Dong mine, one of the oldest in Cornwall. During the visit, Jesus is said to have addressed miners in the parish of Gulval, near Penzance. Proper job.

CHAPTER SEVEN

GIGS AND SHANTIES

'Thank you very much,' says Cleavey after we finish singing 'The Mollymawk'. 'Ladies and gentlemen, we're the Fisherman's Friends. The men who did for singing what Vice-Admiral Horatio Nelson did for binocular sales.'

As he says it, we are singing outdoors, with our backs to the sea, a position that can feel dangerously exposed and which occasionally puts us directly at the mercy of the elements. If it starts to rain, there's little we can do except sing faster and hope we don't get electric shocks from the microphones. If it's raining even before we're due to start, we have been known to pull the lifeboat out of the lifeboat station at the top of the Platt and stand in the doorway to sing. The audience still gets wet, but we're under cover and – most importantly – our pints of beer at our feet aren't diluted by rainwater.

There's also always the danger that our beer consumption plays havoc with our performance. Our strict rule of no more than two pints before a performance is never breached, but let's just say we're not the youngest group of singers on the circuit. With our combined age of 561, we're more buoy band than boy band. But accumulating those centuries of experience and wisdom comes with a physical cost and it's not unusual for one or more of us to feel an urgent need, probably not experienced quite so acutely by younger musicians, to relieve ourselves of the ale's well-known side effect before our performance is finished. At times it can be murder, particularly to those who are about to lead a song, and it's not unknown for one of us to slip off stage and disappear into the lifeboat house, the Slipway, or even one of our homes nearby. The relief we've all experienced at times like that is something quite special.

However, the biggest threat to our wellbeing on stage comes from behind us: the approaching tide. In any season, it might have us two or three times. It's not that we misjudge when it's going to come in or how high it will be. After all, we can consult the tide tables. Our problem is that we have to perform at 8 p.m. every Friday in the season, no matter what the tide is doing. And the tide doesn't wait for anyone. On occasion we've been like King Canute, trying to command the tide to stop and not wet our feet, nervously glancing over our shoulders and praying it's about to stop its advance. And, of course, on those occasions the tide doesn't stay back and we get our feet wet. For Billy, whose guitar is plugged into an amplifier with 240 volts coursing through it, the advance of the tide can be terrifying. 'If that wave comes over here,' he once muttered between songs, 'I'm going to blow up like a bloody pinball machine.'

Our battle with the tide has been made more acute since we signed our recording contract and the weekly audience has swollen from a few hundred to maybe a couple of thousand people on a particularly nice evening in the middle of the summer. There have been nights when the lanes running up the hills on either side of the Platt have been crowded to bursting point, pushing the front row of the audience to within a couple of feet of us. We're thrilled to attract such large crowds, but it's very unnerving when we can see the colour of the eyes and state of the teeth of the people to whom we're singing.

However, worries about crowds, the tide or the weather must be cast aside when faced with hundreds or even thousands of expectant listeners, so Cleavey moves on, introducing the second-tallest man in our line-up, Johnny Mac.

'We're extremely proud Cornishmen in this group,' says Cleavey.

'Nine out of ten of us are from Cornwall, but we do have one outsider. And he's here for all the best reasons.

'Many years ago, Cornwall Council realised there was a bit of a genetic imbalance in Port Isaac, so they trawled the country for someone to come down and try to redress this a little bit. To do this, they brought down Mr John McDonnell, who has done his very best since his arrival. He was entered on a Stalinesque five-year breeding plan. And perhaps, as you can see, it's not had a lot of use.

'Seriously, though, ladies and gentlemen, Mr John McDonnell came down to us from Yorkshire nearly forty years ago. *Forty years.* What a long time. And he fitted in straight away with us, like he'd been part of the furniture for ever, so we thought we ought to honour him and recognise this fact. A few weeks ago we took him aside and made him an offer we thought he couldn't refuse.

'"John," we said, "we're going to make you an honorary Cornishman."

'"Bugger off," he said. "I'm from bloody Yorkshire."

'Well, that's gratitude for you,' says Cleavey as John immediately strikes up with 'Noah Built the Ark', an old spiritual.

Sittin' by the river on the levee, waitin' till the steamboat comes down,
Them cotton bales are rollin' mighty heavy, miles and miles around.

Cleavey's right about us being proud of our Cornish heritage. It's a big part of our identity. Whenever anyone crosses the Tamar they think they've come into the Duchy of Cornwall, but really they've entered a Celtic nation with its own language, food, customs, traditions, folk-lores, sports and peculiarities. Even the name – Cornwall – indicates we're a nation apart from the rest of Britain. 'Wall' is an Anglo-Saxon word meaning foreigner. 'Corn' comes from the English word, horn (and the Latin equivalent, *cornu*), and relates to the shape of our peninsula. So Cornwall means the horn-shaped peninsula of foreigners. That just about sums us up.

Love him or loathe him, the former Deputy Prime Minister John Prescott got it right when he said that Cornwall had the strongest regional identity in the UK. But it's an identity that perhaps doesn't conform easily to a stereotype in quite the same way as a Yorkshireman or a Cockney or a Scouser. Partly that's because we're tucked away out of sight in a distant corner of the country and partly it's because historically we have always looked outside the country as much as into it. For thousands of years we've traded with other maritime nations, selling our copper and tin to civilisations going back to the Phoenicians, who brought us saffron in return. As a result, we have absorbed blood, culture and traditions from far afield, including the eastern Mediterranean, Spain, Brittany, Ireland and Wales, and you can see their influence today in even the most mundane Cornish products, such as saffron cakes.

These outside influences mixed with a bloodline that over time became quite different from the rest of England. At heart, we are the remnants of the ancient Britons, the Celts, who inhabited most of this island until the Romans invaded in 43AD. While the inhabitants of what is now England largely became Romano-Brits, in the far west of the country the Roman influence was relatively minor, so we remained Celtic.

After the collapse of Roman rule in about 410, Saxon, Angle and Viking invaders overran England, pushing Celtic culture further west into our remote and inaccessible corner of the country, which became a semi-autonomous territory in which we were known as the West Britons. Then, under the Normans, who invaded in 1066, the Viking and Anglo-Saxon influences blended to form the English people, but in the northern and western peripheries of the island – Scotland, Wales and Cornwall – the ethnic stock remained relatively unchanged.

Cornwall remained very separate from England until the sixteenth century, when the first of two events conspired to end our independence. In 1549, the old Latin Liturgy was forcibly replaced by the Book of Common Prayer in English. The Cornish, many of whom did not speak English at all, rebelled against the imposition of a new liturgy in a foreign tongue. The English crown stamped on their rebellion, slaughtering around 4,000 West Country men in the process and making it clear who was now ruling over Cornwall.

A century later, the English Civil War broke out and the Cornish wholeheartedly backed the King. But Charles I's defeat by the Parliamentarians in 1646 crushed Cornwall again, this time to an extent from which our ethnic identity struggled to recover.

Still, even after we became fully annexed by England, Cornwall kept its own language, customs, dress and culture. Foreigners who visited Britain in the seventeenth and eighteenth centuries often regarded Cornwall as one of three provinces of England, the other two being Wales and England itself. When an Italian scholar visited Britain, he declared that Britain was divided into four parts inhabited by the English, Scots, Welsh and Cornish people.

We were rightly regarded by outsiders as a separate ethnic group, defiantly different from our English neighbours. Our mining, fishing and farming heritage, our toiling and living close to nature, made us a hardy and independent race. And our isolation, clinging to a rocky peninsula jutting ninety miles into the Atlantic Ocean, ensured we appreciated the value of community and co-operation, making us a courteous and hospitable people (we like to think), quick to appreciate and return acts of kindness. But if there is one characteristic that defines a Cornishman it is his nonconformity and independence of mind and spirit. In the mid-nineteenth century, a writer called Francis Talbot O'Donoghue published a novel called *St Knighton's Keive*, named after a natural archway cut into rock at Tintagel, through which men had to pass to become knights at the table of King Arthur. In this novel, he described the Cornish personality as accurately as anyone has ever achieved it.

The Cornish have been often compared to the Irish, and again to the Welsh, and there are, no doubt, many points of resemblance between them, with an important difference however to be mentioned.

Like all people of Celtic origin, the Cornish are impulsive, imagin-
ative, poetical ... They are quick at learning, and much given to
herding together; they like a crowd, whether it be at funerals, wed-
dings, or what not. They have got the natural politeness and
courtesy of the Irish, and are free from the irascibility and stub-
bornness of the Welsh.

In one important point, however, they fall short of the Irish, and
even the Welsh; and that is, they are totally deficient in the organ
of veneration which would lead them habitually to look up to a
superior. The Cornishman thinks himself quite as good as you, any
day; and doesn't care who knows it.

Maybe it's because we have been lucky enough to have been born
in God's own county that we aren't easily cowed by other men. After
all, nowhere else has anything quite like our combination of stunning
coastline, lush fields, dramatic moors, abundant minerals and natural
resources, gentle climate and lobster-rich waters. Whatever the cause
of our freethinking nature, disregard for authority and irreverent attitude, it's summed up nicely in a couple of Cornish jokes.

In the first, a visitor to Cornwall comes across a local and strikes up
a conversation.

'How do you do?' says the visitor.

'Ow be 'e, yerself?' says the local.

'Isn't it a lovely day?' continues the visitor.

'I s'pose it be.'

'This is a lovely place to live.'

'Ayse.'

'Have you lived here all your life?'

'Not yet, me 'andsome.'

In the second, an Englishman asks an old Cornishman, 'What do
you say in this part of the world, "neye-ther" or "nee-ther"?'

And the old Cornishman replies, 'Nather. Us dawn't use thet word.'

With such a strong identity, it isn't surprising that we have our own
customs, folklores such as pixies, sports such as Cornish hurling and

wrestling, foods such as fudge, splits and fairings, and recipes such as Stargazy Pie, Figgy 'obbin and Hevva Cakes, named after the huer's cry in the days of pilchard fishing. But the best-known Cornish delicacy is probably the pasty. We even write poems about it.

> *I dearly luv a pasty,*
> *A 'ot 'n' leaky wun,*
> *Weth taties, mayt 'n' turmit,*
> *Purs'ly 'n' honyun.*
>
> *Un crus be made with su't,*
> *'N' shaped like 'alf a moon,*
> *Weth crinkly hedges, freshly baked,*
> *E'z always gone too soon!*

Among Cornwall's oldest traditions, of course, is our love of singing. Like other Celtic nations, music and song are at the core of our culture. Our fishermen, miners and farmers liked nothing more at the end of a long day's work than to go home, wash up, then head to the pub to tell stories, sing songs and drink beer. It's no different today, which is why the Fisherman's Friends were born out of our shared enjoyment of a yarn, a pint and a singalong.

That Christmas Eve, when the Brown brothers, Trevor and a few of their mates started singing Christmas carols in the Golden Lion, they were following in a Cornish tradition of striking up a 'curl' that has its roots in the Middle Ages. Medieval European carols that were lost elsewhere were preserved among Cornish people, partially because of our connections with other Celtic communities but also because of our strong but isolated culture. As a result, public singing over the Christmas period is still a big thing in Cornwall.

In Bodmin, 'wassailers' visit homes, public houses and shops on the twelfth day of Christmas in a tradition that dates back at least to the sixteenth century. These wassailers dress in gentlemen's hand-me-downs of top hat and tails and move from home to home, singing the

Bodmin Wassail ('wassail' means hail and hearty good health in Anglo-Saxon) as well as various carols and Cornish songs to collect money for charity. Wassailing goes on in other Cornish communities, such as Truro and Penzance, but in many places it evolved into singing 'curls', a distinctive set and style of carols that were often particular to the town or village. One of the biggest carol traditions is in Padstow, where the carollers follow a route through the town, singing carols, sometimes to crowds of onlookers, but often simply among themselves. One of the carols, called 'Harky Harky' and based on 'Hark the Herald Angels Sing', is unique to Padstow and supposedly isn't even written down. Instead, its words and tune have been handed down from father to son and mother to daughter.

Wassailing and curl singing fed a Cornish tradition that continued in many forms, including male voice and ladies' choirs and pub singalongs, and led to carols in church. It's a little-known fact – and a source of Cornish pride – that formal carol singing in churches began in Cornwall in 1880. Until then, carols were only sung in the street or outside people's homes, but in 1880 the Bishop of Truro devised a service of nine lessons and carols. Intended by the bishop as a means of keeping men away from pubs on Christmas Eve, the service alternates the carols with the lessons, read by an ascending series of church figures, starting with a chorister and culminating with a bishop. All church carol singing originates from the Bishop of Truro's service.

Most famously, during the First World War the Dean of King's College, Cambridge, adopted the service, and the King's College Festival of Nine Lessons and Carols, held at 3 p.m. every Christmas Eve, has become an annual tradition that is now broadcast by hundreds of radio stations around the world. Within pubs, the singing wasn't limited to carols, of course, and it expanded to include Cornish folk songs, such as 'Camborne Hill', which tells the tale of the first outing of a steam carriage invented by Cornishman Richard Trevithick and tested on the sloping high street of Camborne. So when, buoyed by their experience in the Golden Lion, the Brown brothers and Trevor met up early that New Year to discuss singing together again, they were tapping into a long and noble Cornish pub singing tradition. It's such a long time ago that none of us can remember exactly who said what, but one of the Brown brothers, probably John, wondered out loud if anyone wanted to meet for a regular weekly session.

'We've been meeting every now and then,' he said, referring to his brothers, 'trying to learn a few songs, trying to put a singing group together.'

It turned out that John and Julian had been singing on the boat while they were working. John had a tape of a group from Cadgwith, a working fishing village that was very much like Port Isaac, but on the south coast of Cornwall. John and Julian had taught themselves some songs from the Cadgwith Singers' tape and John knew a few more nautical songs, mainly Irish tunes he'd picked up in the merchant navy. More recently, John and Julian had picked up on The Spinners, an English folk group that had released an album of sea shanties called *The Spinners Sing Songs of the Tall Ships*.

A few months earlier, John and Julian had been in the back of a van, returning from a pub quiz night with Johnny Mac, a member of their team at the time, but who hadn't started singing with us. Sitting on a sofa in the back of the van, John and Julian started to sing.

'Have you been practising?' said Mac.

'No,' said John. 'We just know a lot of songs.'

'You're good.'

It was the first time that John and Julian had been told their singing was good. Now they were keen to encourage other singers to join them, but Trevor wasn't even sure if he could sing properly. He didn't have a clue and, as far as he was concerned, joining in with a few carols in the pub didn't really count. Trevor reckoned he'd never sung anything properly, but he was determined to find out if he could.

In the midst of this ramshackle meeting, someone suggested we should all meet at one of our homes each week and have a go at learning some Cornish folk songs. Having weighed it up, we found ourselves congregating a week later in Julian's kitchen, feeling self-conscious, but committed to giving singing a go because we'd enjoyed Christmas Eve so much. After that, we met at Johnny Rowe's place, out on the cliff, then down at Trevor's house, when he lived in Trewetha Lane, and at Mark Provis's place. People dropped in and out of this small group, but it always had Mark Provis, the Brown brothers and Trevor at its core.

Our wives had a mixed response to a bunch of men turning up at their homes, wanting to sing. Some went out for the evening, others stayed home, but they all thought a group of men approaching middle age, meeting to sing, not to drink or to throw darts or to play poker or do any of those things men are supposed to do together, was a bit strange. Thankfully, they let us get on with it.

At first, we all sang together, without any harmonies or separate parts. Our voices blended well together and week by week, line by line, we learned a few old Cornish songs. Songs like the Cornish national anthem, 'Trelawny', or the old Cornish standard, 'Camborne Hill'. And traditional tunes such as 'Lamorna', 'Truro Agricultural Show' and 'Come, All Ye Jolly Tinner Boys'. We'd sing for an hour or two, then go down to the pub, where initially for fear of ridicule, our weekly activity would rarely be mentioned.

It didn't take us long to exhaust the pool of songs that we already vaguely knew. When that happened, we started to piece together lyrics and tunes that we remembered from our childhoods, but often there were more gaps than complete lines. Fed up with singing tunes with whole verses missing, we decided to approach the old boys in the pub, who we were sure would know the words. With the help of two of the old singers called Cogsy and Barry, we pieced the songs back together bit by bit. Our conversations with the old boys in the pub inevitably led to pub singing sessions, so it didn't take long for us to be back where the first spark of the Fisherman's Friends flickered – in the snug – supping pints and singing together.

We'd been getting together for nearly a year and the next Christmas was approaching fast when we bumped into Cleavey at a party. Cleavey was still living in Bristol at the time, but whenever we saw him he'd talk about wanting to move back to Port Isaac. He was happy living in Bristol, but Caroline had just given birth to their first child, a boy called Jacob, and he'd started to feel the pull of home.

That evening, after we'd had a few drinks and the party was in full swing, a few of us started to sing in the front room. From the bewildered look on Cleavey's face, we could tell exactly what he was thinking and it was something like 'What the fuck is going on here?' In a way, he had a point. Although we do it all the time now, in those days it was a bit strange for a bunch of men to launch into song in the middle of a party. But that's what we liked doing – nothing sophisticated, just a few mates singing the melody line with no ornamentation or harmonisation – and so we continued in the same vein.

Making no attempt to join in with us, Cleavey gave no indication that he had any interest in or aptitude for singing. All we knew was that he had been thrown out of his primary school choir because his voice was too low, even as an eight-year-old. When Cleavey turned up for a second attempt at the following year's auditions, the teacher didn't even give him a chance to sing.

'No, thank you,' she said as soon as little Jon walked in. 'You're a growler.'

By the time he hit puberty and his voice broke, Cleavey knew his destiny. He was going to be a bass. Whenever he listened to records on the radio, he was unable to sing along to them because they were too high for his voice. Instead, he taught himself to harmonise and to listen for the deepest notes that were being sung and copy those. This experimental, self-taught approach to harmonising gave Cleavey the ability to hear or devise an instinctive harmony line beneath whatever anyone else is singing. At the time, it was of little use to him, but it's been a valuable asset to the Fisherman's Friends.

A few weeks after he saw some of us sing at the village party, Cleavey was back down in Port Isaac for Christmas. With Caroline, he had hatched a plan to join the police training department and become an instructor. The job came with a police house where they could live rent-free. And with his salary, Cleavey thought he might build a house on a plot of land in the village owned by his parents. When Caroline and he were ready to move back to Port Isaac from Bristol, they'd have somewhere to live.

Back in Bristol, Jon had heard about a Celtic festival. Intrigued, he'd gone along and sat through a lecture on Celtic villages in Ireland, Wales, Brittany and Cornwall. A bit obscure, maybe, but it fascinated him. Afterwards he'd examined a display, then stumbled upon a showing of a film, *The Proud Valley*, starring Paul Robeson. Set in the South Wales coalfield, it told the story of a black American miner and singer, played by Robeson, who got a job in a mine and joined a Welsh male voice choir. It was an odd choice of film, but Paul Robeson was keen on Wales and Cleavey was amazed by his voice. The next day he went right out and bought three cassettes. When he got them home, he played them continuously in the house in Bristol. 'Bugger,' thought Cleavey, 'I can sing to this.' And he did, not as beautifully as Paul Robeson, but nonetheless, it was right in his range. Emboldened by the tapes, Cleavey resolved to join the police choir as soon as possible.

But before he could join the police choir, Caroline and he had come home to Port Isaac for Christmas. Wandering up Fore Street between Christmas and New Year, they noticed that the village post office-cum-shop was for sale. They peered in the window, looked at a notice with the details of the sale, but thought little more of it and just walked past, as they did every time they were in Port Isaac.

A few days later, Cleavey bumped into an old friend whose mum and dad owned the post office.

'I see your parents' shop's up for sale,' said Cleavey.

'Yes,' said his old pal. 'Why don't you bloody buy it?'

Something slotted into place in Cleavey's mind. Maybe it was the answer. Caroline and he went to look at the shop again, then returned to Bristol, talking and thinking about it all the way back to the city. A couple of days later and Cleavey was back in the routine of work, when he was called in front of the chief superintendent from A Division, the superior officer who'd previously told him that he had an overdeveloped sense of humour. This time he was in front of the chief superintendent for his staff appraisal.

With eight years' service under his belt, Cleavey had started taking his police work a little more seriously. The chief superintendent was impressed, but he didn't know that the only reason Cleavey had stopped laughing was because he no longer enjoyed his work.

'Please sit down,' said the chief super as Cleavey came into the room. When Cleavey had taken his place, his boss continued. 'Now, about your promotion board . . .'

'Yeah . . . erm . . . sorry,' said Cleavey. 'I'll have to stop you right there as I won't be going for it. I'm returning to Cornwall.'

For a moment, there was silence. Cleavey couldn't quite believe he'd blurted out his intentions, just like that, and he expected the chief superintendent to react angrily, to snap something like 'Why have you been wasting our time?' But instead, the chief looked calmly at Cleavey.

'Oh, really?' he said. Then he smiled. 'Oh, well, congratulations then, well done.'

Cleavey stood up, shook his senior officer's hand and through his grin tried to conceal his true thoughts: 'You bastard! So it isn't all going to fall apart without me?'

A month or so later, Cleavey's final day in the police force arrived. First, he went to the tailor's shop to hand in his uniform. At the hands of Rex, the camp tailor who ran the shop, he had the numbers ripped off his epaulettes. Rex should have waited until Cleavey had removed his shirt before enacting this very symbolic ritual, but then Rex was never an adherent of convention.

Next, Cleavey was called to the deputy chief constable's office. Knocking on the door, he heard a voice from within the office.

'Ah yes, Roger. Come in.'

Cleavey entered the room, now dressed in civvies, to find the deputy chief constable behind his desk.

'Thank you very much for everything that you've done, Roger,' said the policeman, elegantly avoiding any mention of specifics.

'Exemplary service, Roger.'

'Thank you very much, sir.'

The deputy chief constable continued, prefacing or ending every other sentence with 'Roger'. At the end, he shook Cleavey's hand and said, 'You've been a great credit to the force, Roger.'

Cleavey nodded, said, 'Thank you, sir,' and turned towards the door. 'And by the way, sir – it's Jon, not Roger. But thank you all the same.'

Cleavey walked out, now convinced that he'd made the right decision. That night he went out with an old friend from his student days to the Polish Club in Queens Road in Bristol. A reggae band was playing and although Jon knew he didn't look or behave differently, for the first time in eight years he didn't feel self-conscious when socialising in a public place. Leaving the police force was a massive liberation.

On their return to Port Isaac, Caroline, Jon and Jacob moved in with Jon's parents in the village for six weeks, while the flat over the shop was made ready for a couple with a baby still not quite twelve months old. On 28 April 1990, a searingly hot day, they started work on the shop. For the next fortnight the weather was beautiful as they ripped out the insides of the shop and installed new shelving and furniture, feeling more alive than they had for years. One afternoon, after they'd finished some renovation work, Caroline and Jon went back to his parents' house and sat in the back garden, exhausted but ecstatically happy. After those years in the force, Jon felt as if a heavy weight had been lifted off his shoulders. The days of being very aware of being a policeman, even when he was off duty, were over. Leaving the police had been a huge relief and now he could get on with living the rest of his life in the way he wanted to live it.

Jon realised now that serving in the police force was another thing he never should have done, just like teacher training. (When he looked back over his life, the only period that he'd really enjoyed and that he'd thought was worthwhile was the year he spent working in the psychiatric hospital.) But now he was his own boss and hopefully those days were behind him.

The post office provided a salary equivalent to Cleavey's pay in the police force. Even if his ambitions for the shop didn't work out, at least they'd have a steady income. He stuck with it for the best part of twenty years until his branch fell victim to a wave of post-office closures made by the government. Fortunately, the shop did well and grew until his income from retailing could replace his lost post-office earnings. Jon discovered he had a flair for buying stock and displaying it. His mother had been a window dresser, so maybe it was in his blood. Whatever the cause of Cleavey's new-found talents, the early days of the shop occupied too much of his time and attention when he first returned to the village for him to join the fledgling Fisherman's Friends singalongs that were now happening fairly regularly in homes around the village, so we just got on with it without him.

The gradual coming together of the Fisherman's Friends took another step forward in the early 1990s, when the idea was hatched that Port Isaac should build or get hold of a Cornish pilot gig. These six-oared work boats originated in the late seventeenth century, when they were used as one of the first shore-based lifeboats that went to aid vessels in distress. Capable of reaching speeds up to nine knots – gigs were the speedboats of their day – there are stories of gig crews rowing across the Channel to Brittany and returning with contraband. Nowadays they are used for pleasurable purposes, including offshore racing, so blood, sweat and tears still occasionally make an appearance, particularly as the major events can involve anything up to sixty boats on the starting line.

Cornish pilot gigs are an important part of the living history of Cornwall, which is why we wanted to be part of it. To enter races, their measurements and specifications (thirty-two feet long with a 58-inch beam and made of Cornish elm) must be based on *Treffry*, a gig built in 1838 and still used by Newquay Rowing Club. Gigs like

Treffry were originally intended as general work boats, primarily to take pilots out to vessels coming in off the Atlantic. At larger harbours, the gigs would race to be the first to get their pilot on board a vessel, which was often about to run aground on rocks. Whoever was first got the job and the payment, and so the tradition of gig racing began.

Designed and built to go to sea in almost any weather, pilot gigs were often used in preference to established lifeboats, particularly when conditions were too treacherous. For instance, in 1927 the *Isabo*, an Italian grain steamer, hit the western side of the Scilly Rock in fog. An RNLI lifeboat made an attempt to reach the *Isabo*, but grain in the water, floating two inches deep around the wrecked ship, clogged the lifeboat's intakes, so the *Czar*, a Scilly Isles pilot gig, was launched and successfully rescued the crew.

John Brown called the first meeting to discuss us getting a gig in Port Isaac and roped in his two brothers and Mark Provis. Between them, they pretty much ran the operation, raising the money to buy a boat, bringing it to Port Isaac and recruiting the crew. John even got his wife, Elaine, to join. She rowed, while John coxed and their daughter, Laura, lay asleep in the stern of the boat.

The plan was to practise a couple of times a week for several months, then to enter some races. It was all going well, until club politics took over. We had rowing members and associate members, most of whom were wives and all of whom had never seen the inside of a gig in their lives, but that didn't stop them telling us how to row it (putting their oar in, so to speak).

Eventually the gig was ready. With a brand-new gig gleaming on the Platt, we decided to invite other clubs to come up and launch it with us, then have a little race, but first our plan had to be approved by the club committee (oh joy).

'We've got to get in and have a little practice before the race,' said John Brown.

The rest of the crew agreed, but not the associate members on the committee. 'No, no. It's brand new,' they said. 'It shouldn't go in the water until it's time.'

'And how are we meant to race in it if we've never rowed in it before?' said John.

The associate members would not budge. No one, they said, should even set foot in the gig until it had been officially christened and launched. So we held a vote. The rowing members of the club were outvoted by the associate members. A victory for sentimentality over common sense.

When the day arrived, we held a small ceremony on the beach to launch the gig, then jumped straight in it. Being brand spanking new, all the paint was extremely smooth and shiny on the seats, so we slipped straight back out of the gig and into the water. None of us will ever forget it. We made complete fools of ourselves. Then, in the race, out of six gigs, we came in last. In our brand-new gig. It was shameful.

'You were right, John,' said one of the women members afterwards.

'Too bloody right I was,' John muttered under his breath. 'But it's too late now, dear.'

But at least the gig improved our singing. Back in 1991 there weren't many pilot gigs around, so we were always going off to Sennen Cove and other venues along the coast for races. Thanks to racing gigs, we went round more places in Cornwall than we knew existed.

Gig racing and singing went together like scones and clotted cream. After racing, we'd meet in the pub, where after a couple of pints, the singing would always start. But compared to some of the other crews, we felt like we didn't know many songs. We felt inexperienced and under-rehearsed, so John Brown bought some tapes to learn a few more songs. But what we really needed was instruction on how to sing harmonies. The answer came from a Port Isaac woman whose services to music, Port Isaac and the local community led to her recently being awarded an MBE.

Janet Townsend, a lovely woman who was head of music at Wadebridge School, was well known in the village after having led the Port Isaac

Ladies Singers on television in *Opportunity Knocks*, a talent show on ITV that, like *X Factor*, relied on audience voting to pick the winner, although in those days it was postal votes instead of phone calls or texts. In the early 1970s, Janet established a ladies' choir in the village that was very successful, performing at festivals and reaching the semifinals of Choir of the Year. About a year after we started rowing the gig, Janet launched a mixed choir, called the Port Isaac Chorale, and half a dozen of us – Cleavey, Peter Rowe, Johnny Mac, Jeremy, Lefty and Nigel – joined with our wives.

Until we joined Janet's choir, none of us had a clue about singing. It was all about making a din in the pub and getting louder as the pints went down. With Janet, for the first time we got an insight into how to blend our voices. She organised us into four parts: sopranos and altos for the ladies, and tenors and baritones for the men. Occasionally there'd be a proper bass part for Cleavey, but mostly he sang with the rest of us girly baritones.

Janet taught us how to sing four-part harmonies for dozens of songs, such as 'Tom Dooley', 'Pastime with Good Company', and various madrigals and folk songs such as 'I Drew My Ship'. They weren't the kind of songs we would have chosen, but at least it was proper singing. Janet was an excellent teacher and we were learning to read from sheet music. After years of wheezing our way through songs, Janet taught us how and when to breathe. We learned how to apply light and shade to our singing. We owe Janet a lot.

At about the same time, John Lethbridge started coming to our irregular get-togethers in each other's homes, where we'd try to piece together old Cornish songs. Trevor had bumped into him at his father-in-law's garage one day and suggested he joined us. With Lefty, those of us who used to sing on our boats and at house parties had now grown to form a core of six – the Brown brothers, Trevor and Mark Provis made up the other five – plus a few other lads from the village who joined in and dropped out intermittently.

One day, a few of us bumped into Mick Stone, who in a neat example of nominative determinism delivered stone and cement in the village. As chairman of Wadebridge Male Voice Choir, Mick had been badgering us for some time to join his choir, which needed new, younger members. We liked the sound of Mick's offer, but we were nervous. Joining a choir could be intimidating, especially when relatively untrained voices such as ours tried to slot in among very proficient singers. But this time, we egged each other on – 'If you go, I'll go,' we said to each other – and a short time later, the core six of us turned up at Wadebridge School, where the choir rehearsed. Walking into the school hall, we were confronted by a mass of much older men. At that time, most of us were in our mid- to late thirties and our immediate thought was to question what the hell we were doing there. The average age of the choir appeared to be more than seventy. But that didn't stop them instantly welcoming us.

'Come in, boys!' they said. 'Sit among us. Find out where you fit in.'

Gaining six much younger members was a hell of a bonus to a choir like theirs, but the benefits weren't all one way. As soon as we sat among them and they started to sing, we discovered they were very good and that we could learn a lot from them. It was what we would call a communal choir. No voice test. New members just joined in where they felt comfortable. It was very informal and sociable. As they sang and we attempted to join in, we found our natural places in the choir. Trevor started off in a section too low for him, so he moved up to the next section and eventually settled in the second tenors with Lefty, sitting next to an old boy who looked like he knew what he was doing. Jeremy moved up to the tenors, then back to the baritones. Mark started off with the basses, then moved up to the baritones.

Our understanding of the technicalities of singing progressed rapidly with the choir and soon we were taking part in concerts in the Wadebridge area, singing gospel choir, religious and show songs. Several of us are still members and we've been all over the country with the choir, singing in venues as large as Cardiff Arms Park and as prestigious as the Royal Albert Hall in London. And after choir practice we'd always go to the pub, where there'd be a good free-for-all sing-song, often with several of the lads from the Port Isaac Chorale and anyone else who happened to be there. By this time, having learned how to harmonise, the pub sing-songs were less raw and more melodious. And Lefty came into his own, putting notes into the harmonies that nobody else had the guts even to try.

Month by month, we attracted more members to our pub singalongs after choir practice and word of mouth spread that some local pub singers were gathering regularly as a group. Although he never came to Wadebridge Male Voice Choir, Cleavey was a stalwart of the Port Isaac Chorale and soon joined us every week in the pub. Meanwhile, Johnny Rowe was facing up to the fact that he couldn't really sing and he was starting to drop out. He'd always been one of the boys, one of the old-timers with whom we'd grown up, so it was a shame to see him go, but in return we gained his uncle, Peter Rowe. At first Peter said he was too old for us. He was twenty years older than the rest of us, but we insisted, saying he'd been with us all our lives, coaching us at football when we were tackers and looking out for us when we played on the beach, so it seemed wrong not to have him with us now.

As the pub singalongs gained more members, we started to branch out from the pub to sing at other venues. Nowhere large, at first it was just village and town halls, but we were gaining experience and widening our repertoire, which until then had been mainly Cornish songs such as 'White Rose' and 'Lamorna'. Gradually, the Fisherman's Friends was taking shape. Although we hadn't yet thought of a name, most of the eventual Fisherman's Friends had returned home. Only Billy was still away from the village. And that was about to change.

The Cornish Pasty

More than just a hot meat pie, the Cornish pasty is a cornerstone of Cornish culture, revered in poems and song, and worth £150 million a year to the Cornish economy. And since 2011, our humble 'oggie' has been accorded protected status by the European Commission, like Camembert cheese, Parma ham and Cornish sardines.

To be authentic, a Cornish pasty must be produced in Cornwall, have a distinctive 'D' shape and be crimped along one side (never on top). All the ingredients must be raw, chunky and include only beef (at least an eighth by weight), swede, potato, onion and a light seasoning. The pastry wrapper must be robust enough not to split or crack and it must be glazed with milk or egg, then slow-baked.

Nowadays more than 13,500 pasties are eaten every day in Cornwall, but they go back a long, long time. According to some claims, cave paintings on the Lizard peninsula show a woman eating what appears to be a pasty, so the oggie might date back to prehistoric times.

The *Oxford English Dictionary* cites several mentions of pasties in fourteenth-century texts, but the first regional connection is in a note written by a Cornish baker to Jane Seymour, wife of Henry VIII: 'hope this pasty reaches you in better condition than the last one'. It dates Cornish pasties to no later than 1537. The earliest known recipe for a Cornish pasty, held by the Cornwall Records Office in Truro, is dated 1746.

The pasty as we know it today dates back to the heyday of Cornish tin mining in the nineteenth century, when the pastry had to be strong enough to be dropped down a mine shaft without breaking and dense enough to keep the contents warm for up to ten hours. The crimped crust allowed the miners, usually covered from head to foot in dirt (often containing arsenic), to hold and eat the pasty without contaminating the pocket of meat and vegetables. The crust would then be thrown away to appease the 'knockers' – dangerous spirits of deceased miners that haunted the mines.

Traditional Cornish Pasty
Makes 4 large Cornish Pasties

First make the pastry:
500g strong bread flour
120g white shortening
25g cake margarine
5g salt
175ml cold water

Rub shortening and margarine into flour until it resembles bread-crumbs. Add water, pull the pastry together and knead until it's elastic. Wrap in clingfilm and leave to rest for three hours in the fridge.

While waiting, make the filling:
450g beef skirt in chunks
450g firm potato (such as Maris Piper) in slices or chunks
250g swede in slices or chunks
200g onion in fine slices
Salt and pepper

Mix the finely chopped or sliced vegetables together. After resting the pastry, roll it out into four equal-sized discs, about 10 inches in diameter. Spoon alternate layers of vegetables and meat on to one half of the pastry disc, seasoning well between each layer. (Some people add a dollop of butter or clotted cream on the top.) Fold pastry over. Crimp in a rope pattern or use a fork to seal the pastry. Bake for 50 to 60 minutes at 200°C (gas mark 6).

CHAPTER EIGHT

ON THE PLATT

'Well, we hope you've enjoyed this evening,' says Cleavey after Johnny Mac finishes leading the singing of 'Sitting on the River by the Levee'.

By this time in the evening, everyone has led a song and we're all gasping for a pint, so it's time to give the solo singing a rest. We sing the next song together as one, with no one leading the performance. It's a tune we first heard when we used to go down to beautiful Cadgwith on the Lizard Peninsula for the Friday night singing that had long been their tradition. It always raised the roof in their pub, so we thought we'd pinch it (although we'd call it free-trading), but first Cleavey needs to say a few words.

'Congregating here on the Platt really is resonant of the days when people made their own entertainment, when they would sit around in groups, chat to one another, crack a few jokes and sing, maybe around a piano or with a piano accordion.'

Before continuing, Cleavey twists his moustache, which is nearly always a sign that he's about to take the mickey. 'You may have been wondering why those days ever died out. And tonight is your answer ... I bet you can't wait to get home and put the bloody telly on.'

And with a grin we start on the highly appropriate lyrics of 'Cadgwith Anthem', one of the songs that John Brown first heard when he bought that Cadgwith Singers tape nearly twenty years ago.

Come fill up your glasses and let us be merry,
For to rob and to plunder it is our intent . . .

At the end of the song, Cleavey is serious for probably the only time this evening.

'Ladies and gentlemen,' he says, 'we're the Fisherman's Friends and everything you read about us in the papers, about us being old friends and all having gone to the same school, is true.

'We are all old friends and we did – mostly – all go to the same school. We're all from the same village, just about. Port Isaac, of course. We grew up together in these streets and alleys around you. And we've been singing together for nearly twenty years.

'And that really is our safety net. Because when the record industry is tired of us and doesn't want us to make any more records, we'll just go back to singing down by the harbour here and carry on as we always have. And, quite frankly, what a miserable prospect that is. Long may our Warhol moment continue.'

We've now been right along the line, so it's Cleavey's turn again to lead the next song, the 'Mingulay Boat Song'. It's a simple sea shanty, apparently sung by Scottish fishermen as they returned across the Atlantic towards the Isle of Mingulay, part of the Outer Hebrides. It was written to be chanted with the full breaths that it takes to pull long ropes. Like the songs of chain gangs swinging axes, its purpose was to keep physical workers in unison.

'*Heel y'ho boys,*' sings Cleavey.

'*Let her go boys,*' we respond.

'*Bring her head round,*' he sings.

'*Into the weather,*' comes the response.

When 'Mingulay Boat Song' is finished, we toss the lead back to the far end of the line, where the three Brown brothers stand and the whole game starts again – provided the weather's good. If it's a cold, wet or windy evening, we might skip a few. And if it's really blowing a hoolie, we might call it a night at this point. But usually John's up next with a song like 'Drunken Sailor', though first Cleavey, as always, gets his moment in the spotlight (and he's the first to admit that he does like them).

'We're not sex and drugs and rock'n'roll,' says Cleavey. 'We're more socks and rugs and moleskin trousers. Not for us the Lear Jet. Oh, no.

'We prefer to come by refrigerated fish van. I was sat in a box of haddock on the way here. Julian was in a box of halibut. And John, who's going to sing the next song, was in a box of lobster. One of them gave him a nasty nip, which is why he is now able to reach those really high notes.'

And then John opens his lungs to a tune that is probably the most famous sea shanty of all.

'*What shall we do with a drunken sailor . . .*'

And the rest of us join in:

> *What shall we do with a drunken sailor,*
> *What shall we do with a drunken sailor,*
> *Earl-ie in the morning?*

Every August, without fail, it would be the same. One day in the first week of the month, a bloody great bronze-coloured Mercedes would appear parked up by the church and everyone would know: Billy's back for the summer.

Right through the twenty-odd years he was in Gloucestershire, Billy would come back to the village, usually about half a dozen times a year, bringing Barbara and his daughters for a visit, and then in the summer, he'd be down for a few weeks. Regular as clockwork, like the first cuckoo of spring or the starlings coming home to roost at the end of autumn, Billy's bronze Merc in the church car park was a sign that summer had truly arrived.

When the weather gets bleak, everyone battens down the hatches, goes into hibernation, and the likes of Billy wouldn't usually have been seen in the village at that time of year. One such autumn day, Trevor was down on the Platt when he bumped into Billy walking down Roscarrock Hill.

'How's it going, Trev?' he said.

'Fine, but what's wrong with you?' said Trev. 'Down here this time of year? It's not like you.'

So Billy told Toastie what he'd been doing. He'd just come in from mackerel fishing with the Brown brothers' uncle, Ian Honey. As they were returning into the harbour, Ian had pointed at the old Methodist chapel on Roscarrock Hill and told Billy something that most of the village had known for a long time.

'The congregation is so small now,' Ian said, 'that they're selling the chapel.'

Being a builder, Trevor knew all about it. 'It's been on the market a while,' he told Billy. 'Couple of us have looked at it but it's just too much for us. And anyway, English Heritage keeps stepping in and stopping the sale.'

'I've got an idea, Trev,' said Bill. 'And I might have a little job for you.'

'Really?'

'Yeah. I want to come home.'

Bill put in an offer for the chapel and the school rooms next door to it, two handsome slate-roofed stone buildings. Whereas other prospective purchasers wanted to convert the nineteenth-century buildings into flats, Billy wanted to convert them into a pottery, a gallery and a home. English Heritage liked his proposal and indicated they'd approve it. Billy's only problem was to sell it to Barbara. At Christmas, he showed the empty buildings to his wife and his daughters.

'It's a massive project, Barb,' he said, 'but it's doable.'

A few weeks later, Trevor's phone rang. 'Trev, I bought the chapel,' said Billy. 'You're my first port of call. Are you interested in doing it up for me?'

The building work, which involved installing an extra floor in the chapel to create a gallery and pottery, and converting the school rooms to a home, took nearly two years. In 1995, Billy moved back to Port Isaac and opened his pottery. No longer dependent on galleries, he could now sell his ceramics for less, but make more money on them as he wasn't paying commission. He was profitable from the first day.

As soon as Billy returned, we persuaded him and Barbara to join the mixed choir. We knew Billy had sung in rock'n'roll bands for the twenty years that he'd been living in Gloucestershire and that he played various instruments, so we were eager for him to join us singing in the pub after choir. He slotted in straight away and within no time it felt like Bill had been with us all the time.

At this time up to twenty-five choir members would turn up at the pub each week and the singalongs after choir practice grew too big. Between us, we decided we would form a smaller group: the three Brown brothers, Trevor, Lefty, Cleavey, Mark Provis, Peter Rowe, Billy and Nigel Sherratt. With several baritones, several tenors and a good bass man in Cleavey, we fitted well together, although that was by pure luck rather than design. Nigel, our youngest member, was a whole three decades younger than Peter Rowe. Like many of us, he was also a member of the Port Isaac mixed choir and the Wadebridge Male Voice Choir.

Nigel goes back several generations in Port Isaac, but being younger than all of us, we remember him as one of the cheeky little tackers on the school bus. Back in those days we called him Sherbert, or Zippy, because of the way his lips stretched in a straight line when he smiled. These days he runs a tea shop in the middle of the village, so we call him Attila the Bun. But before he became Port Isaac's cupcake king, Nigel was an electrician. He left school at sixteen and went to college in Plymouth. After training, he worked for Dairy Crest at their Davidstow factory, the largest cheddar factory in Europe (it's capable of making a staggering 150 tons a day), and he loved it. For more than twenty years, Nigel was one of the lads at the factory, while his wife ran a bed and breakfast from their home in the heart of the village. In 2006, the house next door came up for sale, so they bought it and Nigel left Dairycrest to start the tea shop. At first he missed the crack with the boys at the cheese factory (and complained that it was all women and cake wars now), but it's made him like the rest of us, his own boss and controller of his destiny.

We'd all known Nigel for years, so we asked him to join us when we pared down the group that had been singing each week at the pub. With the number down to around a dozen members, we started to take our singing more seriously and began to realise we needed more time for practice than we had in the pub after choir practice. The landlord at the time, a bloke called Neville Andrews, was always very supportive of our singing. He'd turn off the jukebox and tell everyone to shut up before we started singing, but we needed a venue where we could experiment with our singing and try out new songs safe from the gaze of other people in the pub. Billy immediately came to the rescue.

'Come on, boys,' he said. 'You can practise in the chapel.'

From that day, Billy has insisted that the chapel is as much our home as his. As far as he is concerned, it belongs to all of us and none of us ever needs to knock on the door if we go round to Bill's; we just walk straight in. And that's the way Billy likes it because that's the kind of guy he is. The nicest, most generous person anyone would ever want to meet – until one of us crosses him. And then he's a feisty bugger, who always plays to win, which is why it's always such a proper laugh when Billy falls flat on his face. It's not a rare occurrence. With John Lethbridge, Billy is the butt of most of our jokes. They think it's because they're the two smallest Fisherman's Friends or because neither of them are known for their sharp wits. But actually the reason is that they take it very well. Some of the other Fisherman's Friends have shorter fuses, but Lefty and Billy just grin and laugh it off (most of the time). Like the time when we went to Sidmouth to play a big gig on the south Devon coast. We'd arrived in the middle of a baking-hot afternoon to do a sound check before the gig that night. As we waited to go on stage, one of us turned to Billy.

'Everything OK, Sid?' he said.

Billy looked confused. 'Sid?'

'Yeah.'

For the rest of the afternoon, we all called him Sid. At first he tried to ignore it, then he started to get wound up.

'What do you mean, Sid? It's bloody Billy.'

Billy's got a good sense of humour, but he doesn't like it if the mickey-taking goes on too long. So we kept it up. It was 'Sid' this and 'Sid' that. And the more Billy got wound up, the more we laughed, because it was one of those situations where everyone's in on the joke except the victim.

After a few hours, Billy leaned down to retie his shoelace and he felt something slip off the top of his head. He picked it up. It was a dead moth that one of us had rested on top of his hair.

'Got it now, Sid?' one of us said.

Billy still looked confused. Then the penny dropped.

'You bastards. Sid. Moth. Sidmouth. Ha! Very funny.'

Then there was the time we went to Launceston to take part in a choir concert. Now Billy has always liked his clothes. He thinks of himself as quite a snappy dresser and on that day he was wearing a particularly fetching pair of clogs, but he got bored waiting for the other choirs to sing before our turn and he fell asleep. As his eyes closed and his chin dropped on to his chest, the rest of us couldn't resist Billy's fancy footwear. One of us – no names mentioned – pinched Billy's clogs off the ends of his feet.

Half an hour or so later, we were due on stage, so someone gave Billy a nudge. Startled and slightly disorientated, he woke up.

'Come on, Billy!' said Trevor. 'Time's up. We're singing now.'

Billy took several steps before he realised he was barefooted and that it was too late for him to do anything about it. He had to walk down the aisle and perform the entire set with his toes poking out from beneath the hem of his jeans.

'Here, you'll be needing these,' said Trevor as we entered the dressing room after the gig. He handed Billy his clogs.

'You bastards . . .' said Billy in his familiar refrain.

At another gig at a local village hall with a very shiny floor, Billy turned up in a brand-new pair of leather boots with leather soles. Believing they made him look very much the dedicated follower of fashion, Billy loved those boots and we could tell it by the way he paraded around outside the hall in them, thinking they looked very cool.

A couple of hours later, the night was going well and our turn to perform was approaching. We entered the hall and took our places in a line in front of the stage. As usual, Billy was at the centre of the line, which put him closest to the stage, so he leaned back against the edge of it. It had been a long day and his legs were tired, but he hadn't realised quite how far in front of the stage he was standing. Although he didn't lose his balance, he leaned back further than expected, putting a lot of his weight on to his spanking-new leather boots with their shiny leather soles.

Shiny leather soles don't mix well with shiny wooden floors and Billy's feet started to slip away in front of him. Very slowly, but very surely, Bill slid down the front of the stage as his feet moved away from him. And there was nothing he could do about it until he ended up flat on his back.

The rest of us laughed so much we couldn't sing. It was Nigel's turn to start the next song, but he was struggling to catch his breath between fits of laughter. Billy's penchant for fancy footwear had literally led to his downfall and it took Nigel five attempts to start singing his song. In the end, he gave up and Peter took the lead.

Not all of Billy's mishaps involve his dedication to fashion. There's the time that John and Julian Brown, Jon Cleave, Peter Rowe's son and Billy went for an audition for the *Eggheads* television quiz at a hotel in Bristol. When they arrived, they were asked to fill out some forms and provide identification, but Billy had left his passport in his car so he went outside to get it.

When Billy re-entered the hotel, he got lost and couldn't find the conference room in which the auditions were being held. Eventually, Billy arrived in the audition room, very late and very flustered.

'Just copy my form,' whispered Johnny Mac. 'It'll be quicker.'

Relieved, Billy studiously copied all the appropriate details from the Macster.

Half an hour later, a production assistant appeared.

'Erm, I'm a bit confused,' she said. 'Am I right in thinking we have two John McDonnells?'

'No ...' said Mac. Then the penny dropped. When Macster suggested Billy copy out his form identically, maybe he should have told him that it didn't extend as far as copying his name.

If Billy isn't at the centre of any mayhem involving the Fisherman's Friends, then it will almost certainly be Lefty. Those two attract trouble like seagulls around a box of bait. And it's not unusual for both of them to be involved simultaneously, like the time we were asked to sing at the magistrates' annual dinner at Bodmin.

Janet Townsend, who founded and led the Port Isaac ladies' and mixed choirs, was also a magistrate, so she put in a special request for us to entertain her colleagues. This was in the early days before we instigated our two-pints-of-ale rule, so Janet asked us to keep our drinking in check. She didn't want anyone from Port Isaac showing her up.

A few weeks later, after a day's fishing and working, we all scrubbed up, put on our best clothes and set off for Bodmin, arriving shortly before 7 p.m. Shown into the Old Court House by a court clerk, we were told we didn't have to sing until half-past nine. However, the clerk made the fatal mistake of suggesting we waited in the bar. Two and a half hours allows a lot of time for damage to be done, especially by the Fisherman's Friends.

With Janet's request to be sensible ringing in our ears, we took it easy. But one pint led to another, and each one that went down tasted better and just made us more thirsty. Gentle conversation turned to banter, which turned to ribbing and mickey-taking, and eventually to an argument, probably about the monarchy, between Billy and Lefty.

Lefty and Billy might be the smallest members of Fisherman's Friends, but they are also the most feisty. Maybe it's something to do with having to stick up for themselves or maybe it's a lifetime of making a loud noise to ensure they're noticed, but when they get going, Billy and Lefty create a hell of a racket. Before long, the noise they were making was probably loud enough to be heard at the magistrates' dinner, but the rest of us were too far gone to notice it. The court clerk intervened, but by then it was too late. Billy and Lefty's argument had reached another level of abuse and they were now scrapping on the floor. In a courthouse, of all places.

With great difficulty, the clerk pulled our two pint-sized bruisers apart. They dusted themselves down and agreed to settle their differences later. Then we went in to sing in front of the magistrates, wondering throughout if they knew what had been going on in the courthouse bar only minutes earlier.

No one holds grudges for long in the Fisherman's Friends. As Cleavey often says, 'They realise they're wrong and I'm right and we go on from there.' We usually patch things up quickly, so Billy and Lefty's altercation at the courthouse was soon forgotten and we were back to choir rehearsals and their accompanying post-rehearsal singa-longs in the pub.

Not long after Billy returned to Port Isaac, we were in the pub one evening, having a good old sing-song after choir practice, when Billy's builder – that's our Trevor – took the momentous step of leading a song for the very first time. It might not sound like much, but it was a significant turning point for us. Until then, we'd all sung in broadly the same way. None of us being properly trained singers, we'd disguised our lack of skill and experience by belting out the tunes. Rollocking and bawdy, rather than tender and sweet. Passionate and full-hearted, instead of subtle and emotional. It worked well enough for us, but it slightly restricted the types of songs we felt we could sing.

While all of us were happy to lead a song, Trevor always avoided it, quite an irony as most of us – and probably all the FFWAGS – think Toastie has the best voice of any of us. Toastie, however, has never seen it that way. He's always been the least confident singer among us, which is why he was the last one in the group to lead a song.

We'd been on at Toastie for years. Almost every time we were in the pub and everyone was singing, somebody would say it.

'Right, Toastie's going to sing now.'

'No, I ain't,' Toastie would say quietly and shake his head.

'Yes, you are.'

'I can tell you, I ain't.'

Then one night we were in the Golden Lion in the snug next to the dartboard. It was just us, sitting around the table after choir practice, having a few beers and chatting away, then deciding to sing.

Everyone had led a song before it came round to Trevor.

'Come on, Toastie,' someone said. 'You're going to sing now.'

'No, I ain't,' he said, as usual.

But that night we kept on at him. And eventually it worked; he just got fed up with us nagging him.

'Oh, all right, then,' he said.

Without much ado, Toastie started singing 'The Grey Funnel Line', a shanty written by Cyril Tawney, a former Artificer Apprentice in the Royal Navy now regarded as the father of the West Country folk revival scene. It captures the longing for shore experienced by a sailor at sea on a long voyage aboard the Grey Funnel Line, a nineteenth-century nickname for the Royal Navy.

Not only was it a hard song to sing, starting off low but with some very high parts alternating with much lower sections, but it was a song guaranteed to make any singer feel very exposed. But most of all, against our raw voices, Toastie's voice sounded very different. Beautiful, even. So good, in fact, that we all just got up and left afterwards. Having heard Toastie sing on his own for the first time, we all went home because the rest of us couldn't hope to sing anything as beautifully as Trev had done that night. It was a moment when the hairs on the backs of all our necks stood up. Even on Cleavey, who's somewhat challenged in the hair department. And soon after it, Cleavey's wife, Caroline, christened Toastie the housewives' choice.

Toastie has recorded 'The Grey Funnel Line' a couple of times, but even now he doesn't sing it very often because there are so many verses to remember. Discovering Toastie's beautiful and very different voice has given us a very valuable extra string to our bow, but strangely, it hasn't made Toastie any more confident about his talent. He's still just as nervous and hesitant about leading a song as he ever was. Even after singing to thousands at Glastonbury and other festivals, if there's any chance to duck out of leading a song, even at a small gig in front of thirty or forty people, Toastie will always put up his hand and happily volunteer not to sing. It's just the way he is: always very happy to join in with the rest of us, but reluctant to sing on his own because it makes him feel exposed.

At about this time we decided that we needed to give ourselves a name, if only so that we had something to call ourselves when making rehearsal arrangements. Like anything else we've ever done, we insisted that choosing a name would have to be a unanimous democratic decision. None of us can remember who came up with the name. It might have been Jeremy or Cleavey. It could have been John Brown or even Julian, but someone suggested Fisherman's Friends and we all agreed it suited us well.

With our name, our rehearsal space and our membership sorted, we were starting to appear and feel quite organised, which was an unusual sensation for us. We played a few small concerts, mainly at village halls and charity fundraising events, then Neville Andrews, the landlord of the Golden Lion, announced he was going to organise a shanty festival weekend. It galvanised us into learning a few more shanties.

Although we also sing folk songs, shanties have always been the mainstay of the Fisherman's Friends and closest to our hearts. These old work songs provide a link to our maritime past and, as John Brown likes to say, 'make us think we are roughy-toughies'.

Singing can sometimes seem a bit effete and namby-pamby, but shanties were conceived to accompany practical and, at times, dangerous work, so they carry a sense of manliness and strength. As necessary to sailors as the drum and pipe to a soldier, most shanties stem back to the days when human muscles were the only power source aboard ships. In those days, the rhythm of the songs was used to co-ordinate the movements of the heavy synchronised labour needed to keep ships and boats operating at sea. In high winds, singing shanties was the only means sailors had to make sure they were working in unison. Even high-risk tasks, like climbing the rigging to fold away sails in heavy winds, had shanties.

Most crewmen worked alternating shifts of four hours on and four hours off, twenty-four hours a day and seven days a week for the entire length of a voyage. Life was tough. Pulling up the anchor, heaving up the sails and adjusting ropes were all done by hand. To help them the sailors used sea shanties that had been sung for generations.

As work songs, shanties had plenty of rhythm but relatively little melody. Most had a lead singer, or shantyman, to keep everyone in unison. The shanties were sung usually in the form of a call and response in which the shantyman would sing the line and a chorus of sailors would bellow the response while performing the work.

Part of the appeal of singing shanties now is that they transport us to the world of the working sailor and connect us with our past. Although they might sound similar, there were many different types of shanty to suit the various tasks on board. The long-haul or halyard shanty was used when the job was going to take a long time; a shanty accompanying the hoisting of topsails, for instance, would have up to twenty verses. Short-drag or sheet shanties were sung when the job of hauling on a line would be relatively quick but would require a lot of force. These would have one word at the end of each chorus that would be strongly emphasised to synchronise with one strong pull on the rope, such as '*Way, haul away*', sung by the shanty-man, followed by the crew singing '*Haul away, Joe.*' All the heaving would occur on the *Joe*.

Capstan shanties were smooth-sounding to accompany the winding of the anchor along a huge winch, called the capstan, a process that involved steady continuous force instead of sudden pulls.

The old favourite, 'Drunken Sailor', was a stamp'n'go shanty, used on ships with large crews. Many hands would take hold of a line and march away along the deck singing and stamping out the rhythm to raise the sail.

There were also pumping shanties, fo'c's'le shanties, menhaden shanties (sung on fishing boats) and several other types of maritime work songs. Although relatively modern, a shanty such as 'Rattle Them Winches', a favourite of ours, perfectly fits the rhythms and speed needed when hauling lobster pots.

> *We're making money with this sound,*
> *Rattle them winches on,*
> *Soon we'll all be homeward bound,*
> *Rattle them winches on.*

Shanties are songs of experience. When we listen to them, we can hear the sea and the salty wind, but they are very different from classical songs about the sea. The people who devised shanties didn't have any kind of musical training, so the tunes, rhythms and lyrics are straightforward.

Although they started as work songs, shanties soon gained more complex tunes and lyrics that told stories of sailors' lives and emotions. Shanties such as 'On Board a Man-of-War' grew to become haunting reminders of lost loved ones and heroes of the sea, providing a looking-glass into our maritime past. They show us how seafarers lived and felt two or three centuries ago.

Well, as I were a-walking a London street,
A press gang there I chanced to meet,
They asked me if I'd join the fleet
On board a Man-of-War, boys.

Said I brother shipmates, tell me true,
What kind of treatment they gives to you,
That I may know before I go
On board a Man-of-War, boys.

Well, the first thing they did they took me in and
They flogged me with the tar of a strand,
They flogged me till I could not stand
On board a Man-of-War, boys.

Then they 'ung me up by my two thumbs,
Then they flogged me till the blood did run,
And that's the usage they gave to me
On board a Man-of-War, boys.

Well I 'ad a wife and 'er name was Grey,
'T were 'er that led me to shocking delay,
'T were 'er that caused me to go away
On board a Man-o'-War, boys.

Ah, but if ever I get me feet on shore,
To see them London girls once more,
I'll never go to sea any more
On board a Man-o'-War, boys.

Many of the men who came up with shanties were uneducated, so they made up their shanties and passed them on by singing them with one another, which gave them an authenticity and quality that were often lacking in other maritime songs. Consequently, there were few rules to shanties. One of them was that shanties that sang of the joys of voyaging and life at sea were only sung on the outward leg. And shanties that spoke of returning home were only sung on the homeward leg.

Sailors were very superstitious, so they'd adhere to these rules in the same way that they wouldn't whistle aboard a ship. Thinking it would bring bad weather and bad luck, sailors called it whistling up the devil, and the tradition of actors not whistling on stage stems from it, the link being the rigging used on ships and stages to hoist sails and scenery.

Another superstition was that sailors never sang shanties on land in front of an audience. Eventually, though, knowledge of sea shanties trickled on to shore, so that almost every coastal community would sing sea shanties in pubs, in homes and at places of work, such as fish cellars. In most fishing communities, the women were just as important a part of the industry as the men. While the men were at sea, the women would be in the fish cellars or net lofts, repairing nets, gutting and curing fish and preparing bait. The women had songs of their own to sing. Some were work songs. Others were fishing lullabies that not only comforted babies, but also provided succour to the mothers while their husbands were at sea.

Somehow, however, shanties fell out of fashion, probably when sails were superseded by steam and diesel engines. There was no longer a need for work songs designed to synchronise the movements of sailors as they toiled at repetitive tasks. The folk song tradition didn't keep shanties alive and moved on to other forms of song. Shanties might have ended up fading away (a lot have undoubtedly been forgotten and lost), but they have been kept alive and fresh by successive generations of enthusiasts and fishermen singing them to ensure this vital link with our maritime past is never broken. Tales of sailors' bravery and achievements are heard in the songs and have always played a part in keeping people wanting to go to sea, so they're worth keeping alive for that reason alone.

Even today, singing groups in many coastal communities continue to write shanties to reflect a seafaring life and to tell stories from their heritage. In Port Isaac, Billy and Cleavey write songs in a group they've formed called Roscarrock. They've written about thirty songs, some of them based on old shanties, while others are inspired by local events or characters. Mostly they perform the songs themselves, sometimes with backing from other musicians, and always with a lad called Mick Dolan, who's worked in the music industry for thirty years.

They asked Trevor to sing the vocals for one of their songs, called 'The Last Widow'. It's about the aftermath of the violent storm of 1697, which brought devastation to Port Quin, then the most populous village in the parish. The entire herring fleet was wiped out by a northeasterly gale, drowning every member of the male population and creating two dozen widows in the village in one day. The women tried to carry on without their men but, eventually, the hardship became intolerable and they all left Port Quin for Port Isaac. The village was left deserted with the fishermen's cottages falling into disrepair and ruin. Port Quin has been haunted by the events ever since.

> *Why do you look, widow woman?*
> *Why do you stare out at me?*
> *It's a secret you keep in your heart, buried deep,*
> *Of a boy on the bed of the sea.*
>
> *In Port Quin there's a clouded glass window,*
> *Panes cracked and frame dusty dried,*
> *And behind the old lace is the sad, weather face*
> *Of a woman whose heart long since died.*
> *In her eyes she still sees the great tempest*
> *Blow fast and furious through the bay,*
> *She sees the fleet sinking down to the deep*
> *Made two dozen widows that day.*

How cruel the past to the present?
Could God really mean it this way?
For if he were kind, sure he'd empty her mind,
Free the sorrow she still feels today.
She sees her love deep under water,
Pale face unchanged by the years;
For the boy that drowned lies in Moul's Island Sound
The last widow still drowning in tears.

There are few eyes without a tear or throats without a lump when Toastie sings that one.

The first sea shanty festival in Port Gaverne was a great success. Neville Andrews, landlord of the Golden Lion, invited various shanty groups including Rum and Shrub and Hearts of Oak. The chairman of the lifeboat in the village knew a group in America, so they were invited too. Called Forebitter, they came from Mystic, a fishing village in Connecticut about 120 miles from New York. As soon as we heard them, we immediately latched on to Forebitter's type of singing. They sang only sea songs in very close harmonies and with a lot of balls.

Straight after the festival, we started to change our way of singing, taking what we'd learned from seeing and hearing Forebitter, but adding our own rollocking Cornish twist.

At about this time, Cleavey bumped into Johnny Mac in the village. The building recession was still in full swing, so Mac was working in London, coming home every second or third weekend. We all knew Mac from the pub and from the gig; he'd been one of the key gig rowers, as well as part of the lifeboat crew. Thinking Mac was a bass, we asked if he'd like to join us as we needed a cover for Cleavey, who couldn't always make rehearsals.

At this time, Cleavey was involved in an amateur dramatics society in Wadebridge managed by Janet Townsend. An only child who liked the limelight, Cleavey was a sucker for Janet's overture to join her drama group and he was soon a leading light in their Gilbert and

Sullivan productions. Over the years, Cleavey kept us very enter-
tained, showing off his range of accents and his deep bass singing
voice in dozens of productions, including *Trial by Jury*, *The Mikado*,
The Gondoliers, *Pirates of Penzance* and *HMS Pinafore*. Then he got the
main role in *Fiddler on the Roof*, which he loved, even growing a beard
for it. The role completely took him over and, thinking he was going
to be discovered, he didn't shave the beard off until months after it.
He can laugh about it now.

When Cleavey took on a part like Tevye in *Fiddler on the Roof*, he'd
tell us he wouldn't be coming to Fisherman's Friends rehearsals for
several months. So it was useful to have Macster to cover for him,
even though it turned out that Macster was a baritone, so he wasn't
that much use as a backup for him. However, Macster was such a
lovely chap and fitted in so well, that we asked him to stay with us.

It wasn't long before it seemed like Mac had always been with us,
especially as he soon showed a talent for mischief-making and pratfalls
that could rival Billy's. Like the time that we were due to leave the
village at six o'clock one morning to take part in a fundraising day for
the Royal National Lifeboat Institution at Appledore on the north
Devon coast, about fifty miles away.

Shortly after dawn, we were all waiting at the top of the village for
our bus to pick us up. We were all there, looking a bit bleary but present nevertheless. Everyone, that is, except Johnny Mac. The bus
arrived and we all got on board. Eager to get going, the driver wanted
to leave immediately, but we urged him to wait for Mac. The clock
ticked and we could wait no longer, so the driver pressed a button,
the door shut with a hiss, and we moved off, unaware that behind us
Johnny Mac was running as fast as his legs would carry him as he tried
to catch up with the bus.

Mac slowed to a halt and cursed. The day hadn't started well for
him. Hung over and still half-drunk from the night before, when he'd
been to a charity boxing event, he'd had less than two hours' sleep after
arriving home at 4 a.m. He'd slept through his alarm at 6 a.m., then
woken, glanced at his watch, and left the house immediately. Running

through Port Isaac's alleys, he'd dashed up several steep paths to get to the meeting place for the bus. And now we'd left without him.

Wanting to collapse back into bed, but determined not to let us down, Macster turned on his heels, ran straight home and jumped in his car. By the time the bus had reached Delabole, he'd caught up with us. Flashing his lights, he overtook us, then pulled over in front of the bus and waved it down. Feeling quite pleased with himself, he climbed on board. It was quite some entrance, but Mac didn't get the reception he was expecting. Instead of cheers and congratulations for not letting us down, Mac was greeted by laughs and pointing. That's when he realised he was still wearing his pyjamas.

Needless to say, Johnny Mac didn't join us in Appledore that day. Another time, he made it to Appledore all right, but still the journey wasn't without mishaps. Again it was a charity gig for the lifeboat. We'd performed well and were in the bar when the shout went out for the bus back to Port Isaac. The Honorary Secretary, who was driving the bus, was teetotal and he'd decided the bus had to leave at two o'clock sharp, just as things were getting going. Most of us had drunk our fill, but not the Macster, who was having such a good time he didn't want to leave. With another five lads, including Mark Provis, he petitioned for us to stay. But eventually, the final call was made and Macster was just about to drain his last mouthful when someone tapped him on his shoulder. It was an undertaker who lived near Port Isaac.

'You lot can come home with me,' said the undertaker. 'I'll give you a lift, although it'll be a bit of a squeeze.'

With a smile, Johnny Mac waved us all goodbye, then settled into a session with Mark Provis and the other lads. They had a few more drinks, then left with the funeral director. But none of them had anticipated the funeral director's return route, which involved stopping for a drink in every pub between Appledore and Port Isaac. By the time they all arrived in Port Isaac, Johnny Mac could barely walk.

Two years after the Port Gaverne shanty festival, a second sea shanty festival, lasting an entire weekend, was organised. Called the Stormalong Weekend and held at Billy's pottery in the spring of 1997, it was the first time that Johnny Mac sang publicly with the Fisherman's Friends and the first time that Nigel sang 'Shanty Man'. It climaxed with a sing-off between us and Forebitter, over from Mystic again. In the pub between performances, we got talking with Forebitter's members, who were astounded that we all came from the same village. Their members lived hundreds of miles apart and had to fly or drive for hours just to get together for rehearsals or performances. By the end of the festival, when many pints had been shared with the lads from Forebitter, they had invited us out to America to take part in an annual sea shanty festival that they organised at Mystic Seaport, a preserved nineteenth-century East Coast fishing village museum on the banks of the Mystic River in Connecticut.

We'd been invited to other shanty festivals at home and abroad, but had never got round to attending. This time we decided to go. Our only problem was that we knew only a very small number of songs, so we set about researching and expanding our repertoire. Galvanised by Forebitter's invitation, we took our rehearsals more seriously that winter. Gradually we added new shanties to our range of songs, experimented more with our harmonies and developed our performance. Towards the end of April, we started to feel confident about our repertoire, but we still lacked sufficient experience of performance. And we needed somehow to raise money to pay for our trip. That's when Lefty came up with a suggestion.

'Lads,' he said, 'how about singing on the Platt?'

Until then, our experience of performance stretched only to a few renditions of single shanties or Cornish folk songs at charity events for the lifeboat or other good causes related to Port Isaac. We'd also sung with Forebitter at the Stormalong Weekend, but we'd had the safety net of a more experienced shanty group then. We'd never performed a proper concert on our own, so the thought of singing on the Platt was very daunting.

However, Fisherman's Friends is nothing if not democratic, so we put it to a vote. And just about everyone agreed it was a good idea, even if they didn't particularly relish the thought of exposing our talents to the outside world. We reckoned that if we were going to sing in front of people in America, we'd have to polish up our act. Singing on the Platt was the obvious answer. It was staring us in the face. So, to raise money as well as gain experience of performance, we thought we'd give it a shot.

On the second bank holiday weekend in May, we congregated in Billy's pottery. None of us felt inclined to expose our meagre talents to the outside world, so Lefty piped up – it's always Lefty; he's fearless – and spoke his mind.

'Right, are you fuckers going to sing or not?'

Silence. A few nervous shuffles.

'I said, are you going to stand here like a bunch of bloody lemons?'

More silence.

'I can see I'm going to have a job to get you lot to go . . .'

Clearly Lefty thought it was a good idea.

'Come on,' he said. 'It'll be just a bit of fun.'

Taking a collective deep breath, we stepped outside on to the Platt. It was the beginning of the holiday season and the streets of the village were deserted. A blessing, really. Wind was whistling off the sea and through the alleys.

We formed a line at the top of the Platt, near the lifeboat station and the Mote Restaurant (nowadays we stand on the beach at the bottom of the Platt). Feeling like a load of spare hands at a wedding, we looked at each other and wondered what the hell to do. All knowing exactly what the others were thinking – there's no bugger here to see us – we shuffled nervously. Then Lethbridge piped up.

'Look, are we going to do it or not?' he said. 'If we're not, let's bugger off home.'

A few of us muttered about maybe trying again when the weather was warmer and the tourist season was in full swing, but Lefty was having none of it.

'Come on,' he said. 'Let's get things bloody moving. I bloody hate standing around, so if we're going to do this, let's bloody do it.'

Being the loudest, Cleavey started. Listening to him boom through the verses, we all felt as daft as seagulls, but by the end of the song, an old lady had stopped in front of us and was listening. If that was all we were going to get, we might have gone home then, but we persevered.

We'd worked out a rough repertoire. Everyone had a song they could lead and we'd sketched out a running order. One of the Brown brothers led the second song and a few more people came out and started to listen. With every song that we sang, more people appeared. And they didn't just walk off after a while. They stopped, they listened and they stayed. Some even sat down, interrupted their chatting, put down their drinks and gave us their full attention. On occasions when we'd sung in the choir, there had been more people in the choir than listening, and even then half the audience would be family or friends. But here on the Platt we'd attracted a crowd several dozen strong. It was a result.

We were singing without amplification, but luckily the wind was coming from behind us. It doesn't often come directly off the sea – the prevailing wind is southwesterly – but that evening the northerly wind carried our voices through the alleys and up the village. It was almost as if the elements wanted to give us a helping hand.

More and more people appeared. By the end of our performance of nine or ten songs, quite a sizeable crowd had gathered. They even cheered and clapped.

'Well, we'll do this again next week, won't we, boys?' said Lefty as we moved off the Platt into the familiar shelter of the Golden Lion.

Having seen that we could attract a crowd, we realised we needed to be better organised if we wanted to keep them coming. Peter volunteered to make a sign, so we decided to set a weekly time: every Friday evening at eight o'clock, come rain or shine. *Eight Bells Me Hearties*, it said.

The ultimate proof was that most of the audience had stayed until the bitter end. It had been bloody freezing and they'd been dressed in strappy tops, and yet they'd sat there for an hour or so, stoically grinning it out all that time. It was much more than we'd hoped for and a kind of proof that we were doing something right.

Cornish Place Names

The names of Cornish villages, towns and geographic features are often highly literal descriptions (in Cornish) of their very rural environments. Any place name starting with *Tre-* refers to a farm; *Ros-* means heath; *Res-* refers to a ford; *Porth-* or *Port-* indicates a cove; *Pon-* is bridge; *Pen-* means a culmination such as end, top or head; *Park-* is a field; *Nans-* is valley; *Mar-* is market; *Lis-*, *Les-* or *Liz-* is court; *Lan-* is settlement; *un-* is downs; *Eglos-* means church; *Chy-* is house and *Car-* is fort and *Carn-* is rock pile; *Cam-* is curved or crooked; *Bal-* is mine and *Bos-* is dwelling.

Baldhu – Black mine
Balnoon – Mine on the down
Bodmin – Dwelling of monks
Boscastle – derived from *Kastell Boterel,* meaning Bottrel's castle
Boscawen – Dwelling by an elder tree
Camborne – Curved or crooked hill
Camelford – Curved or crooked river
Caradon – Fort of Edon
Carharrack – Fort on a higher place
Carn Brea – Rock pile
Carrick – Huge rock (boulder)

Carthew – Black fort
Chyandour – House by the water
Chycoose – House by a wood
Chykembro – House of the Welshman
Egloshayle – Estuary church
Godrevy – Small farms
Goonhilly – Hunting downs
Halwyn – White moor
Lanhydrock – Settlement of Hydrek
Lesnewth – New court
Liskeard – Court of Kerwyd
Lizard – Court on a high place
Marazion – Small market (Thursday market)
Minack – Ground
Penhale – End of a moor
Pennance – Top of a valley
Penryn – End of a valley
Penwith – The very end
Penzance – Holy headland
Polperro – Pyra's harbour
Polzeath – Dry pool
Porthcurno – Cove of horns
Porthleven – Smooth harbour
Port Quin – White cove
Redruth – Red ford
Rosemorran – Heath of brambles
Tredinnick – Bracken farm
Tregear – Farm by a fort
Trenalls – Farm on a cliff

CHAPTER NINE

ON THE ROAD

Within a few weeks of our first outing on the Platt, the word spread locally and we started to see new faces turning up most Fridays to watch and hear us perform. When the holiday season got under way in early July, these familiar local faces were joined by a few hundred tourists each week. Each Friday, the crowd was a little larger and by the end of the first season, singing on the Platt felt like a tradition, so we vowed to continue it the following year. Now it's an established thing, part of the fabric of Port Isaac. Every Friday from May to September, everybody in the village knows the score: you'll find us on the Platt at eight o'clock, glasses in hand, singing shanties and telling tall tales.

Right from the first time on the Platt, Cleavey acted as our master of ceremonies. Although we were very happy to sing in front of an audience – we were used to doing it in the pub – none of us felt comfortable talking in front of a crowd. Only Cleavey, the eternal extrovert, was eager to say a few words, so we let him get on with it and since then he's always done us proud. That's not to say he doesn't get a bit temperamental at times, like the time we were singing in Exeter and Lefty threw an orange at Cleavey that spilled his pint all over him.

Thrown from ten feet away, it was a beaut of a shot, but it splashed Cleavey, who had had a busy week, and he went off on one.

'If you feel like that about it,' said Lefty, 'I'm going home.'

Lefty'd also had a busy week. He walked out the door, climbed in his van and was just pulling out of the car park when his mobile phone rang. It was Cleavey.

'I don't want you to have an accident. I want you to come back,' said Cleavey. 'Come on, come back.'

Spats between all of us are nearly always like that. A quick flare-up, but soon forgotten. When we first started, Cleavey simply introduced the next person to sing. He's never said much about the songs (we prefer to let them speak for themselves), but Cleavey is a natural story-teller and he likes a joke, even if it's at the expense of the rest of us. So it was no surprise when he started to include what we now call Cleavey's nonsense.

'We've had a very exciting couple of years,' says Cleavey as he pre-pares to introduce the next song. 'Last year, we recorded our album, part of it up at Abbey Road and part of it at the churches at St Kew and here in Port Isaac. It was released in April and went straight into the Top Ten. A few months later, the album went gold, which we were thrilled about. We've been on *GMTV* and Steve Wright's show on the radio. We've sung at the Festival Hall, the Albert Hall, the Cambridge Folk Festival and Glastonbury Festival. We've eaten Rick Stein's lobster pie on his Christmas programme. They're making a documentary about us and they're writing a book about us. And at the end of this year, unbelievably, they are making a movie about us.'

Cleavey pauses and smiles. 'But the marvellous thing is, we still don't mind singing to ordinary people like yourselves.'

Usually the audience gets Cleavey's joke and they laugh. But once – again, no names mentioned – there was an uneasy silence and our toes curled as we realised they'd taken Cleavey's comment seri-ously (OK, it was Milton Keynes). You can't win them all.

Jeremy Brown always sings the next ditty, a song which we regard almost as our signature tune, which is why we all sing the first verse and chorus.

Come, all you no-hopers, you jokers and rogues,
We're on the road to nowhere, let's find out where it goes,
It might be a ladder to the stars, who knows,
Come, all you no-hopers, you jokers and rogues.

Leave all your furrows in the fields where they lie,
Your factories and offices; kiss them all goodbye,
Have a little faith in the dream maker in the sky,
There's glory in believing him,
And it's all in the beholder's eye.

Turn off your engines and slow down your wheels,
Suddenly your master plan loses its appeal,
Everybody knows that this reality's not real,
So raise a glass to all things past and celebrate how good it feels.

Awash on the sea of our own vanity,
We should rejoice in our individuality,
Though it's gale force, let's steer a course for sanity.

'Well, rock'n'roll is not all it's cracked up to be,' says Cleavey, preparing to introduce the next song. His introductions have all evolved naturally over time, so in the last year they've started to reflect the changes that have happened to us since we signed a recording contract.

'We've been waiting in vain, as men of a certain age, to become embroiled in a sex scandal or two,' continues Cleavey. 'But nothing's happened at all. It's been absolutely useless.

'So if anyone is interested, we've left a few application forms in the foyer. If you'd care to fill them in and maybe attach a photo, we'll be pleased to see the ladies as well. Actually, if anyone out there is harbouring any homoerotic delusions, there are clubs you can get that sort of thing – apparently.'

Julian Brown leads 'Paddy Lay Back', a capstan shanty. Sung to accompany the turning of the capstan, its sound is a bit smoother than other types of shanty, with a full chorus in addition to the call-and-response verses. In its full version, it has nineteen verses, but we don't inflict all of them on our audiences.

'Twas a cold and dreary morning in December,
All of me money, it was spent,
Where it went to, Lord, I can't remember,
So down to the shipping office I went.

Paddy, lay back, take up the slack,
Take a turn around the capstan, heave aboard!
About ship for England, boys, be handy,
We're bound for Valparaíso 'round the Horn!

That day there was a great demand for sailors,
For the colonies, for 'Frisco and for France.
So I shipped aboard a limey barque, the Hotspur,
An' got paralytic drunk on my advance.

Now I joined her on a cold December mornin',
A-frappin' o' me flippers to keep me warm,
With the south cone a-hoisted as a warnin',
To stand by the comin' of a storm.

Now some of our fellers had been drinkin',
An' I meself was heavy on the booze.
An' I was on me ol' sea-chest a-thinkin',
I'd turn in to me bunk an' have a snooze.

I woke up in the mornin' sick an' sore,
I knew I was outward bound again;
I hears a voice a-bawlin' at the door,
'Lay aft, ye sods, an' answer to yer names.'

We continued singing through the summer of 1997, gaining experience and collecting donations to help fund our trip to Mystic Seaport that autumn. At some point during that summer, Mark Provis dropped out. It was a shame to see him leave as he'd been with us since the beginning and he'd been a good mate since childhood, but his personal life had become complicated and he could no longer spare the time.

Most of us had never been to America before we flew out to Boston that October. Not only was it our first time on American soil, it was also the first time we went away together. But being from Port Isaac, we couldn't just go away on our own. Wives, girlfriends, partners and friends from the village joined us, including Janet Chadband and Joan Murray, a lovely old dear who came along to show the Americans how to make pasties and other Cornish baking specialities.

Mystic Seaport was a maritime museum built around a nineteenth-century coastal village. There were clapboard buildings, musicians, shipsmiths, woodcarvers and 'chanteymen', as they called shantymen. On paper it sounded like an American version of Port Isaac, but that's where the similarity ended. Mystic Seaport was entirely recreated on the bank of the Mystic River in the 1930s. The buildings were historic, but they were from elsewhere and had been reassembled and restored at this new location. The polar opposite of Port Isaac, it was a curious place, but still interesting, so we spent a day looking around. There was a whaling ship with a crew and someone explaining what everyone did on board the vessel. The old buildings were Shaker in style and had demonstrations of net-making. In one building a baker was making pasties, so Joan stepped in and showed him how *we* made pasties. Proper job.

We played a couple of concerts on successive nights, which seemed like a lot to us in those days, when we were used to singing in public no more than once a week. At the second gig, Johnny Mac took to the stage slightly more well-oiled than any of us would be nowadays. Macster might deny it now, but we all remember him hanging on his microphone, swaying like Mick Jagger and singing just a touch louder than the rest of us. No harm was done, but it was funny.

We then travelled around Connecticut and Massachusetts in two minibuses for a few days, which is where things got out of hand. We always tell people that we formed Fisherman's Friends to give us an excuse to meet for a few pints and some yarns. So with two weeks to spend together, you can imagine the mayhem – and unsurprisingly Billy was at the centre of most of it.

We were in a bar one night. It might have been Cape Cod, although the amount we'd had to drink and the number of intervening years have combined to make us all hazy on the precise details. For some reason Colin Shepherd, one of the Yarnigoats who'd come along from Port Isaac for the ride, had a pair of handcuffs (please don't ask why; you wouldn't want to know). Colin was annoying everyone with his handcuffs when he spotted Billy sitting in a chair with his back to most of us, so he tiptoed up to him and handcuffed him to the chair.

Billy went ballistic. The red mist came down so fast and furious that we thought steam would come out of his ears. Trevor remembers Barbara coming up to him and yelling for him to help set Billy free.

'For God's sake, get the key, Trevor,' said Barbara. 'Get them off. He'll kill Colin if he gets hold of him.'

Behind Barbara, Billy was bellowing a cry that we all knew well: 'Barbs! Baaaarbs!'

'He'll be all right, Barbs,' said Toastie. 'It's just a game.'

'It's not!' said Barbara. 'It's not a game at all. Bill's very claustrophobic. He hates being tied down or chained down or sat on. Anything sets him off. He hates being confined.'

When Trevor looked at him, he could see that Billy was almost delirious. Billy looked liked he was about to foam at the mouth. Not that it made us release him any quicker. We all got our fill of laughing at Billy and eventually, when there was no more laughing to be done, we released him. Billy wasn't pleased. Not at all. But it wasn't his first or last shenanigan of the tour.

We'd only just arrived in America, when it had started. Standing outside a car-hire office, Bill had spotted a drinking fountain and decided he wanted some water. But being Billy, he couldn't work out where the water came out. Anyone else would have spotted the hole and assumed that would be the source. Not Billy, who thought it would be best to take a closer look. Bending down, he pressed the button. The fountain shot him straight in the eye.

'Barbs!' the cry went out. 'Baaaarbs!'

A day or so later, we all stopped off at a branch of Walmart. Some of us went into the supermarket to buy some snacks. Like any supermarket, there was an obvious entrance point through which any pedestrian could walk. In this case, it was a turnstile. Beside it was a channel with a low barrier, beneath which trolleys could be pushed as you walked through the turnstile. And for some inexplicable reason that made sense only to him, Billy decided the only way of entering the store was to limbo-dance under the trolley-channel barrier. That's Billy.

A few days after the handcuff incident in the Cape Cod bar, we arrived at Plymouth in Massachusetts, the town where the Pilgrim Fathers established their first colony after landing from the *Mayflower* in 1620. Having pulled up outside a bar, our hearts sank when we saw the sign: English Bar. Usually that implied a glitzy overlit overpriced sports bar, but on this occasion we were pleasantly surprised when we walked through the door. Called the British Beer Company, the bar was a carbon copy of an English pub, so we immediately felt totally at home.

The Beer Company was a tiny place with a barmaid who was chatting to one of the customers seated at the bar. The customer turned out to be a prison guard and a great conversationalist. Lefty and Trevor stood near him with Billy between them, dipping in and out of the yarning. The afternoon was proceeding nicely into early evening, the beer and the crack were good, thoughts were turning towards maybe having a sing. And then someone mentioned the Royal Family.

Bill has never been a great fan of anything related to royalty. And he's never been good at keeping his opinions to himself. Jabbing his index finger in the air, he let loose with his dislike of some members of the Royal Family. We like to think we're a democratic, free-thinking lot in the Fisherman's Friends, tolerant of all points of view, but sometimes that tolerance wanes when beer is involved. And by that time in the afternoon, several beers had been taken.

'Don't you point at me,' said Lefty, grabbing Bill's finger.

We all held our breaths while waiting to see what was about to happen. Lefty didn't let go of Billy's finger. Instead he started to twist and bend it. Billy got the red mist again and within seconds the pair of them were on the floor, wrestling one another.

'We don't do this sort of thing over here,' said the prison warden.

We all smiled as if it was quite normal for wrestling matches to break out in English pubs.

'For God's sake, get those guys off each other,' yelled the barmaid. 'I'll have to get them arrested for fighting if you can't stop 'em.'

But we'd seen it many times before, so we thought it was funny – standard procedure when Billy lost his rag. And to be fair to Lefty and Billy, they were laughing too. Lefty was on his back on the deck, laughing wildly while Billy sat astride him, his hands around Lefty's throat, also howling with laughter. Eventually they gave up, thankfully before the barmaid called the cops.

Somehow Bill doesn't see trouble coming, even though it always involves him. Towards the end of the trip, we were walking down the street in Boston, yapping to one another. Ahead of us, smack in the middle of the pavement, was an advertising billboard. Although we were all yarning away, we all spotted the billboard and avoided it. But not Bill, who walked straight into it and flipped head first over the top of it.

'Barbs!' This time it was all of us calling the familiar cry of the hapless Billy. 'Baaarbs! Pick him up.'

Billy is a walking disaster, but to his credit he'll always admit that if something's going to go wrong, he'll be the cause. And he always laughs about it afterwards, once he's sworn several times, muttered something like 'What the heck's going on?' and yelled for 'Baaarbs!'

After we got back from America, we returned to rehearsing in

Billy's pottery and learning some new songs. Our trip abroad had done our reputation no harm and we were soon being asked to play more gigs. Nothing huge, but good all the same. Events such as golf club dinners, village hall fundraisers and magistrates' dinners (yes, that one – the one where Lefty and Billy had another fight).

We'd learned a lot from touring to America and playing at Mystic. It had given us more confidence and we'd pinched a few songs while we were there – not that the songs were theirs for the keeping. Lefty pinched 'A Sailor Ain't a Sailor' from a bunch of shiny-booted US Coast Guard cadets in New London. John Brown pinched 'Bully in the Alley' from one of the bands at the shanty festival, although he's got no idea exactly where he heard it first. And Nigel thieved 'One More Day' from the Yankees of New England, who'd half-inched it from some sailors who sang it before being paid off at journey's end.

Pinching songs has always been a big part of the Fisherman's Friends, and of most other shanty groups in coastal communities. In part it's because we had to go out and grab them for ourselves; they weren't going to simply fall into our laps. In the late 1990s, which for most of us in rural Cornwall was the pre-Internet era, gaining access to heritage music was difficult. In these days of Wikipedia and Wikilyrics, it's much easier to research the lyrics and tunes of old half-forgotten shanties. But back then, pinching songs from other groups was often the only way of getting hold of new material. Coastal communities have a long history of making things out of jetsam and flotsam found on the beach. In a way, pinching shanties was no different from looting wrecks for their precious cargoes and timbers.

Beachcombing and wrecking have always been a big part of our local culture. Not for nothing is the rugged coastline between Pentire Point (north of Polzeath) and Westward Ho! called the Wreckers' Coast. According to some accounts, at one time all Cornishmen derived a significant portion of their living from looting shipwrecks along our shoreline. Although that's unlikely, it's certainly true that our rocky coastline, fierce sea and the strong prevailing southwesterly onshore winds were ideal conditions for merchant ships and warships to founder close to shore. Hence the localised version of the old proverb, ''Tis a bad wind that blows no good to Cornwall.'

No coast is more notorious for wreckers' tales. Charles Kingsley, a clergyman and novelist who grew up in Clovelly, described locals as 'merciless to wrecked vessels which they consider as their own by immemorial usage, or rather right divine'. Even as recently as 1982, a freighter wrecked at Hartland Point was stripped of all its contents and fittings amid torrid scenes of looters fighting among themselves.

There are stories of nineteenth-century Cornish tin miners descending on shipwrecks like locusts to 'cut a large trading vessel to pieces on one side ... [and] strip half-dead men of their clothing'. Once the cargo had been removed, the wreckers would strip the ship of every saleable asset, right down to its timber and sails, often with the crew looking on helplessly as every item of value was dragged from the hold or prised from its mountings.

Tin miners on the Lizard, in West Cornwall, reputedly became 'mad people, without the fear of God' when a ship came to grief, so much so that mariners were said to recite a nervous prayer: 'God keep us from rocks and shelving sands, and save us from Breage and Germoe men's hands.'

In response, the wreckers reputedly had their own prayer: 'Oh please, Lord, let us pray for all on the sea, but if there's got to be wrecks, please send them to we.'

According to another story, a vicar of a parish in the southwest was approaching the end of a particularly dull, dry sermon, when the door of his church was thrown open. It was blowing a hoolie outside and through the door came one of the male members of his parish. This man walked straight up to the vicar and whispered urgently in his ear, immediately silencing his sermon in midflow.

'There's a ship ashore between Prawle and Pear Tree Point,' the vicar announced to his slumbering congregation. Tugging at his cassock, the vicar insisted sternly that his parishioners all remain seated until he had removed his vestments 'so that we can all start fair'.

Then, with the vicar at its head, the congregation rose as one and charged straight down to the beach.

Whether this particular story is true or not, the clergy was just as involved in wrecking as any other members of their parish. Wrecked booty would be hidden in crypts, pulpits, bell towers, even tombs, and several rectors and vicars were caught red-handed in possession of contraband. Some, such as the Reverend Richard Dodge of Talland on the south coast of Cornwall, even went so far as to spread stories of demons and ghosts around their parish to keep prying eyes away from their illicit activities.

It's said that Cornish wreckers would often use false lights on the shore to lure passing ships on to the rocky coast, then purposely drown the crew to prevent them testifying against them. There's no evidence at all to support such claims and it seems unlikely that the locals, who were themselves only too aware of the dangers of seafaring, would cynically cause or hasten the death of fellow seagoers, particularly as they would have to bury the bodies of the drowned crew. Nevertheless, a cautionary rhyme that warned sailors that 'From Pentire Point to Hartland Light, a watery grave by day or night' reflected the sorry statistic that in the mid-nineteenth century, for instance, around 200 vessels were shipwrecked along this stretch of the coast.

At the heart of the wrecking tradition was a twelfth-century law that stated that if no man or animal survived a wreck then the owners had no claim on it. This gave coastal communities little incentive to aid stricken vessels. Instead, the contents and fittings of any ship that hit the rocks or beached were regarded as fair game for wreckers. Although there are stories of coastal communities watching greedily from cliffs as a ship foundered on rocks, this is a rather unfair portrayal of the wreckers' intentions. It would be fairer to say the villagers turned the misfortune of the storm to their advantage, using it to supplement a very meagre income and a tough way of life in a particularly harsh environment.

According to the Reverend Sabine Baring-Gould, who wrote

The FFs in 1997, still full of youth and vigour, and unaffected by the excesses of the rock and roll lifestyle that was yet to come . . .

In foreign waters. Singing on the old boat in Brest, Brittany, circa 2003.

Cleavey and Johnnie Mac, or is it Charles Bronson and Ronnie Wood?

'Sailing at 8 bells' – hand crafted by Pete in his sheltered workshop, using no sharp instruments.

Singing on the Platt at Port Isaac: FF HQ and spiritual home!

Recording in the vast Studio One at Abbey Road.

Outside the world-famous Abbey Road Studios,
March 2010.

Possibly not the first band to do this?

On stage with Phil Beer (far left) and Steve Knightley (far right) of Show Of Hands at Trowbridge Village Pump festival, 22 July 2010.

The three Brown brothers giving it some at Trowbridge. From left: Julian, Jeremy and John.

On stage at Birmingham Town Hall, on 25 January 2011.

Performing at the
Southbank Centre in
London for *This Morning*,
22 April 2010.

Receiving our 'homemade'
Gold Disc for UK album
sales of 100,000. *GMTV*,
17 June 2010.

On stage at the
Celtic Beer Festival,
27th November 2010.

Thrown to a baying mob of real ale enthusiasts at the St. Austell Breweries Celtic Beer Festival, 27 November 2010.

Filming our advertisement for Young's early in 2011 – fish finger millionaires one and all!

On board the Padstow
lifeboat.

All washed up on Port
Isaac beach.

Julian's boat *Helen Clare* in
the foreground with
Jeremy's boat *Free Spirit II*
moored behind.

First time at Glastonbury Festival, June 2010, on the acoustic stage – and we thought this was exciting!

Performing hours after Coldplay (the next day!) and 'supporting' Beyoncé on the pyramid stage at Glastonbury Festival, June 2011.

extensively about Cornwall and Devon in the late nineteenth century, 'the coast dwellers believed they had a perfect right to whatever washed ashore'.

He explained that 'by the turn of the century, the coastguard kept such a sharp lookout after a storm that very little could be picked up'. But even so, the wreckers still managed to acquire the contents of shipwrecks, often for next to nothing. Anything found would be heaved up on to the shore, Baring-Gould wrote, and secreted 'in some hidden or inaccessible part of the beach'. The government would then hold an auction on the beach for found articles. If the salvaged object was spotted, it would usually be auctioned for 'a trifle' of its true value 'and the man who found it could then have a lawful claim on it'.

'If the item was not observed, then he could fetch it later at his convenience,' Baring-Gould went on. 'It was generally considered too unsafe to try to make off with anything of size after a wreck.' Instead it was easier 'to obtain it by means of the auction because the auctions were not well attended and the bidders did not compete against each other vigorously'.

Customs officers, or preventive men as they were known then, worked hard to deter wreckers from looting wrecks. Under the law, any dutiable goods were subject to customs charges, no matter how they came ashore, but the preventive men rarely had any chance of securing anything that washed up or was carried on to dry land against the sheer numbers of wreckers plundering a shipwreck. And even when the preventive men had impounded cargoes in government storehouses, the locals had no qualms about breaking into the depositories and reclaiming what they considered to be rightfully theirs.

Being a preventive man was a bloody business, with many wreckers and customs men regularly killed in pitched battles over the booty. The pickings from wrecks could be substantial, and some of the preventive men could not resist the temptation to help themselves. Even John Knill, Collector of Customs at St Ives from 1762 to 1782, Mayor in 1767 and publisher of a scholarly pamphlet on the prevention of wrecking, was said to have dealt in looted cargo as enthusiastically as the next man.

Pick anywhere at random along this coast and the relics of wrecking are all around. Cemeteries contain dozens of graves belonging to the sea-dead. Memorials to shipwrecked crews, often beside their shipwreck's figurehead, surround churches with high, square towers built tall to serve as landmarks for passing mariners. Fences erected as recently as seventy years ago show signs of being built from shipwreck timbers. Gardens contain wreckers' trophies, including even ships' figureheads. Older cottages and barns show signs of being repaired or built entirely from wreck timbers, pit props and beached cargoes. Many of the pubs are named after local wrecks, some of them containing wreck timbers or displaying flotsam and jetsam as decoration, and the local beers they serve are called Wreckers' Ale and Doom Bar.

In Port Isaac we're no strangers to a bit of wrecking. When we were kids, we'd always bring home any timbers we found washed up on the rocks. They'd be used for repairs around the house, or burned in the range, or Billy would use them to make skivers. The Brown brothers grew up in a house in which many of the timbers in the kitchen had numbers carved into them. They had obviously been in a ship.

When Peter was a baby, the *Bessemer City* smashed into rocks at Trevalgan, about fifty miles down the coast. Among her cargo were thousands of cans of food, which were liberated by the locals. Unfortunately, by the time the wreckers got their hands on them, the labels had washed off, so although the food inside was unharmed, opening the can for dinner was always a bit of a lottery.

Closer to home, Julian Brown remembers spending most of a day in the late 1970s watching the *Skopelos Sky*, a large Greek cargo ship, dodging the rocks aound Port Quin in a hell of a storm. With some mates, he watched as the lifeboat and several helicopters pulled the last man off just before she hit the cliff. 'The sound of tortured metal will live with me for the rest of my days,' Julian always says whenever he talks about it. 'And she broke in two shortly afterwards.'

Julian and his mates wasted no time in going aboard and they soon grabbed themselves some gear. It was mainly brass tubes that they sold for scrap. A few days later, Julian was back at Port Quin, climbing down the cliff again to get aboard. The aft section had broken off and fallen on its side, so he was climbing around in the stern when he bumped into a fellow fisherman.

'There's nothing down there,' said the fisherman, pointing into a lower section of the ship.

At first Julian trusted the other fisherman, who had been in the merchant navy, which led Julian to think the fisherman knew what he was talking about. But then Julian noticed a large padlock on one of the hold doors. Surely no one would padlock a door if there was nothing beyond it worth taking, Julian guessed, so he moved on.

By the time Julian got back to the village, a rumour was going around that the salvage people would be arriving the next morning. That night, several gangs descended on the *Skopelos Sky*. A local builder smashed the lock on the hold room and discovered its booty of paint and grease. By the time dawn broke, all the paint had been removed, enough to fill several trucks. For years after that, we would spot the same shade of blue appearing occasionally on houses, boats and other features in Port Isaac.

A few years after the *Skopelos Sky* broke up at Port Quin, a small bulk carrier hit the rocks on Lobber Point, just beyond the Port Isaac harbour. She'd put her anchors out, but somehow still washed on to the rocks. She wasn't carrying much but when the lifeboat pulled alongside to rescue the crew, they found she had six undeclared passengers aboard, all of them women.

The next day, Julian Brown went to Pine Hawn, the next little beach down from Port Isaac. When he arrived, all the other fishermen were there already. Together, they hauled a large booty of timber that had washed on to the beach from the bulk carrier, and landed it up. On the north coast of Cornwall (and maybe elsewhere) there's an old tradition that if anyone carries a piece of timber above the high-water mark, then it's considered to be 'landed up' and it's their property.

The fishermen got so much timber, most of it hatch covers, that Julian sold his share to a local farmer. He didn't make much money, but it was enough for a few rounds in the Golden Lion. And he kept one of the timbers, planed and sanded it, then polished it. It now rests on top of his mantelpiece as a memento.

In case these stories of scavenging from wrecks make us (and maybe our fellow Yarnigoats) sound mercenary and ruthless, we ought to explain that, like anyone who fishes or who lives in a coastal community, we understand and respect the perils of the sea only too well. Cargoes and ship fittings are fair game for wreckers, but fishermen are very precious about their friends, family and fellow mariners. The traditions of the sea dictate that if someone is in danger, you go out to save lives. Most of us are or have been members of Port Isaac's lifeboat crew. Between us, we've served several centuries on the lifeboat. John Brown, for instance, was in the lifeboat for twenty-seven years and seven months. In that time, the Port Isaac lifeboat saved 103 lives from shipwreck. Johnny Mac was in the lifeboat for fifteen years, and most of us have done similar stretches.

However, not all sea rescues rely solely on the lifeboat. In 1995, a few weeks before the first shanty festival at Port Gaverne, John and Julian Brown were out fishing off Hartland with Julian's regular crew member, Paul, when John saw the *Maria Asumpta*, the oldest surviving sailing ship, go past under full sail. Launched at Badalona in Spain in 1858, she was a handsome two-masted, square-rigged brig that had been involved in the textile trade between Argentina and Spain. With a painted white hull, she'd also transported slaves and salt, but now she was a private yacht and sail training ship on a reach from Bideford to Padstow.

A couple of hours later, and Julian, John and Paul had worked their way down the coast. They were about four miles off Port Isaac when they heard a garbled message on the radio. It sounded as if someone was talking through water, possibly calling 'Mayday'. Although it was distorted, Julian could hear panic in the voice. It sounded serious.

Listening to the transmission, Julian could understand only the coastguard's response to the barely audible message, but from it he deduced that a boat, possibly the *Maria Asumpta*, was in distress near the Doom Bar. A notorious sandbank at the mouth of the Camel Estuary, the Doom Bar had accounted for more than 600 wrecks in the last 200 years. A government report published in 1858 even stated that the place was regarded as so dangerous that vessels would risk being wrecked on the coast in a storm, where there was a chance of leaping on to solid land, rather than negotiate the entrance to the Camel Estuary for fear of hitting the Doom Bar in the middle of open water.

The wind was northwest, force four to five, on a flood tide, which meant only one likely outcome for a vessel in distress on this stretch of coast. The wind and tide would sweep her on to the rocks.

Straining to hear the transmission, Julian listened for clues to the vessel's whereabouts and condition, but all he could hear was a burbling sound, like water. Then it cut off completely.

'It sounds like the *Maria Asumpta* has gone aground on the Doom Bar,' he said. 'We'll go down and see if we can help her.'

They'd heard Maydays before, but this was the first time Julian, John or Paul had been close enough to help. Julian put the throttle down while John got fenders and ropes ready in case they needed to pull off passengers. Steaming along the coast, they were the first boat on the scene. And what a scene. At eleven o'clock that morning, the *Maria Asumpta* had passed by majestically under full sail. Now, at 4.30 p.m., she was little more than matchwood in the Sound of Mouls, a gap between Mouls Island and the Rumps, a few miles short of the Doom Bar.

A notoriously dangerous stretch of water, particularly on a flood tide and with an onshore wind, Mouls Sound was not a route recommended by the Admiralty and would rarely be attempted by anyone without extensive local experience. Once the captain made the decision, there was really only one outcome for the *Maria Asumpta* if her engines failed or the wind dropped. Swept on to Rumps Point, a double headland jutting into the Atlantic at the northeast corner of

Pentire Head, the *Maria Asumpta* had been sawn into thousands of little pieces.

With John at the bow of their boat, Julian edged his way through fragments of timber, a mass of wood like straw in the water. None of the pieces was longer than a kitchen table.

They spotted one of the crew on life rafts, waving. But knowing he was safe, they ignored him. There was no sign of anyone on what remained of the *Maria Asumpta*'s hull, now slammed against the rocks, but as they moved through the debris, they spotted four grey heads floating with the tide.

They came back down along the wreckage and with Paul hauled three casualties out of the water and another from the life rafts. Covered in oil, their hair and their faces were so grey with bilge muck that Julian and John could hardly make out their features.

Julian's boat was a catamaran. As they moved in towards the wreckage to attempt to rescue another person, John saw a body floating face down about six inches beneath the water. It slipped silently between the catamaran's two hulls. He didn't want to look, but he needed to keep an eye ahead to avoid hitting rocks.

They picked up another survivor, but they didn't see the body again. On the boat, the survivors were shocked, shaken and very cold. Exhausted and on the point of hypothermia, they were huddled together. None of them was wearing a lifejacket, a sign that none of them were real sea people.

When they'd heard the Mayday call, they had thought they would maybe turn up, throw a rope to the *Maria Asumpta*, tow her off and maybe get some salvage money for helping rescue a stricken vessel. They hadn't even considered the possibility that there would be nothing much to salvage, only people to pull out of the water. None of them had anticipated the havoc they found all around them.

'Can you see them? Are they OK? They were over there,' one of the survivors muttered, pointing at the rocks.

Julian could see a few figures clambering up Rumps Point. 'I think they're safe,' said Julian. 'What happened?'

Listening to the survivors talk, John, Paul and he pieced together a picture of the last hour on board the *Maria Asumpta*. It was later confirmed in greater detail when Mark Litchfield, the captain and owner of the vessel, appeared in front of a court charged with manslaughter.

At about 3.30 p.m., about forty-five minutes before the ship hit the rocks, Litchfield was standing beside his helmsman, John Howells, as they approached Pentire Point, the entrance to the Camel Estuary and their eventual destination, Padstow. They had been making good time towards their rendezvous with the Padstow pilot, so Litchfield, a former Royal Navy officer, had ignored conventional wisdom and plotted a course only one mile off the rocks. Although advised against it by several more experienced crew members, Litchfield wanted to give his crew a chance to view the picturesque coast, as well as allowing people ashore to admire his beautiful ship. He told police later that it was 'a nice coast and I thought everybody else would like to look at it'.

Litchfield's watch leader, Adam Pursar, the boat's most experienced crew member, had urged Litchfield to tack out to sea, away from the hazards of Mouls Rock and the Rumps. Likewise, the Padstow harbourmaster had advised Litchfield to take the *Maria Asumpta* into safer waters, but Litchfield insisted on maintaining his course.

But as they approached Mouls Rock, Litchfield became alarmed by the extent to which the wind and tide were directing his vessel towards shore. With the ship veering off course, he ordered the engines to be started and she skirted around the rock, her engines running smoothly.

Just past Mouls Rock, with a lee shore and the tide against them, the engines suddenly stopped.

'This could be serious,' said Litchfield to Howells. It was some understatement.

Although he hadn't informed his crew, Litchfield had four days earlier been warned by marine engineers who had serviced the engines that he ought to replace the sailing ship's fuel as it was contaminated by water.

With the *Maria Asumpta* drifting fast towards Rumps Point, Litchfield called all hands on deck and gave orders for the sails to be set full to gain speed. He also sent two engineers below deck to attempt to restart the engines. But already most of the crew knew it was too late. Pursar realised the ship was now doomed, as did several other experienced crewmen. Litchfield, too, knew the ship was unlikely to make it. 'I think I started to pray,' he said later.

Although there were sufficient lifejackets on board, no one was advised or ordered to put them on. Instead Litchfield posted one of the crew to the bows to watch for reefs, then he began broadcasting Mayday calls.

Ten minutes after the engines failed, Howells turned to Litchfield and attempted to assure him that all was not lost.

'Mark, I think we're going to make it,' he said.

Seconds later, the *Maria Asumpta* struck a submerged rock that the lookout had failed to spot. She heeled dramatically to starboard, then swung to port. Immediately her hull began to splinter and crack.

'Oh my God, she's struck,' yelled Litchfield to his crew. 'Save yourselves and make land by the rocks.'

Some of the crew members ran to the bow to jump on to the rocks, but not everyone on board found it quite as easy to abandon ship. More concerned by the prospect of being crushed by timbers crashing from above than by the danger of drowning, Howells attempted to find refuge on the foredeck, where he got his legs tangled in ropes by the rail. With the *Maria Asumpta* listing by up to sixty degrees every time the swell hit, the deck was almost vertical at times.

As he cast around for help, Howells could see 51-year-old Anne Taylor, the ship's cook, on the deck, apparently petrified with fear. A widow, she had given up her job as a secretary to sail on the ship. Now she was rooted to the deck as the ship split at the point where she was standing. The last Howells saw of Anne Taylor on the ship, she was being pulled down into the churning sea.

Howells worked himself free of the ropes, then reached the bows, from where he caught sight of Anne again, in the water, looking directly at him, terrified. A wave crashed over Howells and he lost sight of her. A few minutes later he saw Anne on a rock. Thinking the cook was safe, he turned his attention to helping others.

With another crew member, Howells leaped on to the rocks, timing their jump with the movement of the swell. As he landed, a wave crashed over him, but the other crew member grabbed Howells's collar, saving him from being swept away.

Near them, the second engineer, John Shannon, also made it to a rock but lost his grip as the waves washed him back out to sea. A few minutes later, Howells spotted Shannon in the sea about fifty or sixty metres out, clinging to a coolbox. But the coolbox kept on spinning over and although they had a fix on him, no one could help Shannon as he lost his grip on the box and slipped under.

Meanwhile, the first engineer, Jamie Campbell, had made it safely on to a rock, but when he looked back at what remained of the *Maria Asumpta*, he spotted Emily MacFarlane, a nineteen-year-old assistant bosun and a very poor swimmer, still on the deck. Bravely, he jumped back into the sea and made it to the shipwreck. Campbell and MacFarlane were later seen in the sea together. Both went under a couple of times but came up again. Then they went under and disappeared for a while. Campbell was spotted about a minute later on the other side of the ship, but MacFarlane was not seen again.

As well as John, Julian and Paul, another fishing vessel and the Rock lifeboat, the *Jubilee Queen*, had assisted in the rescue. The lifeboat crew unloaded one of the survivors they had rescued on to Julian's boat. Realising the five survivors they had on board needed swift assistance, Julian decided to go into Padstow. He radioed Falmouth Coastguard.

'We're coming into Padstow,' he told the coastguard. 'We've got five people here and we need an ambulance on the quay when we get there.'

John put on the gas ring to keep the survivors warm, but when they arrived in Padstow, no ambulance was waiting. All of the ambulances were on the Polzeath side of the estuary, in spite of Julian informing them they were coming in at Padstow. It's not the first time we fishermen have despaired at the inefficiency of some of the professional members of the coastguard, a bunch of desk jockeys behind computers, sometimes hundreds of miles away, but this time it was particularly galling.

The ambulances took an age to arrive, but eventually the five survivors were taken off to Truro hospital. Meanwhile, we sailed back to Port Isaac, where about twenty or thirty villagers were waiting for us to arrive. It was a moment of which we could be proud.

That evening, a navy helicopter winched the body of Anne Taylor from the sea. The bodies of Emily MacFarlane and John Shannon were found twenty-five days later by the Port Isaac lifeboat off Carnweather Point. They were identified by their clothing.

Julian had smashed a rudder and bent a propeller in the course of the rescue, so his boat was out of action for a couple of days. Two weeks later, Mark Litchfield rang up Julian, wanting to know where his life rafts were.

'I thought you might've phoned some time before this and thanked me for picking up five of your crew,' said Julian. After all that he and John had done to save the lives of the crew of the *Maria Asumpta*, Julian was outraged.

A few days later, a policeman arrived in Port Isaac.

'I hear you've got two life rafts here,' he said to Julian. 'I'm going to have to impound them.'

Assuming the police would eventually want them for evidence, John and Julian had hauled the two large twelve-man life rafts, worth a couple of thousand pounds apiece, up the beach, deflated them and put them over beams in the fish cellar for safekeeping. The police took them away as evidence. A while later, John found out that Litchfield had gone in to Bodmin police station, got the liferafts back and taken them to a friend who had a farm nearby. Julian went to investigate and discovered one of the lifeboats abandoned on the farm, its canopy removed for use as a kid's paddling pool.

In fact, Julian had wrecker's rights on the lifeboats and could have sold them. Instead, his only souvenirs are a belaying pin from the base of the *Maria Asumpta*'s mast, the ship's clock, a cheap old battery thing that stopped at the time the boat sank, and a clinometer, which measured how far she had listed over.

John and Julian were called as witnesses at Mark Litchfield's trial a few years later. Although he pleaded not guilty, Litchfield was jailed for eighteen months for the manslaughter of the three crew members who died due to his gross negligence in navigating too close to the shore, knowing that the diesel was contaminated. The judge told Litchfield he had shown a profound disregard for the lives of his crew.

It emerged in the trial that Litchfield had previously owned the *Marques*, a dilapidated square-rigger that sank with the loss of nineteen lives in 1984.

A beautiful slate memorial to the three crew who died in the wreck of *Maria Asumpta* was erected at St Enodoc's Church in Trebetherick, about two and a half miles from where she hit Rumps Point.

It was a tragedy that needn't have happened. Mostly amateurs, the crew were the kind of people who had a romantic image of putting to sea on a sailing ship. That was all very good, but it meant they hadn't been brought up to respect the ocean like a local. Anyone experienced on a boat the size of the *Maria Asumpta* would have had an anchor rigged and ready to bang away. We frequently sail closer to the cliffs than most of the route taken by the *Maria Asumpta*, but we always take precautions. We'll have an anchor ready to go in case we need to drop it away. Anyone who comes from a fishing family, or who has anything to do with the sea, has it trained into them. You treat the ocean with respect. You don't take chances. It's not a theme park out there. There aren't lifeguards at every turn. There's no health and safety.

As for the body that floated between the hulls of Julian's catamaran, it weighed heavily on John's mind long after the *Maria Asumpta*'s fateful final voyage.

Cornish Legends

Giants, piskies, mermaids, spriggans and knockers. Cornish folk tales are full of legendary creatures, some of which are thought to have developed as supernatural explanations for the frequent cave-ins of Cornish tin mines. Another interpretation is that they were the hallucinations of oxygen-starved exhausted miners returning from underground.

Whatever the origin, Cornwall has a rich heritage of tales of strange and beautiful creatures. The Mermaid of Padstow is said to have cast a curse on the mouth of the Camel Estuary after she was shot from a visiting boat. Diving for a moment, she reappeared with her right hand raised and vowed the harbour would from that day forth be desolate. A storm immediately blew up, wrecking several ships and throwing up the sandbank known as the Doom Bar, upon which hundreds of ships have foundered.

Piskies were identical inch-tall old men in red caps, white waistcoats, green stockings, brown coats and trousers, and brightly polished, buckled shoes. Although mischievous, they were generally well-meaning and helped the old.

With large heads on small bodies, spriggans were ugly and feared. They stole babies, raised whirlwinds to damage crops, and terrified lone travellers. Knockers were elfin creatures that lived in the mines. Believing that anyone who was disrespectful to knockers would suffer bad luck, miners left food out for them and threw them their pasty crusts.

Stories of giants meeting pixies are thought to have originated from the encounters of tall Celts with the small Bronze Age peoples. According to one legend, St Michael's Mount was constructed by a giant. Another story tells the tale of Bolster, a giant with a stride that spanned six miles. He fell in love with the beautiful St Agnes, who insisted he proved his love by filling a hole in the cliff at Chapel Porth, a cove near the village of St Agnes, with his own blood. Not knowing the hole was bottomless, Bolster continued until he was so weak he fell into the sea and died. Even today the cliffs at Chapel Porth are stained red, supposedly with Bolster's blood.

Another giant, the Wrath of Portreath, lived in a huge cavern known to sailors as his cupboard. Wading out to sea, he grabbed whole ships and took them back to his cupboard, tied to his belt, where he would devour the sailors. The stones he hurled at ships trying to avoid him can still be seen at low tide forming a dangerous reef off Godrevy Head.

CHAPTER TEN

BIMBLING ALONG

Cleavey doesn't like to admit it, but he's always slightly relieved when he's got past having to introduce the Brown brothers. It's not their fault, but he finds it difficult to think of anything to say about them that takes the mickey. And as far as most of us are concerned, taking the mickey is half the point of the Fisherman's Friends. The other half is equally shared between drinking and singing.

Maybe Cleavey struggles for appropriate words because the Brown Brothers are the closest thing the Fisherman's Friends have got to founding fathers. Or maybe it's because they're real fishermen, whereas the rest of us are part-timers, or former fishermen, or wannabe fishermen, or hobby fishermen. Or in Cleavey's case, never-really-been-that-interested-in-fishing ('I'd rather be singing Gilbert & Sullivan') fishermen.

So when Cleavey can't think of something to say about one of the Browns, he'll move on swiftly to the next song, usually another heart-string-tugging tune from the housewife's choice – touchy-feely Trev. This time he's going to sing 'Shenandoah', a capstan shanty that has many different lyrics. One version tells the story of a roving trader in love with the daughter of an Indian chief. Another tells of a pioneer's nostalgia for the Shenandoah River Valley in Virginia. A third version is about a Union soldier in the American Civil War, dreaming of his country home to the west of the Missouri river, in Shenandoah, Iowa. And the song is also associated with escaped slaves, who were said to sing it in gratitude because the river allowed their scent to be lost.

Our version steals from several versions, but one thing's for sure, it's a tear-jerker when Toastie sings it.

> *Oh, Shenandoah, I love your daughter,*
> *Away my rolling river,*
> *Shenandoah the white mulatta,*
> *We are bound away from the world of misery.*
>
> *For seven years I told the ocean,*
> *Away my rolling river,*
> *For seven years I never rode her,*
> *We are bound away from this world of misery.*
>
> *I courted Sally, no pen, no paper,*
> *Away my rolling river,*
> *I courted Sally on foolscap paper,*
> *We are bound away from this world of misery.*

And so it continues until there's barely a dry eye left on the Platt. At which point, Cleavey steps in.

'Thank you very much,' he says. 'Anyone who's been affected by any of the issues raised in the singing of this song, if you'd care to contact us afterwards, we'll give you a number for the Fisherman's Friends helpline. A trained counsellor will help you discuss your problems.

'Actually it's a looped tape that says: "Get over it. Pull yourself together and move on."'

As the millennium turned and we built on the lessons we'd learned from our tour to Mystic Seaport, the Fisherman's Friends continued building our repertoire and our reputation. Every summer we played on the Platt on Friday evenings, now raising money for local charities as we no longer needed to find funds for a trip to America.

In the winter, and in between Platt appearances in the summer, we played small gigs anywhere they'd have us. None of these were paid engagements; if we were lucky we'd get a few free drinks. But mostly we did it for the enjoyment of being together and taking part in a small folk festival or a summer seaside event. And whenever we could, we'd agree to sing at charity fundraising events, particularly if the money was going to a local or maritime charity, such as the RNLI. With no grand master plan for the Fisherman's Friends, we kept doing it simply because we liked getting together to sing in Billy's chapel once a week before moving on to the Golden Lion for a few pints and a yarn. We called it bimbling along.

Early in the new millennium, Show of Hands asked us to support them on some larger gigs. They're Britain's leading folk duo and Billy had known them for several years, ever since he saw them in a concert somewhere and invited Steve Knightley and Phil Beer to Port Isaac to play a gig in his pottery. We all went down to listen to them and since then, Billy has become very friendly with them and their families.

We backed Steve and Phil at Sidmouth Folk Festival, at the Phoenix Theatre in Exeter, and at several other events around the West Country. At first, we sang as their support, a few songs and shanties before Show of Hands took the stage. After a while, we started backing them during their set, singing on the choruses of certain songs, such as 'Cousin Jack'. We stole that one off them — well, actually, Steve asked us if we'd do it — and unlike most songs that he introduces on the Platt, Cleavey explains what it's about.

'We think ourselves very lucky to live in Cornwall,' Cleavey says. 'We do consider it God's own country. Actually, if you search through the ancient text of the Bible, you will probably find that God actually was a Cornishman. Although, like a lot of us, he did actually have to move away to find work at one time or another. And that's what this song is about. It's a song about the Cornish diaspora, which is a posh way of saying the scattering of the Celtic peoples.'

This land is barren and broken,
Scarred like the face of the moon,
Our tongue is no longer spoken
And the towns all around face ruin,
Will there be work in New Brunswick?
Will I find gold in the Cape?
If I tunnel way down to Australia,
Oh, will I ever escape?

Where there's a mine or a hole in the ground,
That's what I'm heading for, that's where I'm bound,
So look for me under the lode and inside the vein,
Where the copper, the clay, the arsenic and tin
Run in your blood and under your skin,
I'll leave the county behind, I'm not coming back,
Oh, follow me down, cousin Jack.

The soil was too poor to make Eden,
Granite and sea left no choice,
Though visions of heaven sustained us,
When John Wesley gave us a voice,
Did Joseph once come to St Michael's Mount,
Two thousand years pass in a dream,
When you're working your way in the darkness,
Deep in the heart of the seam.

Where there's a mine or a hole in the ground,
That's what I'm heading for, that's where I'm bound,
So look for me under the lode and inside the vein,

Where the copper, the clay, the arsenic and tin
Run in your blood and under your skin,
I'll leave the county behind, I'm not coming back,
Oh, follow me down, cousin Jack.

I dream of a bridge on the Tamar,
It opens us up to the East,
And the English they live in our houses,
And the Spanish they fish in our seas,

Where there's a mine or a hole in the ground,
That's what I'm heading for, that's where I'm bound,
So look for me under the lode and inside the vein,
Where the copper, the clay, the arsenic and tin
Run in your blood and under your skin,
I'll leave the county behind, I'm not coming back,
Oh, follow me down, cousin Jack.

Of all our repertoire, 'Cousin Jack' is probably the most political song and it's a favourite with a lot of us. So when, in 2002, Show of Hands asked us if we'd accompany them at the Royal Albert Hall, of course we immediately said yes. Proper job.

When the day came, we were like a bunch of kids we were so excited. With a coachload of supporters following in our wake, we left Port Isaac nearly empty that weekend. By early afternoon we'd arrived at the Thistle Hotel on the edge of Kensington Gardens, about a quarter of a mile away from the Albert Hall. We'd just checked in when Steve from Show of Hands walked in with a surprise. Ralph , he said, wanted to sing his most famous song, 'Streets of London', that night on the Albert Hall stage with us.

Although we all knew the song well, especially Ralph's original version, we needed to rehearse it before singing on stage in front of a crowd of more than five thousand. Steve got in touch with him and less than an hour later we were singing 'Streets of London' with

Ralph, a lovely, lovely man, in the foyer of the Thistle Hotel. As we rehearsed, a crowd gathered to watch. It was a surreal moment.

Some of us had been to the Albert Hall previously with one of our local choirs, but to be on the stage as the Fisherman's Friends was a very different experience for all of us. The stalls were solid with people; the boxes were packed and most of the top balcony tier was occupied. The biggest gig we'd played until then, it was a real buzz.

That night, we accompanied Show of Hands on four songs. Then, as previously arranged, we were going to sing 'South Australia' on our own. As the big moment loomed, we looked along the line to where Jeremy was standing. Nominated to sing the lead, he was so nervous he was shaking, but he managed it. What a night!

Three years later, Steve and Phil asked us to accompany Show of Hands again at the Albert Hall. Of course we immediately agreed, but by then we'd also been asked to sing with them at the Radio 2 Folk Awards at the Brewery, a major turning point in our story.

In 2005, we weren't sufficiently well known to have been nominated for an award; our role was to back Show of Hands on stage and to entertain the nominees and all the nobs as they arrived at the event. Jeremy and Billy were meant to be going on holiday with their wives, Liz and Barbara, but they didn't want to miss the chance to sing at the awards, so their wives went ahead and Jeremy and Billy joined us in London.

Having arrived in the early afternoon at the Brewery, an events venue near the Barbican in the City of London, we were asked to take our place on the stage in the main hall for a sound check. Arranging ourselves on the stage, we looked out at a small army of table layers, technicians, sound engineers and electricians busily preparing the hall for that evening's awards and entertainment. Like a silent army of worker ants, they were laying out cutlery, glasses and crockery, cleaning the floor, unfurling cables to loudspeakers, checking table settings, putting flowers on tables and undertaking all the other tasks necessary to make a big event proceed smoothly.

Feeling slightly self-conscious in front of the silent workforce, we started singing a shanty so the sound technicians could check the sound level settings on their public address equipment. Before we finished the first verse, all the worker ants had stopped what they were doing. Every single one of them was still, their eyes and ears directed at us. These were people who saw different bands almost every day and night. They'd seen much bigger bands and choirs than us perform live in some of the best venues in the country. And today, they had busy jobs to do. With a hectic evening ahead, they couldn't afford the time to stop and watch a bunch of middle-aged Cornish chancers singing centuries-old sea shanties. But that's exactly what they did. And at the end, they all clapped.

That applause meant more to us than probably any recognition we'd received until then. These were hard-nosed catering and events staff, used to ignoring entertainers. And here they were, stopping in the middle of their busy day, to applaud the Fisherman's Friends. For the first time since we'd started singing together, we realised we might have something special, something that resonated with an audience.

That evening, as the nominees, guests and various celebrities arrived at the Brewery Centre, we took our place in the entrance foyer, where we sang as the arrivals came through the door. Dawn French, Charles Dance and various other celebrities stopped to listen to us. Some of them stopped for a minute or two to listen properly before taking off their coats and moving on into the reception; others did little more than glance our way. Having only ever seen these kind of people on television, it was a great thrill to see them in real life, in the flesh. Then Sir David Attenborough arrived. As soon as he came into the entrance area, Sir David stopped talking to the people with whom he'd arrived and stood stock still, looking at us. He listened to one song, then clapped. We thought he'd move on, but he didn't. A couple of people in his party whispered in his ear and appeared to urge him to move on, but he refused. For more than twenty minutes he stood in front of us, all of his attention directed at the Fisherman's Friends, a warm smile on his face, looking at us as if he'd just discovered a new species. And compared to the crowd pressing into the folk awards in their dicky bows, dinner suits, long dresses and jewellery, we were a very different breed: *homo rollockus shantius*, you might say.

The evening went like a dream. It was a proper job to sing in front of some of the best folk bands and singers in the country. After the awards were finished, we were invited to a hotel nearby where many of the nominees and award-winners were staying. Relieved that it all had gone so well, we were buzzing as we got a few drinks and sat down with some of the musicians we'd admired. Jon Boden, lead vocalist with Bellowhead and a fine fiddle player, came over for a chat. He used to sing shanties, so we asked him if he wanted to join us in a sing-song. As ever, it started with our traditional call to song.

'We'll have a sing, shall us?' said John Brown.

'Yeah, yeah,' said those closest to John. 'All right, then.'

Then we rounded up the rest of the reprobates, drinking further down the room.

'Hey, hey!' we shouted. 'Come on, we're going to sing.'

After we sang a shanty, Jon Boden led 'The Alabama', which Cleavey usually leads when we sing it on the Platt. Then he sang a shanty that he had written, which was fantastic, and after a couple of choruses, we joined in where we could.

From midnight to four in the morning, we kept at it nonstop. Singing and drinking, yarning and rollocking. At 4 a.m. we poured Jeremy into a taxi, feeling ill, and pointed him in the direction of Gatwick airport so he could catch a plane to join his wife in Egypt. The rest of us kept going until 6 a.m., partying with musicians and people from Radio 2, including Eddi Reader from Fairground Attraction and Sally Traffic. We'd all heard Sally read the traffic news on Radio 2, but to see her drinking and singing along with us until sunrise was a surreal experience, especially as she had a lovely singing voice.

For some reason we always sing best when we're all together having a few drinks after the main event. It's looser and less pressurised and we've had a few pints and a little bit of a dig at each other, so often we try something different, just to make it more entertaining for us.

And it's better because we're happy singing to ourselves. Even if nobody wants to listen, that's fine.

Few of us got to sleep that night before we had to catch the train back down to Cornwall to get home to Port Isaac. By the time we arrived back at our cottages in the village, we all looked wrecked, but we managed to placate our wives by convincing them that the source of our exhaustion was all hard work and no play. It was all going swimmingly – some of the FFWAGS had even brought us painkillers and cups of tea as we wallowed around at home, moaning about our headaches and tiredness. They looked sceptical, but they had no reason not to believe us. Until, that is, Sally Traffic came on Radio 2 and the DJ, Johnnie Walker, teased her about her stinking hangover. Sally explained that she'd met a bunch of sea dogs from Port Isaac at the Radio 2 Folk Awards and told the nation she'd been drinking and singing with them until sunrise.

Suddenly we all needed to go fishing.

A few weeks later, we were all out in Guernsey for Peter Rowe's seventieth birthday. Through his connections with the RNLI, Nigel had arranged a trip from St Peter Port on a Severn-class lifeboat, the largest type used by the RNLI, but other than that, nothing out of the ordinary was planned. Some sightseeing, a dinner, a few drinks, maybe a sing together.

Waiting on the quayside near where the boat was moored, Billy was sitting on a long set of railings, swinging his legs. Most of us were leaning against the railings either side of Billy, waiting for our excursion on the lifeboat. Behind us, over the top of the railings, was a twenty-foot drop on to the hard stone of a lower level of the quay. The rest of us were leaning against the railings because, quite frankly, none of us wanted to risk a fall that would almost certainly be fatal. Sitting on the top, swinging his legs and yarning with the rest of us, Billy was the only one tempting fate. All of a sudden (and somewhat inevitably), his legs flipped over his shoulders as he disappeared over the back.

Expecting to hear a scream or maybe the dull thud of bone on rock, we all whipped around to see where Billy had fallen. But instead of a scream, we heard the hefty clunk of a middle-aged man striking metal, followed by a long, loud giggle. A tall van had parked directly behind him and he had fallen only about three feet on to its roof, leaving a big dent in the sheet metal beneath a nervously giggling Billy.

Along the entire length of the railings, no other vehicles had parked. If he'd fallen anywhere else, he would almost certainly have died. But Billy, whose brushes with danger were starting to rival a cat's, had escaped yet again relatively unharmed.

Of course, it was no surprise to find Billy at the epicentre of mayhem. Even when he didn't create trouble, it came looking for him. Like the time he decided to go away for a long weekend with Barbara. It was such a good tale it even made the national newspapers. It started with Barbara and Billy going off to Paris for a few days, then stopping off for a long weekend in Torquay, leaving John Brown to house-sit their cat and dog.

Now, John has never been one of Port Isaac's early risers. He likes his sleep and was thoroughly enjoying a doze in bed at Billy's house one morning when the phone rang. It was a mate with a pick-up truck who needed some slate moving. There aren't many things that will get John out of bed, but the offer of money for old rope is one of them.

'I'll have some of that,' he said.

A cup of tea later, John was off down Roscarrock Hill and past the Platt on his way to work. An hour later, he returned, only now the street was full of police and the lifeboat crew. Robert Sloman, a Port Isaac farmer, was among them, looking very worried. But his worried frown immediately relaxed into a beaming smile when he spotted John.

'Thank God you're alive,' said Robert.

John was just about to ask Robert what he meant when he noticed something poking out of the top of Billy's house. It was a Land Rover – Robert Sloman's Land Rover. Somehow it had speared through the roof. And judging by how its wheels were pointing into the air, its cab must have landed directly in the bed in which John had been sleeping.

'We jumped out less than a hundred yards before it went over the edge,' said Robert. 'It was the most terrifying experience of my life.'

Robert had been rounding up sheep in a steeply banked field at the top of the cliff above Billy's house. After weeks of dry weather, a sudden downpour had raced off the surface, making the grass as slippery as a skating rink. The slope above Billy's house is as steep as anything. Difficult to negotiate in dry conditions, it was lethal in the wet.

'Nothing went wrong with the Land Rover,' said Robert. 'It started to slip and I lost control. It aquaplaned and took off down the field.'

Robert and his shepherd, Tony Wickett, jumped free of the vehicle just before it hit the first small hedge. Then it hurtled 300 feet down the hill, rolling over and over, gaining momentum and bouncing like a tennis ball until it nose-dived through Billy's roof into the very bedroom in which John had been sleeping. A fireman told John that had he indulged in his customary late lie-in, it would have been curtains for him.

As he stood outside Billy's house, the extent of his lucky escape slowly dawning on him, John spotted Nigel in his RNLI kit, emerging from the house with a wrench in his hand.

'What's going on, Nigel?' said John.

'Boy, am I pleased to see you,' replied Nigel.

Nigel explained that he'd been working in the village when a maroon went off, the signal for a lifeboat shout.

'That's a bit strange, I thought,' he said. 'The sea's as flat as a pancake.'

He ran down to the lifeboat station, but no one else was there. The launch authority hadn't been mobilised. So he phoned Falmouth Coastguard.

'We've just raised your team,' the coastguard said. 'There's an incident in your chapel.'

'What?'

Nigel ran over to Billy's house and the old chapel, only about fifty yards from the lifeboat station. From where he was standing, he couldn't see the Land Rover poking out of the roof. The only sign of anything untoward was a river of water cascading down the steps leading up to Billy's front door. Nigel opened the front door gingerly (we rarely lock our doors in Port Isaac because we all keep an eye open for each other) and entered. Water was everywhere, but otherwise nothing was out of place. Thinking John might have left the bath running, Nigel ran upstairs and immediately came face to face with an upside-down Land Rover surrounded by collapsed roof timbers, crumbling plaster and snapped pipes. He checked John wasn't in the bed beneath the Landy, then turned off the stopcock. As he related the story, the flood of water on the steps behind him finally dwindled to a trickle.

'You know what you've got to do now?' said Nigel.

'What?' said John.

'Phone Billy, of course.'

Billy and Barbara were stepping out of the Palace Hotel in Torquay when Barbara's brand-new mobile phone rang. The first mobile phone Barbara had ever had, she still hadn't used it.

'Billy, it's ringing,' she said. 'What will I do?'

'I'd answer it,' said Billy.

Barbara tinkered with her phone, trying to figure out how to get it to work.

'Barbs? What's that thing say?' said Billy, who was getting impatient with Barbara's fiddling.

'It's John,' she said. 'He's left a voicemail. He said a Land Rover's landed in our roof.'

'That's bollocks, Barbs. You can't believe that,' said Billy. 'It's the boys winding us up. Just because you've got a new mobile phone.'

Billy had good reason to think it was a practical joke because we were always playing them on each other. Just before he and Barbara had left for Paris, Cleavey and Lefty pulled a stunt on an old boy in

the village. The chap had a Robin Reliant that he used to park outside Cleavey's post office and shop. While the old boy was in
Cleavey's shop, Lefty and Cleavey jacked up his three-wheeler and put
some bricks underneath it so that the wheels were an eighth of an
inch off the ground. The old boy came out of the shop, got in his car
and fired it up. When he went to drive off, the wheels span around
but the Reliant went nowhere.

So it was understandable that Billy thought the phone call was just
another of our many practical jokes. But Barbara was curious, so she
phoned Port Isaac. By then, everyone in the village had seen what
had happened. They confirmed the accident to Barbara.

'It's true, Billy. What are we going to do?' said Barbara. 'A Land
Rover has gone through our roof. Everyone says it's so.'

'They're all in on it, Barbs. It's a practical joke. Don't believe a
word of it.'

But as Billy was speaking the news came on the radio. One of the
first reports described the scene in Port Isaac as the village struggled
to cope with the incident of a Land Rover that had fallen off the cliff
on to a house.

'Bloody hell, Barbs,' said Billy. 'That's us. It's true.'

Billy immediately pulled a U-turn and drove straight back to Port
Isaac, arriving late in the afternoon. As they drove into the village they
could see from the scarred cliffside where the Land Rover had torn
through hawthorn hedges before plummeting through the air on to
their home. Greeted by the emergency services and shown the devastation the Land Rover had wrought, Billy shrugged.

'But Billy, we've only just finished decorating the bedroom,' said
Barbara.

'I know, Barbs, but there's nothing we can do. It's only bricks and
mortar. No one's hurt.'

Already the insurance assessors were on the scene, vying like vul-
tures to represent Billy and Barbara's claim.

'I've had enough of this,' said Billy, turning to one of the assessors
at random. 'Right, you sort it out.'

He turned to Barbara. 'And we can't stay here, Barbs, so we might as well go back to Torquay and worry about it on Monday.'

So Billy and Barbara returned to the Devon Riviera to enjoy the rest of their mini-break.

The next morning, the story of John Brown's lucky escape from the sudden arrival of a Land Rover through Billy's roof was splashed all over the fronts of all the Saturday national newspapers. 'Land Rover That Went a Little Too Far Off Road,' said the *Daily Mail*'s headline. '£200,000 Home Wrecked as Farmer Loses Control in a Downpour.'

The story started: 'Off-road ventures are what they are built for. But not even a Land Rover could take the direct route from the clifftop to Bill and Barbara Hawkins' listed Cornish home without making a mess . . .'

The *Guardian* also had a report. 'From Here to Down There – Runaway Vehicle's Rampage,' said the headline above a picture and a report that started, 'Barbara and Bill Hawkins yesterday returned from a break in France to find that a runaway Land Rover had devastated their Cornish home.'

While we were all poring over the newspaper reports, a loss adjuster from Billy's insurance company turned up in the village. John showed him the damage.

'It's a new one for me,' he said. 'Land Rovers through roofs aren't covered in our guidelines.'

With much head-scratching and sighing, the loss adjuster tried to work out how to get the Land Rover out of Billy's roof. His first idea involved driving a line of stakes into the cliff above the house, then winching the Landy out of the roof and up the cliff. But he then realised it would be slow and tortuous with a risk that the stakes might dislodge, releasing the Land Rover to cause even more damage. And with diesel from the Land Rover spilled all over Billy's house, the assessor couldn't risk using heavy machinery.

John Brown was standing nearby, a wry grin creasing his face as he watched the loss adjuster's antics. 'I'll take it out for you,' he said.

'Yeah, yeah.' The loss adjuster looked very sceptical.

'No, really. I'll do it.'

'How?' said the loss adjuster. 'This won't be easy. We'll need heavy machinery to remove the back wall and then maybe we can lift it out with a crane.'

'No, you don't. I'll take it out for you. On my own. No heavy machinery. No removing back walls. Just me on my own.'

With a tight smile, the loss adjuster ignored John's solution and turned his attention to working out a different scheme. 'I know,' he said. 'We could get a helicopter down and use it to lift the vehicle straight out of the roof.'

'I wouldn't if I was you,' said Peter Rowe, who had ambled over from the harbour to listen in on the loss adjuster's increasingly madcap methods. 'You'll take off half the roofs in Port Isaac with the downdraught.'

Looking despondent, the loss adjuster nodded in agreement.

'I'll take it out for you,' said John. 'Proper job.'

Struggling to hide his exasperation, the loss adjuster turned to John. 'And what exactly are you going to do that a helicopter or a crane can't do?'

'It's simple,' said John.

'Really?'

'Yup. Don't need any special equipment.'

'Oh?' The loss adjuster raised his eyebrows. 'And what exactly do you propose?'

'Dismantle the Landy with a few spanners.'

'And then what?'

'Take it down the stairs.'

'Really?'

'Yeah. No problem. Land Rovers are all bolted together.'

'You couldn't do that. It . . . it wouldn't work. Surely?'

'Yes it would.'

The loss adjuster appeared flummoxed by the simplicity of John's proposal. No helicopters. No heavy cranes. No removal of back walls. Surely the answer couldn't be as simple as taking it all apart?

'I'm going to have to go away and think about it,' he said. A few days later the loss adjuster phoned John. 'How much would you want?'

'Two and a half thousand.'

'Pounds?'

'What else?'

'I'd have to see your insurance.'

'I can get that sorted.'

In less than a week John went from lucky accident survivor to accident salvage engineer. First he removed the wheels and axles, an easy job with the Land Rover upside down. Then he unbolted the aluminium body panels, cut them up and carted them downstairs. The chassis was next. When he was finished, John got a few of us to help him carry the engine block out on two scaffolding poles.

After two and a half days' solid labour, the Land Rover was fully dismantled and in hundreds of parts, all stacked up in the street outside Billy's place. By the time the loss adjuster arrived to collect the bits, John was in the pub buying all the drinks, financed through flogging the wheels and some other items to one of the Port Isaac fishermen. The fisherman was proper made up with his newly acquired spare parts, the Land Rover from Billy's roof being almost new.

Of course, the rest of us rallied around Billy and Barbara to help them out. They rented a cottage at the top of the village from a friend and we all did whatever we could. Looking after each other is one of the things that has held us all together over the years. Like the time that we noticed Peter Rowe was struggling in his garden. Pete's garden is one of the wonders of Port Isaac. Arranged on one of the steepest slopes in the village, most of it is a series of narrow terraces stacked above each other until the top, where there's more space and it opens out. Pete collects a lot of seaweed from the beach to fertilise his garden, but he was struggling with it. One day, he mentioned to Lefty that he was having trouble hefting the seaweed up the slope.

'Get away, boy,' said Lefty. 'I've got a mate who will sort that out for ye.'

A few weeks later, Lefty's mate turned up. He works on forklift trucks and had found some spare parts to build a lift to carry up to two tons of seaweed up the side of Pete's garden. It took us a while to get it made, but anyone who passes Pete's house now might see Pete ascending the side of the hill with his barrow beside him. We call it his stairlift to heaven.

But it's not just the little things that pull us together. We also keep a lookout for each other when big changes rock our lives, like when Lefty sadly lost his wife, Mary. It was a sudden tragedy that came as a great shock to all of us, a bolt from the blue. Billy and Barbara were returning to Port Isaac and as soon as they came down the hill and started approaching the village, they could sense that something wasn't quite right. In a small community, events reverberate very quickly and profoundly through the place. It affects everyone.

We all sang at Mary's funeral – the choir did as well – and over the next months and years, while their two children were away at university, whenever we could we rallied round to help Lefty get through it. In those days, he used to work on a crane a lot. Sitting in a crane cab all day with only your thoughts for company can be a lonely job, and returning to an empty house even worse, so if there was something going on, we made sure we invited Lefty along, whether it was dinner at someone's house or a party or whatever. At times like that we all need our friends.

Similarly when Mark Provis died we were all profoundly affected and we all leaned on each other for support. By then, Mark had left the Fisherman's Friends, but we all used to see him almost daily around the village and Peter maintained his very close friendship with him. He'd always been very grateful to Mark because he'd fixed Peter up with his second wife.

Driving his car one day, Mark had felt strange, so he'd pulled over by the side of the road, then passed out. When he came to, he went to the doctor. It was a brain tumour and it killed him within about six months. It was a tragedy. Mark had two lovely boys and he'd just remarried. And because he had been so popular, a lovely big fella who was great fun, witty and good at swimming and rugby, an all-round super bloke, it was very hard on the entire village.

It was a hell of a funeral because Mark knew so many people. We were all there; some of us were bearers. Mark had been with us at the very start of the Fisherman's Friends and although he dropped out in about 1995 because rehearsals interfered with complications in his private life, we still regarded him very much as part of our history. His death hit us all very hard.

Living in a coastal community on a very dangerous stretch of shoreline, the prospect of injury, distress and, at worst, death is always present. Across the centuries, the ocean's danger has been the one constant in the life of anyone who lived in Port Isaac. Maybe that's why the village instinctively rallies together at times of sorrow or loss. It's also the reason why many villagers automatically volunteer for lifeboat service as soon as they are old and able-bodied enough. As Johnny Mac says, 'You can't live in Port Isaac and not be part of the lifeboat.' For many of us, the lifeboat and the weekly training exercises are as much a part of village life as Fisherman's Friends singing on the Platt on summer Fridays and rehearsing in Billy's pottery on winter Tuesdays. In fact, there's no one in the Fisherman's Friends who hasn't at one time been a member of the lifeboat or the coastguard cliff rescue team.

Port Isaac has had a lifeboat since 1869. For most of its history, our lifeboat was housed in the building that is now Cleavey's shop and former post office, halfway up Fore Street hill – not the most obvious or convenient location for a lifeboat house. In those days, the lifeboat was a ten-oar 32-foot boat, a fairly standard design called the Original and found in lifeboat stations around the country. However, the Port Isaac vessel had a narrower beam than most, just seven feet seven inches, so that when it was launched it could be squeezed around the tight corners of the buildings surrounding the Platt and run down to the slipway. A famous photograph of 1925 shows the *Richard and Sarah III* being pushed through the alleys of Port Isaac with only inches to spare. Mounted on its launching trailer, its gunwales ran level with first-floor windows as it passed through the village.

Our first three lifeboats, all called the *Richard and Sarah*, were rowing boats. With a crew of thirteen – ten oarsmen, a coxswain, a second coxswain and a bowman – they relied entirely on human power, which bears thinking about now that we have a modern 'D' class lifeboat, powered by a single 40hp engine.

Getting out of Port Isaac harbour in a storm is no mean feat. A big groundswell and a northerly or northwesterly gale will bring twenty-foot waves into the harbour, crashing over the Platt and against the doors of the lifeboat house. In a particularly big storm of the kind we'll get once or twice a winter, the spray from the waves will even carry as far as Cleavey's shop and the old school building halfway up Fore Street hill. As for the fish cellars, they'll be drenched, with the water escaping out of the doors on to the Platt. At high tide, any-where in the centre of the village or along the lower parts of Roscarrock Hill and Fore Street might be deluged with seawater.

In 1927, a new lifeboat house was built in Port Isaac, opposite the Slipway, but it was used only for six years, when the service was withdrawn because it hadn't been called out for some time. The lifeboat was reintroduced in 1967, which is when we got our 'D' class vessel. An inflatable rib capable of 23 knots, it's only one of 444 lifeboats in 235 lifeboat stations around the British Isles, which in 2009 rescued an average of 22 people a day. Unlike the RNLI life-guards on beaches, who are paid, almost all lifeboat crew members are unpaid volunteers. We regard it as a privilege and a duty to serve. Since the charity was founded in 1824, lifeboat crews and lifeguards have saved more than 137,000 lives. The biggest single rescue was in 1907, when lifeboats from Cadgwith, Coverack, the Lizard and Porthleven on the south coast of Cornwall rescued 456 people from the liner *Suevic*.

At Port Isaac, we've also got a volunteer cliff rescue team, which is part of HM Coastguard. Most coastal rescues will involve both the lifeboat and the coastguard cliff rescue, such as the time Peter Rowe was involved in a rescue from a cave at Hole Beach, an area up Tintagel way, rich in slate quarries with high cliffs that drop sheer to the sea.

As usual, the alarm was raised with three maroons fired above the harbour, signalling a sea-and-cliff rescue (one for cliff rescue; two for sea; three for both). Peter, his brother Jack, and Mike Scott, another villager, were the first three lifeboat members to arrive at the Slipway, so they took the boat out. Mike was a good lifeboat member, but not sea-experienced at all, so Jack went on the helm, with Pete on the radio. Racing up to Hole Beach, he received details of the rescue over the radio. Somebody was trapped in a cave. They'd been seen entering it ahead of the tide and they hadn't come out. It was now close to high water.

As they approached, they saw a helicopter hovering above the cliffs. Beneath it, the coastguard cliff rescue team was in place. Jack turned the lifeboat inshore, towards the cave, hoping maybe to get inside it to rescue the stranded man, but he turned the boat away at the last moment. A heavy ground sea and strong onshore winds made the going dangerous.

'We aren't going to get in there,' Jack yelled.

'I'm damn certain we won't,' said Pete. 'If we do get in there, we'll never get out again. That's a certainty.'

Jack eased the lifeboat away and kept it idling nearby while the helicopter descended for a closer look. Although the sea conditions were bad, they kept watching the entrance to the cave, hoping they might spot a chance to get in and out of it cleanly. But with the sea rough and at its highest, it was impossible to tell how much time they might be allowed for a rescue attempt. Having never explored the cave at low tide, they had no idea how much space they'd have inside it for turning the lifeboat.

'What the bloody hell's the lifeboat doing?' said a voice over the radio in Peter's hand. It was one of the lifeboat controllers, probably at RNLI headquarters in Poole. 'Why don't they go in and get him out?'

Pete was enraged. The controller had no concept of the local conditions. 'We may get in there,' he said over the radio to the controller, 'but there's no chance on Earth we shall get out again with this guy on board. We wouldn't stand a chance in hell.'

Jack yelled to Pete, asking him what he'd heard over the radio, so Pete explained.

'He doesn't know what he's talking about,' said Jack, shaking his head.

For a few minutes, everyone held their positions, then the helicopter descended and started to lower an inflatable dinghy. Pete and Jack assumed one of the helicopter crew was going to make an attempt at entering the cave. But as the dinghy dangled ten or twelve feet above the water, a huge sea came in, seized the dinghy and snapped the cable like a bootlace. The helicopter shot up like a rocket.

'There you are,' said Pete to his fellow crew members. 'What chance do you think we've got in there with the sea running like that? We'd be dead by now if we'd had a go.'

Then, from the top of the cliff, Bill Pink, Port Isaac's chief coastguard, started to climb around the cliffs with his crew. Driving pitons and anchors into the cliff walls, they made their way down and around, eventually arriving above the cave. They abseiled down the last section of cliff and disappeared inside.

Bill Pink was awarded a medal for the cliff rescue team's successful operation, but Pete's crew wouldn't have stood a chance. The cliff rescue team's decision to go in from above turned out to be the right one, and an example of why the amateur volunteer crews at the scene of the rescue almost always know better than the professionals ensconced in their cosy offices hundreds of miles away.

It might sound harsh, but many local fishermen or lifeboatmen on the spot have little time for chairbound professionals. We're the ones who are out at sea day in, day out, so we inevitably know much more about how the sea behaves. We're the ones who do the actual work when a rescue's on, so we're invariably the ones who are better qualified to make decisions about the safest and most effective course of action. In fairness, some fishermen have reservations about the knowledge of the so-called experts. As the Brown brothers' father used to say, the Meteorological Office's weather forecasts would 'either drown you or starve you', which is why we prefer to rely on our appraisal of the conditions. After all, it's our own lives that are at risk. Likewise, there's little respect for some Coastguard officers, who sit in offices that can be hundreds of miles away. They use computer programs to work out where the lifeboat and cliff rescue teams should position themselves to intercept a boat being carried on computer-simulated tide and wind projections. But they have insufficient experience or knowledge of local conditions, so we prefer to work it out for ourselves.

If Pete's crew had heeded their controller's insistence to enter the cave, they would most likely have joined the casualty list, turning a rescue operation into a minor disaster. Something like that happened a few years later, when the maroon was fired and the shout went out for a crew to undertake a rescue from a cave at Bossiney Bay, a cove between Tintagel and Boscastle.

A big groundswell had come in on a spring tide, catching a father and son unaware on the beach at Bossiney and sweeping them into a cave. In the time it took to alert the emergency services, the weather had turned nasty. When the shout went out, we all ran to the lifeboat station. Nigel's son-in-law, Kevin Dingle, was the first helmsman to arrive, closely followed by Mike Edkins, the landlord of the Golden Lion, and Paul Pollington, who had recently moved to Cornwall. As the first complete crew, they launched the lifeboat, while we watched them head out into mountainous seas.

Bossiney is a long shout from Port Isaac and its caves are one of the most inaccessible and difficult spots for a lifeboat to reach. In that weather, it would have taken about twenty-five minutes, all of them very uncomfortable. In thirty-foot seas, it's not nice being on a lifeboat. It hurts.

The North Cornwall coast gets a lot of northerly wind, particularly when there's a storm. It makes the sea very confused and generates a lot of northerly chop. A big breaking sea will flip the boat over if the crew doesn't meet the waves head-on, so they would have pushed the lifeboat directly into the waves. And meeting a sea like that at twenty-five knots makes the boat slam against the water. The crew gets pounded, which translates into pain. Kneeling in drysuits with integrated thick-soled boots, their arses slam into their thick-soled heels every time the boat hits a wave. Any lifeboatman who experiences a shout like that, knows about it the next day. We see them hobbling around the village for a week afterwards.

Having braved mammoth waves, the crew arrived at Bossiney on their own. There was no sign of a helicopter or a cliff rescue team. With no other option available, Kevin pointed the lifeboat at the cave entrance and tried to enter it. The boat got as far as the entrance, but just as it was going in, the backwash of a wave that had slammed into the cliffs flipped her over. Paul Pollington was washed out to sea in his lifejacket and later winched from the sea by helicopter. His two crewmates were swept into the cave, where they found the father and son cowering on a ledge.

Outside the cave, the ground sea was increasing in strength minute by minute. Inside, the swell was banging further and further into the cave with every wash of the waves. Kevin and Mike looked round for somewhere safe, but before they had a chance to pull themselves out of the water, the overturned lifeboat was picked up by the sea and swept into the cave – engine first.

Thinking they were about to be killed by the collision, Kevin and Mike prepared themselves for the impact. But at the last moment, the boat twisted on the swell and hit them side on. That sudden, unexpected change in orientation meant the difference between being struck by sharp metal or the softer inflatable chambers of the boat. It spared their lives.

Within seconds of the boat entering the cave, the groundswell cut off all light. Then the lifeboat's fuel tanks ruptured. Hallucinating in the fumes of the leaking fuel, and with the sea pounding on the cave entrance with a force that threatened to burst their eardrums, the lifeboat crew helped the father and son climb to the top of a crack in the cave, where they managed to survive until the sea subsided and they could be rescued.

With most of us in the Fisherman's Friends in our fifties and over, our days in the lifeboat have largely come to an end. We remain members of the RNLI, but we're no longer active crew members. However, Nigel (our youngest member) is still very much a part of the crew. In the lifeboat for two decades, he's been a helmsman for the last eight years and took charge of Port Isaac's response to possibly the biggest shout on this coast for a very long time.

On 16 August 2004, Nigel was working outside the village when he got a call on his pager. It said: 'Help with flooding in Boscastle.'

Nigel looked outside. It was bright sunshine. The sea was flat and calm. No sign of rain, let alone floods. He rang the station to check the message wasn't a mistake. 'Do you really need me?'

'You better come down, Nigel,' said the deputy launching authority. 'We haven't got many hands here.'

'All right, I'm on the way. It'll take me five minutes. Get the boat in the water.'

'Thanks for that. It's coming up as a major incident.'

Nigel grabbed a drysuit as soon as he arrived, got changed in the boat, then took over at the helm. The sea was as flat as a dish. He was making thirty knots when he came around Tintagel Head and the boat hit something in the water. It felt like a dolphin or a whale, so he turned back to investigate. Just under the water's surface he spotted it: a green velour sofa. With a great big slice out of it where the boat had hit it.

Looking around, Nigel realised he and his crew were in the middle of a great brown muddy soup that was flowing out of Boscastle. As for Boscastle itself, it was like a biblical scene. A foreboding black cloud was thundering directly over the valley. Lightning flashes lit up the harbour. But around Nigel's lifeboat, a mile or so offshore, the sky was clear and the sea calm.

Nigel's crew was the first lifeboat on site. The only other rescue service was a single helicopter. The storm was so severe that nothing else could get close, so Nigel moved in towards the harbour, under the cloud into rain falling with a force that he thought was impossible. He had never seen or experienced rain like it. It was incredible.

At first, Nigel's crew couldn't do anything but keep the lifeboat moving to rid it of water. Then a few other helicopters arrived and another lifeboat.

The crew was assigned to work with a helicopter from the Royal Marines base at Chivenor. At one point the conditions became too severe for the helicopter to move, so Nigel sat at the edge of the harbour directly under the helicopter, trying to use the downdraught to shelter from the rain. But even beneath the Sea King helicopter, the rain was so strong that the lifeboat was filling with water. Lifeboats have to be kept moving to drain them, so Nigel spun her around in a hard circle underneath the helicopter in an attempt to get the water out.

Then, as the rain eased just a little, Nigel's crew worked nonstop for eight hours, rescuing stranded people from flooded buildings. After some time they were assigned to checking that no one was trapped in the cars that had floated out to sea, which presented them with a problem if they found someone in a car. Their dilemma was that the cars were floating only because their cabins were sealed. If anyone was trapped in a car, they'd need to break a window. But breaking a window would break the seal and immediately reduce the air pressure inside the car. Water would push in past the door seals and the car would plunge into the depths.

Nigel's crew spent hours checking the cars. Fortunately all were empty. Having arrived at two o'clock in the afternoon, they were still working at 10 p.m. Eventually their lifeboat broke down. Silt and detritus in the water had blocked the propeller and she had to be towed back to Port Isaac.

It had been a surreal day, but they were called out again the next morning. This time, their task was to sink the vehicles that were still floating. Nearly forty cars had drifted out to sea. Flipped over, upside down, their tyres in the air, they could only be sunk by smashing their windows. It took Nigel's crew all day but they got it done.

Nigel has a reputation as one of the more fearless helmsmen that Port Isaac has seen, as Johnny Mac discovered on the shouts he's been out with Nigel. On one shout on a Saturday evening, Mac arrived at the lifeboat house to be told they had a report that a body had been spotted in the water. With Nigel at the helm, they were just passing Trevose Head, almost out of our area, when Mac spotted the body in the distance, wearing an orange jacket. As they approached it, Mac leaned out over the edge of the boat, thinking this would be the first body he would have to pull out of the water. Feeling very apprehensive as they pulled alongside, Mac leaned right out and gave it a tug. With a startled yell, he discovered the 'body' was nothing more than a huge plastic bag. A proper relief.

Interrupted occasionally by lifeboat shouts, we Fisherman's Friends meanwhile kept going, rehearsing, singing on the Platt, playing occasional gigs and, of course, fishing and working. Bimbling along from year to year.

Over the years we recorded two self-produced mail-order-only albums. *Suck 'em and Sea*, our first album, was recorded in St Peter's Church at the top of Port Isaac after audiences on the Platt repeatedly asked us for a recording. Built in the nineteenth century, the church suited our sound perfectly, although the faint squawking of seagulls in the background was a bit of a distraction. We recorded the second album, *Another Mouthful From* . . . , in a home-made studio in a garage behind Julian's house. We also recorded a third CD called *Home from the Sea*, providing our services for free on the understanding that all profits would go to the RNLI. As current and former members of lifeboat crews, launching authorities and lifeboat committees, we were eager to provide any possible support. Consequently it was a considerable disappointment to discover that our contracted efforts resulted only in a relatively small proportion of the profits benefiting the RNLI. In fact, we've no idea how many copies of any of these three CDs we actually sold. On one occasion we took a box of CDs to a gig in Clovelly, but forgot to sell them afterwards and then forgot to bring them home. When we went back to collect them a week later, all but one of the CDs were still in the box. That's how good we were at marketing.

Some of us branched out into other projects. Cleavey and Billy formed a duo called Roscarrock to sing and play folk songs set in and around Port Isaac that they'd written together. They recorded a CD called *First and Last*, with Trevor singing one of the songs. Johnny Mac formed a blues and rock'n'roll covers band with some mates. They rehearsed every Monday evening and played a few gigs in the village every year, covering songs from Buddy Holly and Elvis Presley to David Bowie and Thin Lizzy.

However, by 2007 or 2008, several of us were starting to ask ourselves where and what next for the Fisherman's Friends? Some of us wanted to start singing shanties and folk tunes that we'd composed ourselves; others thought this went against Fisherman's Friends' original ethos of singing traditional songs with plenty of rollocking good cheer.

At the Golden Lion, a change of landlord had a profound effect. In the early days, Neville had really helped us and pushed us on. He used to turn down the jukebox when we wanted to have a sing-song, but his successor was less encouraging. Over the years, we'd always turned up for a practice at Billy's pottery, but on many occasions we never actually got around to singing. We'd be having too much of a laugh and joke at Billy's to buckle down for a rehearsal. Then we'd move on to the pub, where the larking would continue. It would only be at the end of the night, when a few pints had been sunk, that we'd get around to singing at all. At times like that, the pub was sometimes the only place we sang all week, so when a new landlord became less supportive of our sing-songs, we lost some of our impetus to keep things going.

Towards the end of 2008, Julian Brown announced he'd had enough. For various reasons, he said he needed a change.

'I can't do this any more,' he said. 'I've got too much on my plate. I'm going to finish.'

Although devastated, we respected Julian's decision. 'Don't finish,' we said. 'Just take six months off.'

'No,' said Julian. 'I've had enough. This is it for me.'

The following summer on the Platt was the first in the Fisherman's Friends' history that we sang with only two Browns in the line-up. We understood Julian's decision, but by the end of 2009, we were starting to miss the cantankerous bugger (only joking, Julian), so someone put out a few feelers.

'We've got a few things on this winter,' we said. 'Do you want to come?'

And Julian replied in typically succinct style: 'Yeah, I'll come. I've got nothing else on.'

Within a few weeks of Julian's return, it seemed like he'd never been away. He said he hadn't missed us at all, but somehow we all knew, Julian included, that it hadn't been quite the same without him. It was good for him to have had that time away, but it was even better for us to get him back.

But even with Julian back in the fold there was still a lingering feeling that we needed something to happen, that we needed to move on and progress somehow. As 2009 approached 2010, many of us were wondering if the Fisherman's Friends in its current form had maybe run its natural course. It was hard to face up to it, but maybe something that had been the centre of our lives was starting to fall apart. To stop it falling apart, maybe we needed to change fundamentally. None of us had the answer, so we kept going. Winter nights in North Cornwall are long, cold and dark, and the village battens down its hatches in the face of harsh weather. There's not much to do but work. And compared with working, the prospect of going down to Billy's, having a practice and a few pints, was something to which we all looked forward. We had to keep it going.

In early 2009, when Billy had returned from his skiing holiday, we steamrollered ourselves into recording a third mail-order-only album. It followed the same formula as our two previous albums, only this time we weren't ready for it. We hadn't practised enough and we weren't in the right frame of mind. Again, we recorded it in the studio in the garage behind Julian's house, but it didn't go well. A couple of us had colds. Some of us sniped at each other. We knew we weren't doing a good job or doing ourselves justice. When it was finished, none of us were happy with it.

For the next few months, we sat on the album, wondering whether we wanted to start selling it after gigs and appearances on the Platt or whether we should just forget we had ever made it. And then, just when we were at our lowest point in twenty years of singing together and in ten shared lifetimes of living in each other's pockets, the phone rang at Cleavey's house one Sunday morning.

It was half-past eight and Cleavey had just sat down with the *Sunday Times* and a cup of tea.

'Hello,' said an unfamiliar voice. 'My name's Simon King. I manage a record producer called Rupert Christie.'

Simon explained that Rupert had seen us performing on the Platt that summer and had been very impressed.

'He filmed you on his cameraphone and sent the video immediately to me,' said Simon. 'When I saw it, I was blown away.'

Having worked with U2, Echo & the Bunnymen, Coldplay and Lou Reed, Rupert now wanted to make a record with us.

To be honest, Cleavey didn't quite believe it – none of us would have – but that didn't stop him turning up the next Friday at our weekly practice, his moustache twitching and eyes sparkling, like they always do when he's trying to suppress a smile.

'Lads,' he said, 'you aren't going to believe this. Some record producer guy from up London wants to record us. He said he's going to get us a record deal . . .'

Stargazy Pie

One of British cuisine's more unusual offerings, Stargazy Pie makes a feature of fish heads poking through pastry so they appear to be gazing at the stars. Not for the faint-hearted, the pie is traditionally eaten during the festival of Tom Bawcock's Eve, held every year on 23 December in Mousehole.

According to legend, Mousehole was facing starvation one sixteenth-century Christmas after a particularly stormy December prevented local fishermen from taking to sea. On the night before Christmas Eve, Bawcock, one of the fishermen, ignored all advice, went to sea in a storm and returned with enough fish to make a pie that fed the entire village.

The pie in the legend contained seven fish (including sand eel, horse mackerel and dogfish), but the modern pie usually contains pilchards as the primary ingredient. Herrings and mackerel are frequently used as substitutes for pilchard and many other variations on the recipe exist, including one with rabbit and venison.

Stargazy Pie

6 to 8 Cornish pilchards, gutted, cleaned and boned, but with heads
    and tails intact
2 soft-boiled free-range eggs, finely diced
1 beaten free-range egg
3 rashers bacon, finely diced
Juice of 1 lemon
1 medium-sized onion, finely chopped
Sea salt and pepper
1 tablespoon finely chopped parsley
1 tablespoon finely chopped tarragon
4 tablespoons double cream
500g shortcrust or flaky pastry

Line an eight-inch shallow pie dish with half the pastry. Mix together
all the ingredients except the pilchards and spoon into the dish.
Cover with a pastry lid, trim and crimp the edges. Cut slits into the
pastry lid. Gently push whole pilchards into the slots, leaving just the
heads or tails showing. Seal the slits and coat the pie with a beaten
egg. Bake at 200°C (gas mark 6) for 30 minutes or until the crust is
golden brown.

CHAPTER ELEVEN

SUCCESS

After Trevor sings 'Shenandoah', we run through a few more numbers. Between Lefty singing 'Yellow Girls' and Billy singing 'When the Boat Comes In', Cleavey can't resist the temptation to take the mickey out of the shortest members of the line-up.

'We're all very excited about the Fisherman's Friends movie,' he says. 'We are all going to be movie stars as well as rock stars. It's absolutely fantastic. And we are all going to star in a film . . . well, I say all, but sadly not Bill and Lefty, who are currently contracted to *Snow White*. And the nasty precious bitch won't let them go. Anyway, we are going to be OK because our management team have brought in Janette Crankie and Toulouse-Lautrec to replace them.'

Then Pete leads 'The Corncrake', a lovely shanty written by Nobby Dye and his daughter, Erin. Nobby's a charming Bristol fella who sings in a shanty group called the Harry Browns. Pete heard them giving 'The Corncrake' some at a dinner aboard the SS *Great Britain* (we assume he was invited). He got Liz, his wife, to pop it into her handbag, along with some sachets of sugar and foil-wrapped butter pats, and he free-traded it home for us to sing. We're very grateful to Nobby for letting us pinch his ditty, particularly as it's one of the most melodic tunes we sing all night, so

much so that Cleavey remarks at the end that it 'was almost musical. We'd better be careful we don't hurt ourselves.'

Depending on the time and the weather (and the hankering of our
thirst for a fresh pint), we'll slip in another couple of shanties. Johnny
Mac will lead 'The Union of Different Kinds' and the Brown brothers
lead 'Cousin Jack', after which we usually take a little break. If we were
a proper act on a proper stage, this is the point at which we'd walk off
and wait for the audience to demand we return for an encore. But we
stay on stage, just in case the audience doesn't want to call us back on.
After a brief pause, Cleavey introduces the first of our encores.

'A few years ago,' he says, 'we were highly excited because we were
invited to the Brest Festival. Imagine our excitement as men of a
certain age.

'We turned up there only to be so disappointed to discover that it
was in fact just a port in France. Earlier this year we were invited to
the Cockermouth sea shanty festival and clearly we weren't going to
be had twice, so we didn't go there either.

'Anyway, while I was over in France, I did pick up this dirty little
song.'

Jon then leads 'Capitan [sic] de St Malo', a supposedly French
shanty, but something that sounds quite different when sung with our
Cornish vowels. After that it's 'Sloop John B.', a traditional West Indies
folk song that most people know best in a slightly different
arrangement made famous by the Beach Boys, although we stick to the
original lyrics.

> *Come on the sloop John B.,*
> *My grandfather and me,*
> *Round Nassau town we did roam;*
> *Drinking all night, we got in a fight,*
> *We feel so break-up, we want to go home.*
>
> *So h'ist up the John B. sails,*
> *See how the mainsail set,*

Send for the captain – shore, let us go home,
Let me go home, let me go home,
I feel so break-up, I want to go home.

We finish on one of our standards, 'South Australia'. Arguably, no song has more resonance with the people of Cornwall than this old capstan-and-pump shanty from the great emigrations. Jeremy solos it and we give it plenty of roaring and stomping and hollering to build a fierce, driving rhythm to finish off our live shows with a bang. And we didn't even have to pinch it because we think it's ours anyway.

'South Australia' finishes the set in a suitably rollocking style and at last it's time to quench thirsts. But first we have to break down all the equipment (a roadie would be a fine thing). After that we chat to the crowd. And in the last year, since we signed a recording contract, a lot of people want to talk to us.

For the next half-hour or so, we sign CDs and chat. For us, it's a lovely part of the evening. In Cornwall, there's a spirit of togetherness, a sense of 'he's one of us', and so lots of people come forward for a yarn and we always enjoy meeting the crowd. It's a real kick, a chance to meet our audience, and occasionally we'll get a tap on the shoulder from someone we haven't seen maybe since we were tackers. It's happened to all of us in the last year and it's been a real pleasure and privilege to make contact again.

Eventually we get to the bar, and then we spend our time doing what we like doing most: standing around on the Platt, yarning, slipping into the Golden Lion or the Mote or the Slipway for a top-up, and simply enjoying the evening. Often this is the best part of the day. Sometimes the Padstow boys come over on a bus with their accordions and drums, so we start an Irish session, playing jigs and reels. Ten years ago it would have been unthinkable for Padstow and Port Isaac fellas to get together like this. But since Billy's daughter got involved with a Padstow lad, a lot of the old Yarnigoat and Town Crow rivalries have slipped away, and we're now the best of friends.

Depending on how the evening goes, gradually we start to drift off home, or in some cases, stagger in the general direction of our houses. Sometimes we'll be fairly sober; on a good night, a couple of us might be completely legless. It all depends on how we feel. If it's a lovely evening, the sun's been out and it's warm, and we've been in good voice, then it tends towards the latter. After all, it is only once a week.

At the time that Rupert first got in touch to say he wanted to record an album with us, we already had an offer from a small independent record company called Proper Records. Out of the blue, Proper Records made us an offer to record an album for them. Then Rupert called. After years of never attracting (or seeking) any interest from record companies, suddenly we had two parties vying for our services. We felt almost like the hot new thing.

Proper Records specialised in re-releasing classic old recordings and recording new releases of artists at a more mature stage of their careers. We spent a long evening in the pub discussing Proper Records' offer (well, that's what we told our wives we were doing). We were flattered and decided to tell them we were interested, but within days of Billy giving Proper Records a call, Rupert called. We couldn't quite believe that we'd attracted the attention of someone of his calibre and experience, so we invited him down to Port Isaac to see if he lived up to his reputation.

As soon as we met Rupert, we could tell he understood us. A lovely, easy-going man, he brought his manager Simon with him. They'd made a long journey to meet us in our home environment. We were impressed.

That afternoon, just after lunch, we sang to Rupert and Simon outside the Slipway, just us in our fishing gear and work overalls in front of them, listening to us intently. Then we buggered off back to work and they returned to London, trailing promises of imminent recording contracts and the trappings of showbiz life. We took it with a pinch of salt, but at least there was no harm in dreaming.

A few days later, Rupert called to say he thought he could get us a deal with Decca. It sounded impressive. But as self-employed Cornishmen, we'd heard a few tall stories in our time. So we told Rupert it sounded interesting and decided to wait to see exactly what came of it.

A few weeks later, we were in the height of the holiday season. The village was busy with tourists and we were singing to large crowds every Friday evening on the Platt. One Saturday evening, Jeremy heard through the grapevine that Johnnie Walker, the Radio 2 DJ, was touring locally in his campervan and had stopped for a few days in a friend's guesthouse. A long-time Johnnie Walker fan, Jeremy called his mate Nigel Andrews on Sunday morning.

'I hear you've got Johnnie Walker staying,' said Jeremy. 'Can I come up and have a chat with him?'

'Yeah,' said Nigel. 'When'll you be up, boy?'

'Dreckly.'

Jeremy immediately hit it off with Johnnie Walker, then they got talking about singing.

'Oh, this guy here can sing,' said Nigel.

'Do you sing?' said Johnnie.

'Erm,' said Jeremy. 'Just a little bit of mucking about, every now and then.'

'You weren't part of that bunch singing down by the pub on Friday night?'

'Oh . . . yes, that was me.'

'That was very good.'

So Jeremy told Johnnie all about Proper Records and Rupert Christie. 'I'll go and get you an album,' said Jeremy, and he nipped down to Bill's place, got a copy of *Another Mouthful From . . .* and gave it to Johnnie.

'What you need is a manager,' said Johnnie. 'You've got a good sound. It's marketable.'

'Get away. We don't need a manager.'

'You do. They'll eat you alive otherwise.'

On our behalf Johnnie called his manager, Ian Brown, to suggest he got in touch with us. 'You've got to listen to them,' he told Ian. A few days later, when Johnnie had moved on in his camper, he called us to see if Ian had been in touch. Ian had not. 'Leave this to me,' said Johnnie.

Johnnie called Ian, who was in Hyde Park, listening to a band. 'Have you heard the lads in Port Isaac that I told you about yet?'

'No,' said Ian.

'Look, you need to get your arse down there and see these guys and get them signed up.'

A few evenings later, on a Friday, Ian appeared on the Platt just as we were getting ready to sing. A big, round, jovial guy and very nice, Ian introduced himself. 'I like the look of you,' he said. 'I can get you a record deal.'

'Don't you want to hear us sing?' we said.

We were due on the Platt, so Ian hung around at the back of the crowd. We saw him listen to one, maybe two, songs before he slipped away. At the end of the Platt performance, Ian reappeared, waiting near the Slipway.

'Come in here,' said Ian, beckoning us towards the bar. He bought us each a drink – always a good start – chatted briefly, then cleared his throat.

'I'm just a pig farmer,' he said.

We could see Ian liked to come over as some sort of rural person, but we could also tell he was very switched on. He was the kind of guy who was so full of energy he needed to put his brain on ice just to keep it from exploding.

Ian told us his story. Originally he was a pig farmer who, through singing in his local pub in an amateur band, met a singer called Gordon Haskell who he thought had talent. He offered to manage the singer. Six months later that singer had a number one record and Ian had diversified into a new career as a record company manager with several other acts on his books including The Priests, who have sold nearly three million albums worldwide.

'Now I'd like to manage you boys,' said Ian. 'I know some record companies. We'll record a CD and I'll get you a million-pound deal ...'

To be honest, we took it all with a very large pinch of salt, but Ian continued.

'... then we'll take you out on tour,' he said. 'The best venues and then the festivals ... Glastonbury ... Cambridge Folk Festival ...'

Oh right, we thought. *Us? At Glastonbury?* By this point, we were getting very sceptical. But with nothing to lose, we nodded in agreement. After all, we'd heard a lot of bluster and promises already from Proper Records and Rupert Christie, so we told Ian that we'd had interest from them too.

'Don't do it!' said Ian. 'I'll get you a better deal.'

Startling as it was, this was Ian's manner. In time we'd realise he was like this all the time. Full on and straight down the line.

'Proper Records?' he said. 'Tell them to bugger off. Rupert? Tell him you'll get back to him later.'

A few months earlier we'd been a bunch of mates wondering if our singing still had a future, wondering where we could take it next. Now, out of the blue, we had three parties fighting for us. Surreal didn't begin to describe it.

'We told Proper Records we might be interested ...' said Billy.

'Tell them both to sod off. I'll get you a much better deal.'

'Really?'

'Yes. But I've got to go now.' Ian had been in Port Isaac less than a couple of hours. 'I don't believe in signing anything,' he said before getting into his car. 'Let's just shake hands and I'll be in touch.'

Two weeks later, an email pinged on to Cleavey's computer. He soon passed on the news to the rest of us. 'Ian said he's coming down with three deals from record companies. Universal, Island Records and Decca.'

It didn't sound real. Exciting maybe, but still we were sceptical. After all, none of us is a spring chicken. We all run our own businesses and we all know that no one ever gets anything for free, so we needed convincing. 'Yeah, all right,' said John Brown, voicing all our thoughts. 'I'll believe it when I see it.'

The next day, Ian arrived and this time he had a solicitor with him. We met at Billy's place and the solicitor explained the merits of each of the record company offers. In the end we went with the deal that contracted us to the least time with the company and the fewest obligations to tour and promote the records. None of us had gone looking for a record deal, so none of us wanted it to change our lives. As long as we could still continue fishing, working and living in Port Isaac, just the same as before, we were happy. Anything else that came our way was a bonus, but we didn't want it to change our lives.

That night, we agreed with Ian that he would represent us as our manager and that we'd sign a contract with Universal Records. We'd be labelmates with Lady Gaga, Elton John, Justin Bieber and Take That. Ian hit us like a whirlwind, but since that day we haven't looked back.

In the autumn of 2009, after having signed the record deal, we started recording our first album for Universal. Ian enlisted Rupert Christie and we got to work. Every afternoon, when we'd washed up after fishing and work, we gathered at St Peter's Church at the top of Port Isaac. After a few days, Rupert started to despair of the seagulls that gathered on the church roof, so we decamped a few miles inland to St James the Great Church at St Kew. We swapped seagulls for icicles in the coldest winter we could remember, so Lefty came to the rescue with his space heaters between takes. Fortunately, the St Kew Inn next door saved us from hypothermia, starvation and, of course, dehydration.

Rupert introduced us to a completely new way of working. Previously, we'd recorded each song 'live' with all of us singing the entire song into a small number of microphones. And if it sounded good to us on the first take, we'd immediately move on to the next song.

Rupert was different. Never accepting second-best, he made us sing each song over and over again, often breaking it down to record each verse and chorus separately. We each sang in our own cocoon, with our own microphone and headphones, and blocked off from each other by large baffles, like padded partitions.

It was hard work, but we averaged two songs a night and after a fortnight we had fifteen songs in the can. Rupert disappeared to record musicians playing backing instrumentation at a studio in London and then to mix the tapes. Having purposely avoided any instrumentation, we were very nervous of Ian and Rupert's advice to add backing. But when we heard the first samples with music behind our voices, we liked it. We sounded like a proper band. And for a bunch of Cornish chancers, that was some achievement.

Meanwhile, we continued rehearsing every week at Billy's place. Rejuvenated by the prospect of a proper CD being released in April 2010, we were taking rehearsals seriously (without neglecting the yarning or the pub) and singing better than ever. Later in the winter, a photographer came down to the village to shoot the pictures for the CD. It was a simple enough task, but of course nothing is ever that straightforward when Billy's involved. Having asked him to come into Port Isaac harbour with Trevor and Lefty in a dinghy, the photographer positioned himself to take the picture. As we landed on the beach, Trevor suggested that Billy climb out of the boat. A simple enough task, but not for Billy, who tripped over an oar and fell flat on his face in the water. Some things never change.

The early part of 2010 passed uneventfully. If we'd known then how much our lives were about to change, we might have got all those odd jobs done that always need doing. Then, on one cold spring morning, we travelled up to London to record two more songs at the legendary Abbey Road studios.

For all of us having grown up listening to The Beatles, the prospect of stepping into the studios where the Fab Four recorded most of their albums and singles was almost beyond comprehension. None of us ever thought ten middle-aged shanty singers from a remote

Cornish village would find themselves recording within the same four walls as John, Paul, George and Ringo.

Having stayed the night in a London hotel, Johnny Mac and John Brown decided to mark the occasion by walking from Camden Lock along the Regent's Canal to St John's Wood, where the Abbey Road studios are located. Approaching the studio, they spotted a young Japanese guy bending down scribbling on a wall. Ever the vigilant community-minded citizen, John was about to make a citizen's arrest on a graffiti vandal when he realised that the kid was writing on the wall outside Abbey Road studio, already covered with thousands of signatures and messages all dedicated to The Beatles. Barely a square inch of the whitewashed entrance gateposts and front wall wasn't covered in tributes to one or more of The Beatles. And just beyond the studio entrance was the famous zebra crossing. Of course, we all had to have our pictures taken walking across it like The Beatles on the cover of their *Abbey Road* album.

Walking around inside Abbey Road, we had to keep pinching ourselves. The front reception area was very similar to the entrance hall of an expensive hotel or city bank. There were leather sofas, coffee tables and people turning up with suitcases and instrument cases. Several corridors led off the reception area. The one we were taken down was lined with framed record covers and huge black-and-white photographs of some of the world-famous musicians who had recorded in the studios. About halfway down the corridor, we were shown into the control room of Studio 2, possibly the single most famous studio in the world, the scene of most of The Beatles' recordings, as well as those by Oasis, U2 and countless other musicians.

Pinching ourselves at the mind-blowing fact that we were standing where The Beatles once stood, we got ready to record our two songs. At the arranged time, nine of us were ready and waiting in the studio. Rupert and Ian were in the control room, tapping their fingers on the mixing desk. But no Nigel. The clock ticked and ticked. Two hours later, Nigel arrived. His wife had left her handbag in Bodmin

Parkway Station, so she had to go back for it. Well, there were worse places to be kept waiting and we soon got down to singing.

One of the two tracks we recorded at Abbey Road was 'Sloop John B.'. When we'd finished, Rupert called us into the control room in which George Martin had produced The Beatles. That afternoon we all heard ourselves singing on the CD for the first time when Rupert played us singing 'No Hopers, Jokers and Rogues' through four vast Nautilus loudspeakers at Abbey Road. With smiles as wide as dinner plates, we were like a bunch of kids as we listened to the song, led by Jeremy. The Beatles had come out when most of us were about twelve years old and none of us ever thought we would find ourselves in the same studio that they used, let alone listening to a track we had just recorded in the same room as them.

'The hairs on the back of my neck are standing up,' said Johnny Mac. We all knew what he meant.

Then Johnny Mac pulled out his phone to call an old friend with whom he used to spend weekends in Blackpool at the Majestic Hotel, playing the *Abbey Road* album all through the night. Mac played his pal our recording of 'No Hopers, Jokers and Rogues' down the phone. Then he told his old mate that he was phoning him from Abbey Road studios.

'He loved it that I thought of him,' said Mac when he put down his phone. Mac later said that his mate's wife had phoned later that day to say Mac's mate had gone around all day with a smile on his face.

We rounded off our day inside Abbey Road studios by signing our record contract in the control room of Studio 2. When we'd finished, we all walked out on to the steps at the front of the studio building and paused to take it all in. It was hard to grasp what had happened to us in such a short time. Just six months earlier we'd been wondering where Fisherman's Friends was going. Now, filled with new enthusiasm, we were embarking on the biggest change in our collective history.

Billy turned to Nigel and shook his head. 'What the hell are we doing here?' he said.

'Billy,' said Nigel, 'don't question it. This kind of thing doesn't happen very often to lads like us. *We're just here.*'

A few days later we were back in Port Isaac and Ian phoned to warn us that he was about to announce that we had secured a £1 million recording contract. A few weeks after that, our CD would be released.

'You'll be a bit busy tomorrow, lads,' Ian said. BBC *Spotlight*, the local television news programme for the West Country, wanted to film an interview with us first thing in the morning. 'After that, you'll be free to go fishing and get back to work.'

On 18 March, we were down on the Platt at 6.30 a.m., ready for a *Spotlight* interview at seven o'clock and wondering who on earth was going to be watching television news at that time of the day.

The interview went well. When it finished, we got a message that another television company wanted to do an interview. As soon as that was done and dusted, we were told that another news programme wanted to film us. And so it went on all day. The BBC, ITV, Sky and countless other broadcasters, all asking the same questions and getting the same answers until we were blue in the face. At half-past six that evening – twelve hours after we'd started – we recorded the last interview of the day. Having hardly eaten all day, we should have been exhausted, but we were pumped up on adrenaline. By the time we all got home, every single one of us was completely shattered.

When Trevor walked in, his wife was waiting. 'Where've you been?' she said.

'We went down at six o'clock to do this interview,' said Trevor. 'I thought I'd be on site, building, by eight o'clock, but we've been there for hours.'

'I know. I've been watching it on the telly. It's on every station.'

That night, Trevor's son Mark received a text from Nicky Bradbury, who runs the pasty shop at the bottom of the village. Nicky was in Mauritius and she'd just seen us on the telly. In *Mauritius*. Astounding.

The next morning, our story was all over the newspapers. 'Cornish Fishermen Net £1m Record Deal,' said the *Guardian* headline. 'Cornish fishermen land £1m deal with Take That's label . . . for an album of sea shanties,' said the *Daily Mail*.

To our fellow Yarnigoats, the television reports and newspaper stories were the first they'd heard of our record deal. Sworn to secrecy by Ian, we'd had to keep it quiet until 18 March. They all thought it was fantastic news, but inevitably they also thought we were all instant millionaires.

'Oh, you're rich now,' we heard again and again.

But then we had to explain that nearly everyone gets a million-pound record deal nowadays. That million pounds is spread across several albums that we are contracted to deliver to the record company. It also has to pay for marketing, promotion, recording, videos and many other costs. When we divide what remains between the ten of us, there's barely enough to pay for a family holiday.

For the next week or so, a steady stream of camera crews, journalists and reporters found their way down to remote Port Isaac to interview and examine us. They came from all over the world, asking questions for their listeners and viewers in languages from all over Europe and in the English-speaking world from as far afield as Australia and New Zealand.

The media attention didn't let up as the day our CD was to be released approached. It seemed like we were spending half our waking hours on the train up to London to appear on a succession of programmes. We did *GMTV*, BBC *Breakfast*, *This Morning* and loads of radio stations. It was very exciting, although most of us didn't have to do much more than sit in the background while Cleavey, Jeremy and Billy, the ones with the best television and radio voices, did the talking. Elements of it were bizarre, particularly in the period when it seemed that every time we came home and switched on the television we'd find ourselves on the screen. Trevor remembers phoning suppliers in Birmingham or Manchester and giving his address for a delivery.

'Port Isaac?' the suppliers would say. 'That's where that shanty group comes from, isn't it?'

Trev didn't dare tell them that he was one of the members of 'that shanty group', not least because, ever the canny Cornishman, he didn't want them driving up their prices.

As the CD launch date approached, Ian started to draw up a list of festivals and other appearances that we were being offered. That's when the idea of playing at Glastonbury was first dangled in front of us. And as various festivals responded, confirming that they wanted to book us, the sense that Fisherman's Friends was about to take over our lives became overwhelming.

Already Fisherman's Friends was becoming bigger than anything any of us had ever dreamed of. Everyone wanted to be a part of us, it seemed. Something that we'd started for the purposes of enjoyment was beginning to rule our lives. The turning point came when we started getting buzzes that we might tour to Australia and New Zealand. For the first time, we started to feel that our commitments would be taking us away for too long from Port Isaac and none of us wanted that to happen.

We'd already put procedures in place to allow us to go to London and spend time at festivals to promote the CD. Jeremy and Julian's sons, Tom and Sam, could take their boats out. Cleavey's shop could run itself for a few days at a time, likewise Billy's pottery. Johnny Mac and Trevor had their sons building with them. Only John Brown and Lefty would lose out if they weren't window-cleaning, mackerel-fishing or servicing boats and fibreglassing milking parlours, and provided the absence wasn't too long, they were happy with it. The only time any of us couldn't go would be if our wife had booked a holiday – none of us would dare chance that. But for a couple of us, the thought of Australia and New Zealand was a step too far. Adhering to our ethos of unanimous agreement, we knocked that idea on the head.

And then, one day in mid-April, suddenly it was out there. The CD was released and we all had one in our hands. After the long wait, it felt slightly strange to see the finished product, especially when we looked at the picture of ourselves on the cover. Johnny Mac had a little moan about how the white jumper he'd worn had itched his neck (that's a Yorkshireman for you), but we all loved it. It took a while to get used to seeing it on the shelves in Tesco and other stores next to CDs by world-famous artists, but before that happened we had to travel down to Truro on the day the CD was released to do a record-signing at the HMV store.

Arriving at five o'clock in the evening, there was nobody about in the street. It was dead. Outside the HMV store, a line of pumped-up burly guys in black suits and black coats were standing behind some crowd-control barriers. Like them, we were all dressed in black reefer jackets. Jeremy approached to ask them what was going on.

'Good evening, sir,' said one of the guys outside the store. 'We're your security.'

'What?' said Jeremy. 'What do you mean, security?'

'We're down from Birmingham. We're your security. Six, as ordered.'

'You mean you're bouncers?'

'That's right, sir. And there's a woman in there in a wheelchair and she wants a signed photograph from you. We'll keep the crowds away from her.'

We fell about laughing. It seemed so unbelievable, particularly as hardly anyone was inside the HMV store.

The manager took us upstairs to a staffroom, where some food, coffee and a couple of beers were laid out. 'We'll give you a shout when you're due on,' he said.

About an hour later, the call came. The plan was to sing a couple of songs, then sign our newly released CDs. But we were concerned more about the lack of a crowd. None of us wanted to sing to an empty shop.

Tentatively we pushed open the door into the shop. Immediately in front was a line of black-clad bouncers with their backs to us. And directly behind them, filling every aisle to the back of the shop, were hundreds of people.

With such a large crowd, it seemed churlish to sing only a couple of songs, so we worked along the line, singing half a dozen shanties. Then, sitting behind a long trestle table, we signed our CD for a long line of people. The first signing we'd ever done, it went on for ages.

It felt really strange, but great. We each signed more than a hundred CDs and at the end the manager said it was the largest crowd for a signing the store had ever had. He probably says that to every act that comes to his store, but it still sounded good.

A week later, Rupert phoned. 'You're number nine,' he said.

'We're what?'

'Number nine. In the Top Ten: number nine.'

'You're not serious?'

'I am.'

'Blimey ... proper job.'

Apparently we were the first folk act to go straight into the Top Ten. Who knows if that was really true? Maybe it would have been more accurate to say we were the first a cappella shanty singers from a small North Cornish fishing village with a Top Ten debut album. A few weeks later, Ian called.

'You've sold 60,000 CDs,' he said.

'Yeah, yeah.'

By now we were used to Ian's grandiose claims – although they seemed to have a habit of coming true.

'Mark my words, boys,' said Ian. 'You're going to sell 300,000. Wait and see.'

'Oh, right.'

Although we were still sceptical – that's the fisherman in us, always scoffing at other seamen's purported catches – it was a thrill to look at the charts and find ourselves in the same company as the big boys and girls. At that time we were outselling Paul Weller and Lady Gaga. What a buzz.

As the weeks ticked on, the CD continued to sell and we realised it wasn't some kind of fluke. People really did want to listen to a bunch of middle-aged fellas singing old sea songs. In a way it was quite shocking. Maybe we needed to start taking it all a bit more seriously.

By Whitsun weekend it was time for our first Friday evening appearance on the Platt after the CD went on sale. By then, anyone entering Cornwall along the A30 was being greeted by a huge billboard at the side of the road advertising our album. So maybe it shouldn't have been such a surprise when several thousand people turned out to see us sing on the first Friday evening.

All the way up by the slopes of Fore Street and Roscarrock Hill, it was solid with people. Even as far away as Lobber Point, we could see them standing. An unbelievable crowd, most of whom we suspected hadn't even heard of us three months earlier.

With several of the songs on the album backed by instrumentation, Universal had insisted we should now have musicians with us on the Platt. Rupert rounded up some instrumentalists, some of whom had played on the album, and we had a few beers with them. Then we rehearsed twice with the band. We'd recorded the album without them – their backing had been added separately, after we'd sung the shanties – so we needed to work hard to get used to having a musical accompaniment.

The musicians were lovely lads and we thought their contributions sounded great on the album, but we weren't sure it was going to work on the Platt. Nevertheless, on the first evening of the summer season we set up their kit, including a full set of drums. Jason Nicholas, an accordion player from Padstow, was on the squeeze-box, and Jonny Bishop, who'd played on the album, was on the mandolin. Then we took a deep breath and went to face the crowd.

It was awful. Our songs just didn't work with a band on the Platt. The musicians performed brilliantly and professionally, but we were not used to singing with accompaniment, so we didn't know what to do and the instruments drowned us out. We might as well have not been there. We could tell from the response of the crowd that they thought it was wonderful, but we didn't like it. Cleavey said he felt like saying, 'You silly buggers, that was awful, we're struggling up here,' to the crowd between the songs, but he didn't and we just pressed on. With so many people watching, it was embarrassing.

After that first night, we had a week's interlude until our next performance. But next time it would be at the Meltdown Festival. Curated by Richard Thompson at the Royal Festival Hall in London, the Meltdown Festival was our most prestigious gig yet. It was a big honour to have been invited and it had to go well, but Cleavey was having sleepless nights, worrying about the instrumental backing. And a week after the Festival Hall, we were due to play our biggest gig ever at Glastonbury.

For days Cleavey fretted, then he let us know about his concern that we would again be dominated by the instruments. That's when we all told him that every single one of us had the same worries. Quietly, we were all very uneasy about the instrument thing. But none of us wanted to let Rupert down. We had a huge regard for him. He was a lovely guy, knowledgeable and supportive to us when we were recording the album.

'We could really muck this up,' said Cleavey at rehearsal a few days before the Festival Hall gig. We had one more opportunity to practise with the band before we went to Meltdown. We all agreed that our reputation was on the line.

That night Cleavey didn't sleep at all. In the morning, he went round to see Billy. 'What do you think, Billy?' he said.

'I've just been talking to Jeremy and we both decided we're not going to do it with the instruments.'

'Brilliant, because I don't think we should either.'

'Well, you'd better tell Ian then, hadn't you?' said Billy.

'Thanks a bloody bunch.'

Under the pretence of talking about something else, Cleavey rang Ian. At the end of a long conversation, he finally summoned the nerve to tell Ian our concerns.

'And the other thing is, Ian, we're all a bit . . . we've tried it with the instruments . . . we've rehearsed a bit . . . we've done a performance . . . and well, it was bloody awful.'

Ian said nothing, so Cleavey continued.

'I spoke to Steve Knightley from Show of Hands. And Steve said: "If you try something new at a big gig and you've not done it before and you're not sure about it, you'll be found out. And it could be embarrassing."'

'Right ...' said Ian.

'So we really don't want to do it with instruments.'

'Great,' said Ian. 'I'll sack all the musicians, then.' Ian was delighted. 'They're costing me a fortune.'

'Really?'

'Yeah.'

'Brilliant. How will you do it?'

'Just like I've always done it.'

It felt like we'd had a weight lifted off our shoulders. Cleavey immediately got busy, working out a list of songs and some gags and links between each one. And we got rid of all the musicians except for Jason. His squeeze-box added something, particularly when partnered with Billy on guitar. At the Festival Hall, they worked brilliantly together, so we kept the same format for Glastonbury.

We played two sets at the Meltdown Festival, one at lunchtime, the other in the evening. Richard Thompson was there and lots of other folkies, so it was quite a big thing for us.

After the lunchtime set, we thought we'd nip away for a few pints. Someone had told us that a wine bar across the footbridge from the Festival Hall was the place to go. Called Gordon's, it was in a dark, busy, low-ceilinged basement near the river. It was a lovely place, but a bit too crowded for us country mice. So, emboldened by a couple of sherries, we thought we'd get taxis and go back to a pub we'd discovered the previous day near the British Museum. It had been quiet in the afternoon and ideal for a couple of peaceful pints.

When we arrived at the pub, it was just as we'd hoped it would be; no more than four regulars propping up the bar. Sitting down, we had a few pints and started chatting away. After a while, we fancied a sing, so one of us got it going. Probably slightly pissed, but we sounded all right.

'Here,' said one of the regulars after we'd sung three or four songs, 'there's a group like you lot out just now. A gang of fishermen. You ain't them, are you?'

There was no point denying it, so we came clean. Then we sang for about an hour. The locals were chuffed to bits. And so were we. It just about summed us up. Quite happy to sing for our own pleasure and if other people got enjoyment out of it, well, that's the key really.

On the Platt, for the rest of the season the crowds remained vast. Some weeks there were so many people in the village we struggled to find a place to sing in between them. With the audience so close, it could be nerve-racking – no hiding place when we could see the whites of their eyes. Some Fridays, when the tide was out, we'd have as many people behind us on the beach as we had in front. And on one of the biggest tides of the summer, we were right up near the top end of the Platt with the audience about two feet from us at high tide, their feet getting wet in the sea.

After Glastonbury, the festivals came thick and fast: Cornbury, the Trowbridge Pump and Port Eliot. Then the big one, the Cambridge Folk Festival.

At Trowbridge, we stayed in a lovely bed and breakfast, although a thoroughly good session after the gig at the festival stopped us making full use of the beds. Likewise, we didn't take full of advantage of the breakfast the next morning, when Trevor sat in front of two pieces of toast, one bite taken, looking rough.

'What's wrong with you, Trev?'

'Ugh . . . just can't face it.'

We all felt a bit like that. It had been a late night, but thankfully our bus driver was staying with us and he'd picked us up shortly after midnight. At half-past midnight, we were still missing three stragglers, Billy, Johnny Mac and Julian. Trevor phoned Julian.

'Julian, we're going,' he said. 'Are you coming or not?'

'No, we're staying, we're having a great time.'

Half an hour later, when we were back at the B&B, Jeremy's phone rang.

'This is Julian. We can't get a taxi. Can you pick us up?'

Jeremy had to knock the bus driver up. Fast asleep and in his pyjamas, the driver wasn't happy, but he did it. As for Jeremy, he went outside to give the driver a hand with sorting out the bus and got locked out, dressed only in a T-shirt and jeans. It took him half an hour to wake Liz, his wife, to let him in. She wasn't pleased either.

In a year of highlights, Port Eliot stood out for Julian and Johnny Mac. Primarily a literary festival with a few bands playing, the setting was beautiful: the seat of the 10th Earl of St Germans on the south coast of Cornwall. As we wandered around, Johnny Mac spotted a blackboard listing the attractions. At the top was Jarvis Cocker. A few lines further down it said Fisherman's Friends. Just a little thing, but it was worth coming for that alone. Mac took a photograph of it. Later, when the Brown brothers sang 'Cousin Jack', and the song came to its climax – '*I dream of a bridge on the Tamar, It opens us up to the east, And the English they live in our houses, And the Spanish they fish in our seas*' – the reaction from the crowd was fantastic. We thought the revolution was starting.

Four days later, we were in Cambridge. Our sixth festival of the season, by then we'd sussed out what they were all about. We chilled out properly and made sure we had decent accommodation. It was only a Travelodge, but we had our own rooms for once. As Billy said, 'I love Jon Cleave to bits, but I don't want always to be stuck in a four-foot-wide bed with him.' As men of a certain age, we need beds to ourselves. Thanks to a good night's sleep, we were very relaxed, so we performed well.

Jon had been to the Cambridge Folk Festival as a punter the previous year with all his Bristol mates. When they left, his mate Roger had said to him, 'Shall I get us tickets for next year?'

Ever the wag, Cleavey replied, 'Don't bother, Rog, we'll probably be here singing anyway.'

At that time, we didn't have Ian on board, but we did have interest from Rupert and Simon, so it was quite a bold statement. Cleavey's mates didn't quite believe it, and neither did Cleavey. And yet, there we were on the Thursday night, playing on the number two stage.

The festival didn't officially open until the next day and only the second stage was hosting bands, so all the attention was on us.

Absolutely rammed, if anything it was busier than Glastonbury. All the sides of the tent were open and people stretched into the distance as far as we could see.

The gig went down a storm. Afterwards Mike Harding – folk singer, stand-up comic, photographer, traveller, filmmaker, playwright, author and presenter of Radio 2's flagship folk and roots music programme (a very busy man) – came up to us and congratulated us on our performance. Mike had always been really nice to us, right back to our gig at the Radio 2 Folk Awards. That night he was as encouraging as ever. We also met Mark Radcliffe, who came over and shook our hands ('pressing the flesh' they call it in the music biz).

'That was fantastic,' he said. 'Really enjoyed it.'

A few weeks later, they played some of our gig on the Johnnie Walker show and Johnnie had Mike Harding in the studio.

'Mike, have you been to the Cambridge Folk Festival?' said Johnnie. 'Was it good?'

'Yeah, it was great.'

'What was the highlight for you?'

'Without doubt, the Fisherman's Friends.'

What a plug. And what a nice man.

Having paid flying visits to all the other festivals, at Cambridge we made a long weekend of it. John Brown, who's obsessed with the great heroes from the golden age of exploration, dragged us all to the Scott Polar Research Institute. Then a bunch of us went for a punt. Happy days.

We played a couple more festivals. Boardmasters at Newquay, the only festival that impressed our kids, and Beautiful Days in mid-Devon. In between the festival appearances, Ian kept the momentum going. Determined not to relinquish that 300,000 sales target without a struggle, he squeezed us into a few more promotional appearances on television.

'Any exposure is good exposure,' said Ian.

And not knowing better, we agreed to almost anything. Or as

John Brown put it one day: 'He's got us by the scrotum, hasn't he? He twists it – "You go to Exmouth. Be on Radio 2. You can't buy that exposure" – and we do it.'

So it wasn't really a surprise when we found ourselves at the offices of QVC, the TV shopping channel, at one o'clock one August morning.

'What on earth are we doing here?' said Billy.

'Oh, you can't buy this kind of exposure . . .' said John Brown.

Having arrived two hours earlier, we'd been ushered into a dressing room that contained a few bottles of water and a pot plant. As far as we were aware, QVC was not a God channel, but it seemed like the people who ran it were fairly godly as they wouldn't allow us to have any booze in the room. And, they made it clear, they would tolerate no swearing. Nevertheless, being good Cornishmen, we managed to smuggle some beer into the building, which elicited a few gasps and a turned-up nose from the production assistants, but what were we to do in the middle of the night with two hours to kill before we went on air?

Of course, it didn't help that we got the giggles on live television. What a nightmare. It wasn't anything particularly funny that set us off. A presenter was demonstrating an alarm for travellers to secure their hotel rooms. It was a long triangular device that a hotel guest could put under a door. If somebody tried to break into their room, the device made a bizarre noise.

At 1 a.m., anything unusual seemed funny. When we heard the alarm, we all started to snigger.

'Thirty seconds,' said a floor manager. 'You're on air in thirty seconds.'

About to go live on national television, none of us dared to look at anyone else. John Brown had to sing 'Haul Away Joe', so he was looking down to the left, away from any of us just to avoid catching anyone's eye. He managed to hold it together without giggling, but it was a close-run thing. At the end of the song, the presenter introduced our album and said it was on sale through QVC's phone lines.

Even more bizarrely, Pete, Cleavey and Billy then had to take part in a game in which they had to fish out plastic ducks from a plastic pond on behalf of viewers who gave them instructions by phone. As they got ready for the game to start, Billy noticed he could see clearly which ducks were tagged with cash prizes, so he corralled all those ducks into his corner of the pond.

The first duck won the first caller a £20 prize. The next won £50. The third won £30.

'Good God, where are you getting all these ducks from?' said the presenter. 'We've never had such a run of prizes.'

Cleavey hadn't sussed out the ducks, so none of his won any money, which was probably a good thing as it quelled the presenter's suspicions.

After an hour on air, we went back to our hotel, where we all shared the narrowest double beds we'd ever seen. Then, having had four hours' sleep and no breakfast, we bundled back into taxis to return to QVC for the 6 a.m. to 7 a.m. shift. Another couple of songs and another game of ducks, then we were free to go. We sold out of QVC's stock of 3,500 albums in those two appearances, so it had been worthwhile. If we'd had more, we could have sold them as well. Afterwards, a couple of us had a little moan to the management about the palaver of appearing on a shopping channel in the middle of the night. It seemed a bit much.

'It'll push you up the charts again,' said Ian.

'Hmm . . .'

'I'll push you to do everything I can possibly get you to do. All you have to do is say "no" when it's too much.'

That seemed fair enough, especially when we appeared on *GMTV* a few days later and they told us we'd just been awarded a gold disc for the sales of our album. More than 100,000 copies sold. We had to pinch ourselves to believe it was true. To us, gold discs were the stuff of proper rock stars. Suddenly all Ian's efforts seemed very worthwhile.

For most of us, winning a gold disc meant more than anything

we'd done since signing a recording contract. An iconic achievement, it was worth more than any amount of money.

A few days after we each received a framed copy of the gold disc,
Trevor was in the Co-op at the top of the village. Standing at the till,
he was tapped on the shoulder by an old lady who lived at the end of
his road.

'What's that hanging on your wall?' said the lady. 'My son came up
the road and said there's something shiny hanging on your wall.'

'That's my gold disc,' said Trevor, very proudly.

'What?'

'It means 100,000 albums sold.'

'No? Really?'

'Yes, but my sons say they're going to put it on eBay the day I
croak.'

The moment Trevor got home, he moved the gold from where it
was hanging on the wall. Now it's somewhere much safer. No point
in taking chances, he thought.

A few days later, he was down at Peter's place, hacking out his fire-
place, installing a new woodburner and building a new hearth. As
soon as Trevor had finished, Pete walked in, complimented him on a
good job, then immediately hung his gold record on the chimney
breast. There was nothing else in the room, no furniture and no curtains, but Pete made sure the gold disc was in place. And that's how
proud we all feel about it.

At the end of the festival season, we were given some dates for a
West Country concert mini-series that the management wanted us
to do in the autumn. Nothing particularly demanding – St Ives,
Tavistock and Ilfracombe spaced over a fortnight – they were going
to be our first ever proper gigs. After twenty years of appearing
for charities, or promoting ourselves unpaid at festivals, this would
be the first time we sold tickets and earned a fee.

'I don't know if I can do that,' said Nigel. 'I'll be really busy in the
tea shop then.'

It was hard to believe that three dates in October would affect a tea shop out of season in a Cornish fishing village, but ever since we had signed the recording contract, Nigel had struggled to make a lot of our commitments. Although he'd made all the big festival gigs like Glastonbury and Cambridge, he'd missed some of the smaller ones. He'd also missed a lot of rehearsals and nine Fridays on the Platt. That was unprecedented.

'Look, Nigel,' said John and Jeremy Brown, 'you can't afford to miss any more.'

Some of us wondered if we ought to suggest to Nigel that he took a twelve-month sabbatical from Fisherman's Friends, like Julian had done a year earlier. A few days later, Nigel pre-empted our decision when a letter arrived from him. In it, he explained that he had decided to resign immediately from the Fisherman's Friends.

It wasn't really a surprise. Out of all of us, Nigel had been most reluctant to sign a record contract. 'What do you want me to do?' he'd asked Cleavey at the time it came to put his name on the dotted line.

'Nigel, I don't want you to do anything,' said Cleavey. 'But if you're going to be part and parcel of this, you have to have signed, for obvious reasons.'

Nigel complied, but for various reasons he couldn't commit to rehearsing and performing as frequently as the rest of us. In the end, it wasn't about the money (because there wasn't much). And it would be precious to say it was about artistic differences, but when Nigel *could* make it, he was under-rehearsed and not used to being on stage. Cleavey was particularly frustrated and disappointed because, like him, Nigel had a very forceful voice. They usually stood together in the line-up because Nigel gave Cleavey something to work off. They sang as nicely together as anyone can sing in shanties, so Cleavey was keen for Nigel to stay.

All of us were saddened by Nigel's announcement that he was leaving. When we played football in the village, it was always Hartland Road against Mayfield Road and he'd been part of that. An old friend who'd played a big role in all our childhoods, forty years later he still added something to our lives. Great fun when we went away, he was always good company and he liked a few beers. So when he left, we all were sad. Not least because after being involved in everything else we'd done through our lives, Nigel was going to miss out on what was coming up.

However, Nigel's departure had a wonderful consequence. It meant we had space for Jason to join us permanently as a proper tenth member of Fisherman's Friends. As well as playing the squeeze-box, Jason had a lovely voice. All he needed was to learn and rehearse the songs. Easy-going, quietly spoken and with a perfect temperament, he slotted straight in and within six months it felt like he'd always been with us. And as a Padstow lad, Jason helped to bridge the divide between the Yarnigoats and the Town Crows.

If any of us had been told five years ago that we were going to have an accordion player in the group, we would have told that person where to go. And if we'd also been told that the accordion player was from Padstow, none of us would have believed it. But everything has to move forward. Otherwise things go stale. And so Jason joined the Fisherman's Friends.

At the end of September we embarked on the mini-tour of the southwest that had prompted Nigel to leave us. Having never asked anyone to pay to see us, we were very nervous that we'd turn up to empty halls. The thought that people were deciding weeks in advance that they'd come to a Fisherman's Friends gig, instead of just wandering down to the Platt on a Friday evening, was quite daunting. But we needn't have worried. When we turned up at St Ives, Tavistock and Ilfracombe, we discovered we could have sold the tickets many times over. The gigs went so well, they passed in a flash.

Even now, quite a few of us struggle to understand why we're popular. After each of the mini-tour shows, we congregated in the foyer of the theatre, not just because of the bar, but because we wanted to meet our audiences. We were hoping to find out from them the gist of why they came to see us. It was all a very steep learning curve for us. Everyone enjoyed it, they said. They liked it all: the singing, the banter, the way we stood in a line, even the way we looked at each other. A lot of it was down to Cleavey, who had worked very hard developing his links and jokes between each song. Nothing was rehearsed; it had developed organically, but we now knew how to put on a performance that came somewhere near to looking like it was somehow professional and well thought out. Our act had become slightly more polished.

After the mini-tour, in early October we were back in Port Isaac to film our contribution to *Rick Stein's Cornish Christmas*. We spent two days in the harbour and on Jeremy's boat, filming with Rick in breaks between lashing rain. A few weeks later, we travelled with the FFWAGs to Little Petherick (between Wadebridge and Padstow) to take part in a Christmas lunch cooked by Rick Stein in the village hall. Overheated in our thick winter coats, it was slightly surreal to be singing Christmas carols in the hall in October, but it was more than worth it for the bloody marvellous lunch that Rick cooked for us, our very chuffed wives, and several other guests.

We'd all met Rick once before about ten years earlier, when we'd performed on the Gloria Hunniford show, one of our first television appearances. We'd been invited on to the show after Gloria and her late daughter, Caron Keating, saw us sing on the Platt during a holiday in Cornwall. We sang 'The Shantyman' and John Brown ended our appearance with his arm around Gloria, a big smile creasing his face.

In early December, we were on the move again. As the worst winter in living memory threatened to engulf the country in snow, we left the village to play our first headlining gig in London. Although no snow fell on Port Isaac (to the dismay of John Brown, who had four new sledges lying unused in his garage – 'Sixty quid they cost me,' he muttered), we travelled up to the capital pursued by a bank of black cloud depositing snow behind us. We arrived safely, but woke the next day to a blanket of at least eight inches of snow. London looked beautiful, like something out of a Victorian novel.

With most of the day off, we dispersed to sightsee, eat and shop before convening that evening at the Union Chapel in Islington. An iconic venue, the Union Chapel was a great place to sing. The acoustics were fantastic and we could see why Radio 3 and Radio 4 used it so frequently. With a deep, resonant sound that bounced back at us from the ceiling and filled the room, we felt like we didn't need microphones. In spite of the weather, the hall was packed and it became the best gig we'd done to date, a very special evening with our families watching us close to Christmas. Although we were in the middle of London, a long way from our usual audience, it felt no different, but we were still baffled by the idea that several hundred people of all ages had paid around £20 a head to come and listen only to us.

On a high after playing the Union Chapel, we left London the next morning for Milton Keynes. With a foot or more of snow on the ground and the threat of cancellation hanging over our next gig, we arrived in Milton Keynes to find the main street empty of cars except for a few taxis. None of them wanted to take us up to The Stables, a 400-seat theatre belonging to Cleo Laine. After calling around all the local companies, we found a 50-year-old Rastafarian driver with a minibus and the nerve to carry us, with our instruments and kit jammed on our laps, up a long sloping ice-packed track to The Stables, accompanied by the strains of 'Have A Reggae Christmas' blasting out of his minibus stereo while our Rasta driver grinned and told jokes.

Arriving to find a bulldozer trying to clear snow and ice from the car park in front of The Stables, we were convinced our sold-out gig would be cancelled. So we had a few beers more than usual and a Sunday roast in a pub. But at half-past four the news came: the gig was going ahead. A few hours later, The Stables was three-quarters full. How most of the audience got there we still do not know, but after that kind of perseverance, they were really up for it and, although the sound wasn't as good as the Union Chapel, we went down a storm.

After the gig, we phoned our Rastafarian minibus driver, who had promised to come to our rescue if no one would collect us. With heavy reggae booming in the background, it sounded like he was at a party, but he agreed to come. Fifteen minutes later our taxi

Rasta appeared, his clothes carrying the faint smell of something not quite legal that we suspected had been in the air at the party. Grateful for his commitment and charmed by his good humour, we stood in a circle in the snow around his taxi after he dropped us off at our hotel and sang him 'While Shepherds Watched Their Flocks'. Then we gave him a tip that was larger than the fare. Without him we would have been stuffed.

We returned home the next day and one or two of us went down to the pub on Christmas Eve lunchtime for a chat, a few pints and some singing. As the New Year beckoned, our thoughts turned to the future. So far, everything had surpassed our expectations and we'd thoroughly enjoyed it. We had no regrets about having committed ourselves to a recording contract, but we also knew that we didn't want it to take over our lives. Long before fame and fortune came blowing into Port Isaac and knocking at our doors, we'd all reached a point in our lives where we were very content with our achievements. We'd worked hard to end up doing exactly what we wanted.

Most of us had come to look on the recording contract as a means to an end, a chance to see a bit more of the world, to become known as the group that helped make shanty singing popular again, and to take part in events to which we would otherwise not have been invited. And if it all ended in six months' time, Cleavey would still be a shopkeeper who wrote a few books and Bill would still be a potter. Port Isaac would still be there, the same as ever. Jeremy and Julian would still be lobster fishermen, and the rest of us would continue as we always have, living side by side, sharing our lives and feeling blessed to be doing it all together on the North Cornish coast in wonderful, fantastic, unique Port Isaac.

It's a Shore Thing

(Or, Weather Forecasting, the Fisherman's Friends Way)

When it comes to predicting the weather, we fishermen have learned through bitter experience to rely more on local knowledge and sayings handed down from our granfers than on the Meteorological Office's forecasts.

> *Fast rise after low,*
> *Foretells stronger blow.*

When the barometer mercury rises fast after being low, you can bet your next catch on a gale soon flying out to the northwest. On our shore, there's no shelter from a nor'westerly, so this is advice that must always be heeded. Every Port Isaac fisherman can check the 'glass', as the barometer is known locally, by opening a small green door on the wall directly to the right of the entrance to Port Isaac fish cellars.

> *Long foretell long last,*
> *Short notice soon past.*

274

If the weather is breaking, a sudden change ('short notice') will not remain for long ('soon past'). But if the transition is slow ('long foretell'), the change of weather will stay for a long time ('long last').

> *Wind before the rain, reef your sails'n'oist 'em again,*
> *Wind after the rain, reef your sails'n leave 'em remain.*

Sudden appearances of wind before rain rarely last long, but wind that appears after rain will persist.

CHAPTER TWELVE

BRINGING IT ALL BACK HOME

The New Year started quietly. It's always best to ease gently into anything new, so we spent the first weeks recovering from the Christmas festivities and preparing for our first foreign tour. When we say foreign, we mean Scotland.

Our largest tour to date – four dates over a five-day period – started with a gig at Queen's College, a public school in Taunton. Picked up from the railway station by school bus, we wondered how and why we had wound up at this very prestigious school. Or as Billy put it: 'What's going on here? We're just a bunch of roughnecks from Cornwall.'

As soon as we arrived, we discovered the answer. Several people at the school were massive fans of the Fisherman's Friends. Only six weeks earlier they had put on a show based loosely around our music. Their show had sold out every night, so when we walked in we were treated with huge reverence.

Ironically, Billy had a couple of childhood mates who had been there and he'd always taken the mickey out of them about going to a posh school. And now we were playing there. When Billy's mates heard about it, they didn't let him off lightly.

Queen's College was a lovely school, the type you'd want everyone to be able to attend. No discipline problems; a row of music rooms, each with a piano at which pupils could practise; classes full of motivated kids. You'd have to be a fool not to thrive there.

The gig went very well. Afterwards we stayed in a boarding house belonging to the school and had a little singing session in one of the school common rooms, during which we discovered Lefty can play the mouth organ. He'd kept that quiet all the years we'd known him. It just goes to show, there's always something new to learn about your mates.

After Taunton, we stopped off the next night at the Town Hall in Birmingham, a beautiful old building with intricate mouldings on the ceiling, a fantastic atmosphere and stunning acoustics. Having been told that Midlanders were frequently indifferent, dour audiences, we were apprehensive when we arrived, but they were marvellous. Enthusiastic, demonstrative and really up for a good night, they were the best crowd we'd ever had, encouraging us to sing our best gig ever. At the end we were rewarded with a standing ovation. It was a very special evening. After the show, we stood in the foyer for more than an hour, signing CDs. The Brummies told us they'd loved every moment of the gig, and we'd loved them.

Our third night away from home took us to the Celtic Connections festival in Glasgow, a celebration of Celtic culture that goes on for more than a week. Booked to appear as support for Seth Lakeman, it's not boasting to say that we took it by storm. Seth was clearly the established star, but the reviews in the papers the next day gave us newcomers nearly all the praise. Later that night, we performed an after-gig set for BBC Radio 3 on a stage that stayed open for performers until the early hours. We saw some brilliant acts there, including the Red Hot Chilli Pipers, three guys on bagpipes backed by a band on electric guitars and drums, and didn't get to bed until 4 a.m. was long behind us.

The next day was our one and only rest day of the tour, so we spent it on an open-topped bus tour of the city, down to the docks and around all the sights. Billy went to see some bands and the rest of us went to the pub, where Cleavey drank so much he lost his voice and struggled to sing at our next stop, Liverpool. In spite of missing the full force of Cleavey's bass, the Liverpool gig went well, but for Trevor it was a nerve-racking affair. His wife is from Liverpool, so he had five relatives in the audience, which added to the pressure. Fortunately it all went well.

Although we enjoyed every minute of our mini-tour, it taught us that we couldn't do a tour that took us away from Port Isaac for much longer than five or six days at a time. With all the travelling, hanging around, sleeping in strange beds and eating at odd times (not to mention the socialising), we were all absolutely knackered by the end of it. And none of us are spring chickens, so we need our beauty sleep. Unfortunately there would be little of that over the next few days.

We arrived back in the village on a Saturday. Sunday was a day off and on the Monday we had to be at the Metropole Hotel in Padstow by 5.30 a.m. to film an advertisement for Young's Seafood. And they say show business is glamorous.

Peter Cattaneo, who was nominated for an Oscar for directing *The Full Monty*, met us and, with the assistance of several storyboard sketches, described the advertisement he had in mind. While singing rewritten lyrics of 'When the Boat Comes In', we would be filmed coming in from a hard day's fishing and swapping our fresh catch for Young's breaded cod.

It sounded a doddle. In practice, shooting the advertisement was the hardest four days' work any of us had ever done for the Fisherman's Friends. We'd had longer and harder days at sea, but then we were our own bosses. For the advert, we had to adhere to the demands of the film crew and they wanted us on set every morning at six-thirty, even if that meant spending a couple of hours standing around, eating bacon rolls and drinking tea while we waited for the crew to get ready. Billy, who's never liked early mornings, told the producer he didn't need breakfast, so he got a lie-in until half-eight. Lucky blighter.

As fishermen, we couldn't understand why it took so long for

anything to happen. We were used to seizing opportunities when the
tide and weather were right, then getting on with it. But a film crew
takes for ever to do the smallest thing, so we had to watch and wait,
marvelling at the sheer number of people needed to get the job done.
Every time the director called 'Turning!' (they rarely say 'Action!'),
more than a dozen people would repeat it. And then if any of us sat
down for more than two minutes, someone would appear beside us,
offering a sandwich, a cup of tea or a biscuit. Lovely to have that attention, but it would drive anyone mad after a while. And after accepting
all the offers of refreshments, just to be polite, consuming all that food
and drink soon felt like hard work.

Under the watchful eyes of around seventy people – the film crew,
the gang from the advertising agency, the clients and countless
others – we spent four days shooting the advert. The first part was
filmed in Padstow harbour, then we moved to Port Isaac to film
other scenes. Singing in synch with the sound of 'When the Boat
Comes In' blaring from loudspeakers on the Platt, we walked up the
harbour countless times so that the director could shoot it from every
conceivable angle. Every time we did the walk, John Brown added a
pebble to a line of stones he'd laid along the beach. When the director was finished with the shot, John turned to Billy.

'What do you reckon, Billy?' said John. 'How many times do you
think we did it?'

'I dunno,' said Billy. 'Ten times. Maybe a dozen?'

'Twenty-seven.' John shook his head. '*Twenty-seven takes.* We're
earning our money, I can tell you.'

If only John had known then what was awaiting him a few days
later on the final day of the shoot, when all of us except Billy and
Jeremy arrived at a warehouse at Basildon in Essex. Dressed in oilskins
and surrounded by fake jellyfish, we climbed into a twenty-foot-
deep tank of tepid water and sank to the bottom, gripping our
microphones. While a plastic model of a hammerhead shark was
pulled back and forth behind us, we pretended to sing an under-
water shanty, wondering if the only purpose of the exercise was to

show how silly we could look. Two and a half hours later, we emerged from the tank, our skin shrivelled by the wet and cold.

'What the hell have we just done?' said John. 'If anyone had told me that when I signed a record contract I'd end up spending half a day in a cold water tank, surrounded by plastic fish, I would never have believed them.'

But it was all part of life's rich tapestry. It had been a good laugh, something to tell the grandkids about, as were the events of the following day, when we were back in London for the Radio 2 Folk Awards.

We had history with the awards, but on our previous visit we'd been there to entertain the nominees and their guests. This time, someone else was providing the entertainment and we were among the winners, collecting the Good Tradition Award for keeping folk music alive and bringing it to new audiences. After receiving our award, we were meant to sing two songs, but Frank Skinner wittered on for so long that we had to cut it down to just one, 'South Australia', which went down very well with the audience. After we sang, Joan Armatrading came out on to the stage to present an award. 'I'd like to hear a bit more of *that*,' she said.

After years of being amateur outsiders, it was strange to look around at the other performers and guests and to realise that we were now a small part of that world. Roger Daltrey was sitting at the next table, Charles Dance was nearby, both looking fantastic for their age, and Billy had a chat with Donovan, with whose music he had grown up. As the evening wound to an end and the guests filtered out of the room, Trevor stood at our table, surveying the room, wondering if such a fantastic event had really happened. It didn't feel real.

In late February, we started recording our second album. Every evening for a fortnight, after the fishing boats had been tied up and the tools put away, we headed over to the church at St Kew to work on a new set of songs with Rupert Christie. Other singers and musicians, we heard, took a year or longer to record an album. Because of our commitments to work, fishing and families, we could afford only ten three-hour sessions, but in the last year we'd become more pernickety.

As ever, we wanted to do it to the best of our abilities, but now we had basic instrumentation from Billy on guitar or mandocello and Jason on the squeeze-box, so we needed more time to work out arrangements. To make the most of our limited time, we'd started rehearsing for the album in January, but with ten of us all having an opinion on melodies, wordings and the rest of it, we would often take several weeks to finish one song. To speed up the process, the harmony section of Billy, Lefty, Trevor and Cleavey started to rehearse separately in an extra session on Tuesday evenings. When they joined the rest of us to try a new song, they already had the harmonies worked out. It made a big difference.

In early March, the festival booking offers started to trickle in. After the previous year's appearances, festival organisers and audiences now knew about us. In 2010, we were mainly offered slots on the first day of festivals, or even on the day before festivals officially started; in 2011, we were offered much better slots on Saturdays and Sundays, often on the most prestigious stage. With work and families still the most important parts of all our lives, we needed to be careful not to let Fisherman's Friends dominate. But we also realised that our brief moment in the spotlight wouldn't last for ever, so we had to seize the opportunity.

In mid-March the news that we had all been waiting for came in: an invitation back to Glastonbury. Instead of playing the Acoustic Stage, this time we were being offered the Pyramid Stage, the largest at the festival and probably the most prestigious venue at any festival anywhere in the world. Two nights before we were due to sing, U2 would be on the same stage. They'd be followed the next night by Coldplay. On the final night, Beyoncé was scheduled, but before that, at midday on Sunday, the last day of the festival, we were going to sing from that hallowed spot. We were thrilled to be asked. To be completely honest, the first thought that actually passed through most of our heads was *'Bloody hell!'* Performing on the legendary Pyramid Stage at Glastonbury was such a nerve-racking concept that we tried to put it to the backs of our minds. Fortunately, before too long something happened to distract us. Something that, in Fisherman's Friends terms, was even bigger and better than being invited back to Glastonbury.

On the Friday of the Whitsun bank holiday weekend, just as we were getting ready to sing our first gig of the season on the Platt, the landlord of the Golden Lion came over.

'I've arranged it with Jeremy down at St Austell Brewery,' he said. 'You've got a ninety-pint keg of beer. And when that one's empty I'll just call up another one.'

Now we knew that we had well and truly cracked it. Free beer. St Austell Brewery had offered to sponsor us and now we could go into our own pub, order ten pints of Tribute and walk away from the bar without handing over a penny. This was without doubt the greatest thing ever to have happened to the Fisherman's Friends!

Not wanting to abuse this generosity – no one wanted to kill the goose that laid the golden egg – we intended to limit ourselves to just a few small pints every so often, but it's fair to say we had a good old session that first night. By the time we left the pub, we were all pretty merry. None of us actually remembers walking home, but we must have somehow rolled up the road and into our beds some time in the small hours.

Eight weeks later, on the Saturday morning of the Glastonbury weekend, we gathered at the top of the village for a trip that a year earlier we thought we'd never repeat. In 2010, we had rented a bus to take us to Glastonbury, but since then we'd hit the big time. Now we were going to do it in style. We'd clubbed together and bought our own wheels. No stretch limo, tour bus or private jet for us: we were doing it Fisherman's Friends style in a ten-year-old white Peugeot Boxer minibus with 107, 000 miles on the clock. Lefty had fitted a new clutch to get it through its MOT and added a tow bar so we could drag our kit behind us in a trailer. The bus wasn't very comfortable, but it was going to save us money. We called it the Fish Van.

Although some of us had watched U2 playing Glastonbury live on television the previous night, somehow it hadn't sunk in that we would soon be following them on to the very same stage. (We'd been promised free beer all weekend in the Cornish Arms tent, so maybe we were focusing on that!) Then, as we crested a hill, the festival site was laid out in front of us like a city and we realised the immensity of what was ahead. The Fish Van was suddenly a very quiet, very tense place.

That evening, after having spent most of the day watching different bands on some of the other stages, most of us convened at the Pyramid Stage to watch Coldplay. Whether you like them or not, no one could deny it was a fantastic show. And that's when sheer Pyramid terror struck us. It was a huge stage, there were thousands of people there, and we were next up. Coldplay was the last act of Saturday night; we were the first act of Sunday morning. It was scary.

Trevor was standing in the crowd with his son, Mark, and Jason, our accordion player from Padstow. As Coldplay finished their set, Trevor's and Mark's eyes met.

'Dad,' said Mark, 'you're going to be on there tomorrow.'

'Don't say it!' said Trevor. 'Just don't remind me. I can't believe we've got to stand up there and do what Coldplay have just done.'

After Coldplay, we ran for the Fish Van, hoping to get to our hotel in Taunton early enough for a good night's sleep in preparation for the morning. But our driver didn't know the way, so he asked a taxi driver for directions. The taxi driver said to turn right, when we should have gone left. We ended up miles off-course in Cheddar. (Lefty, who was staying on the festival site, claims he left us with a map and sat nav for the journey, but perhaps we'd better keep quiet on that point.) Anyway, by the time we found our beds in Taunton, it was 3 a.m., which was not exactly the great night's shut-eye we wanted just before the biggest gig of our lives.

The next morning, with only three hours' sleep inside us, there were one or two grumpies in the hotel car park. Still, by about 9 a.m., we were on site, behind the Pyramid Stage, the Fish Van parked directly beside a vast trailer.

'*Private*,' it said on the door. '*Beyoncé*.'

We decided it was probably best not to knock on the door and say hello, so we all stood in front of it and had our picture taken. Several of Beyoncé's dancers were relaxing in the sun outside the trailer. We gave them one of our CDs, thinking that maybe they'd want to listen to it on the way home. Then one of us noticed the bus parked on the other side of the Fish Van.

'*U2*,' said the sign on the door. '*Bono – dressing room*.'

Like minnows squeezed between two whales, we were trying to come to terms with where we'd managed to land ourselves, when two pantechnicon trucks turned up: it was Paul Simon's stage kit. Beside these giants, our trailer, all nine feet of it behind the Fish Van, felt very, very small.

Backstage there was a lounge with coffee machines, fridges full of drink, and tables laden with just about anything we might have wanted to eat if we hadn't been so tense. While Billy and Jason set up their instruments on stage, the rest of us peeked out onto the field in front of the stage. Nearly empty. We were quite happy with that. It was a relief not to have to play in front of a vast audience like the one we'd seen watch Coldplay.

There was still an hour to wait, so we made ourselves comfortable backstage and quietly sipped a few beers. Ten in the morning was a bit early to start, but we needed some Dutch courage. After half an hour, a few of us had a wander out to the stage again. There was bad news: the field was filling up.

With ten minutes before showtime, the whole front section of the audience was packed, black and white St Piran's flags and fish kites flying in the breeze. After one of the wettest starts to Glastonbury for several years, the weather had turned. It was a glorious day and the crowds were making the most of it.

Looking around at each other, we could see the tension etched into all our faces. We huddled like a rugby team and geed ourselves up to go out and kick arse. If the audience liked it, that was fine. And if they didn't, we'd win them over.

And then the big moment arrived. A stage manager called us onto stage and we found ourselves climbing the steps, wondering how the hell we had ended up on the Pyramid Stage at Glastonbury. When we thought of all the stars who had climbed those steps, and now a bunch of old farts like us, it was just unbelievable.

After the immense build-up, the first few songs passed almost in a dream. It was like an out-of-body experience, with most of us still unable to take it all in. Then our nerves finally settled and we started to enjoy it, looking out over the swelling crowd. People were coming down the hill from their tents and already the number watching had doubled. One highlight was Billy singing 'New York Girls', dedicating it to his new granddaughter Annie, whose name featured in the chorus. By the time we were on our last song of the 45-minute set, the field was full. Something like 30,000 people were watching us, all singing along, cheering, waving flags and whooping. Fired up by the crowd, we were loving it. But suddenly it was over and we were traipsing offstage, slapping each other on the back and feeling like we were walking on air.

'That was great,' said John Brown. 'It's Trevose Golf Club on Wednesday.'

Poor Billy was still on the stage, struggling to pack up his instruments. We'd all buggered off, leaving him to get it in the ear from the stage manager, whose stage hands were bringing on the drum set and kit for the next band, The Low Anthem.

'Where are your roadies?' yelled the stage manager. 'The guys who help you.'

'I haven't got any guys who help me,' said Bill.

'What on earth do you mean?'

'It's just me. I clear up my own kit.'

The stage manager was speechless but his withering look said it all: Who the hell are you and what are you doing here?

Backstage, the rest of us were over the moon with what we'd just done. None of us had ever felt anything like it before. And if we were honest with ourselves, we weren't likely to top it.

When we'd calmed down, we had lunch, did an interview with BBC 6 Music and had a scout around – we saw Don McLean and the keyboard player from Mumford and Sons – before being bundled into a courtesy Range Rover to carry some of us and our instruments over to the Cornish Arms.

As we drove through the crowds, hundreds of people peered into the car at us, their faces turning from expectation to confusion as they realised the stars they wanted to see were only a bunch of hairy Cornishmen in their sixties and seventies. Then, as we pulled up at the Cornish Arms for our next gig, the cheers nearly lifted the tent off the ground. The St Austell Brewery Proper Job and Tribute were flowing and we went down a storm, singing for an hour and a half to a packed crowd that spilled far out of the tent. We certainly brought a little bit of Cornwall into the heart of Glastonbury. Feeling as if we were back home among our people, the pressure was off and we could just relax and rock and roll.

Afterwards, five of us wandered up to the Avalon field to see Steve and Phil from Show of Hands play to another packed tent. Steve spotted us in the crowd and gave a shout-out. It seemed very appropriate. Show of Hands had always supported us, taking us to the Albert Hall and Bristol's Colston Hall, and now we were with them on the bill on the same day at Glastonbury.

By the time Phil and Steve had finished their fantastic set, a golden sun was hanging low in the sky and our mobiles were chock-a-block with messages urging us to get back to the Fish Van, where Lefty was waiting, itching to get back home. Julian was also sitting in the bus, wanting to make tracks: he had to be up in the morning to go fishing. But with all the people stopping us along the way to say how much they enjoyed our gig, it took us nearly an hour to walk the short distance back to the Pyramid Stage.

We made a quick last visit backstage, where Beyoncé's backing singers were warming up and Billy stood a foot away from Jay-Z. Jeremy and Jason had decided to stay on to see Beyoncé perform, but by nine o'clock the rest of us were speeding west, most of us asleep in the back of the Fish Van as Lefty, and then soundman Sam, floored it all the way back home. Tomorrow was another day and most of us had to go to work.

By midnight we were all home, where some of us watched the last half-hour of Beyoncé on TV, totally unable to believe that we had stood on the very same stage that morning. It had been a wonderful couple of days, but coming back down Fore Street hill and looking onto the harbour, we'd all known we were back where we belonged.

With the next morning, inevitably, our thoughts started to turn to the future. None of us knew what would happen next, but everything so far had surpassed our expectations. We'd thoroughly enjoyed it all, although we also knew we didn't want the Fisherman's Friends to take over our lives. Long before fame and fortune came blowing into Port Isaac and battering at our doors, we'd all reached a point where we were very content with our achievements. We'd worked hard to end up doing exactly what we wanted and none of us wanted that to change.

Most of us had come to look at the recording contract as a means to an end, a chance to see a bit more of the world, to become known as the group that helped make shanty singing popular again, and to take part in events to which we never would have dreamed of being invited, like Glastonbury.

Cleavey sat down at his computer to type up our Glastonbury exploits on our new blog. 'Jer and Ju are out harassing innocent lobsters again,' he wrote. 'I'm catching up with me bills and tidying the shop. John Brown's filling up his aquarium with fish, Johnnie Mac's up on a roof, Bill's throwing pots, Jason is up on a roof too, and Lefty sounded on his mobile like he was manically wielding a carving knife in a hen house trying to catch his dinner. Oh, and Pete? He is doing bugger all as usual. He's seventy-seven, you know . . .'

As for Trevor, he was mending someone's porch in Mevagissey, where he bumped into a couple of boys he knew from the local choir.

'I feel very sorry for you boys in the Fisherman's Friends,' one of them said.

'Why's that?'

'Trying to fit all your normal lives in with that.' The bloke shook his head. 'How long do you think it's going to last?'

'I don't know,' said Trevor. 'Nobody can know how long it's going to last.'

If truth be told, all that really matters to any of us is that we maintain our friendships, share our lives and know that Port Isaac will always still be there for us, the same as ever.

'How can you work it out so all this hullabaloo becomes easier for you?' asked the Mevagissey fella.

'It'll pack up one day,' said Trevor. 'And when that happens, we'll just go back to our normal lives, fishing and working all week and singing on a Friday night, sharing a few yarns and a pint of beer on the Platt or in the pub. And then everything in Port Isaac will be as it has always been: just fine.'

PICTURE AND SONG LYRICS CREDITS

Lyric Credits

'Cousin Jack' Words & Music by Steve Knightley
© 1997. Reproduced by permission.

'Sailor Ain't A Sailor' Words and Music by Tom Lewis © 2010.
Reproduced by permission of EMI Music Publishing Ltd, London
W8 5SW.

'No Hopers Jokers and Rogues' Words and Music by Rupert Christie
and Tom Gilbert © Sony/ATV Music Publishing. All rights reserved.
Used by permission © 2009. Reproduced by permission of EMI
Music Publishing Ltd, London W8 5SW.

'Mollymauk' written by Bob Watson © 1987. Reproduced by
permission of Patchworks.

'The Last Widow' Words by Jon Cleave and Music by Billy Hawkins
© Copyright control. All rights reserved. Used by permission.

Picture Credits